TRUE ANGEL STORIES
777 MESSAGES OF HOPE AND INSPIRATION

Also by Diana Cooper

2012 and Beyond
Prepare for 2012 and Beyond
Double-CD (with Rosemary Stephenson)
Enlightenment through Orbs (with Kathy Crosswell)
Ascension through Orbs (with Kathy Crosswell)
Ascension through Orbs Meditations Double-CD
(with Kathy Crosswell)
The Orbs Cards (with Kathy Crosswell)
The Wonder of Unicorns
Unicorn Cards
A New Light on Angels
A New Light on Ascension
A Little Light on the Spiritual Laws
The Wisdom Cards (with Greg Suart)
Angel Answers
Angel Inspiration
Angels of Light Cards (2nd edition)
Angels of Light Cards Pocket Edition
Angels of Light Double-CD
Angels of Light Address Book
Angel Cards for Children
Teen-Angel (cards)
Angel Colouring Book
Discover Atlantis (with Shaaron Hutton)
The Atlantis Cards
Light Up Your Life

available from your local bookstore
or directly from the publisher at
www.findhornpress.com

TRUE ANGEL STORIES
777 MESSAGES OF HOPE AND INSPIRATION

DIANA COOPER

FINDHORN PRESS

© Diana Cooper, 2013

The right of Diana Cooper to be identified as the author
of this work has been asserted by her in accordance
with the Copyright, Designs and Patents Act 1998.

Published in 2013 by Findhorn Press, Scotland

ISBN 978-1-84409-612-1

A CIP record for this title is available from the British Library.

Compiled and edited by Elizabeth Ann Morris
Cover design by Richard Crookes
Interior design by Damian Keenan
Printed and bound in the European Union

Published by
Findhorn Press
117-121 High Street,
Forres IV36 1AB,
Scotland, UK

t +44 (0)1309 690582
f +44 (0)131 777 2711
e info@findhornpress.com
www.findhornpress.com

Contents

Introduction 9

    About the Diana Cooper School 10

    Acknowledgements 11

Part I - True Angel Stories

1. Diana's Experiences 14
2. Guardian Angels 24
3. Angel Signs 32
   - *Angel Clouds* 34
   - *Angel Feathers* 37
   - *Angels and Rainbows* 44
   - *Angels Working Through Names and Numbers* 46
   - *Angel Names* 49
4. Angel Wake-Up Calls 51
5. Angelic Help 56
   - *Angels Answers Prayers* 63
   - *Saved by Traffic Angels* 70
   - *Warned by Angels* 74
   - *Angel Guidance* 78
   - *Angels Give Confirmation* 84
6. Angels Comfort 91
   - *Angel Wings* 98
7. Travel Angels 103
   - *Angels on Aeroplanes and Trains* 103
   - *Angels on the Road* 104
8. Angels and Animals 110
   - *Angels and Cows* 110
   - *Angels and Horses* 111
   - *Angels and Dolphins* 113
   - *Angels and Birds* 114
   - *Angels and Cats* 118
   - *Angels and Dogs* 120
   - *Angels and Insects* 124

9.   Angels Everywhere 128
      Lost and Found 135
      Angels Organize Time 140
      Angel Humour 143
      Dreams 148
10.   Seeing and Hearing Angels 153
      Angel Voices 153
      Seeing Angels 160
      Angels Singing and Angel Songs 165
11.   Babies and Children 170
      Angels and Babies 170
      Angels with Children 174
12.   Angels Help with Finance 180
      Abundance 183
13.   Earth Angels 188
      Vanishing Angels 196
14.   Death and Dying 202
      Angels Help with Passing Over 202
      Near-death Experiences 208
15.   Archangel Michael 213
      Faith 218
      Archangel Michael's Sword and Shield 219
      Archangel Michael Protects 221
16.   Archangel Raphael 230
      Archangel Raphael Looks After Travellers 239
      Healing Angels 243
17.   Helping Relationships 250
      Mother Mary 251
18.   Archangels and Masters 258
19.   Unicorns 265
20.   Elements and Elementals 272
21.   Angel Orbs 278

Part II - Angel Exercises and Visualizations

1. Grounding and Protection 288
2. Your Guardian Angel 290
3. Communicating with Angels 292
4. Asking for Help 295
5. Be an Angel 299
6. Cleansing and Releasing 301
7. Healing 304
8. Spiritual Practices 306
9. Comfort 308
10. Working with Animals and Birds 310

In Conclusion 312
Contributors to this Book 314

Introduction

Angels are beings of light who resonate at a frequency beyond our normal range of hearing and vision. Angels are everywhere and have always been around us. As the vibration of the planet and individuals continues its rapid rise, more and more people are able to connect to them.

This book offers a collection of amazing stories from people who have heard the angels singing, seen them, or received messages or signs from them, as well as hundreds of inspiring examples of their presence. As well as this, we offer visualizations and exercises to help you connect with the wonders of the angelic realms.

The first of the 777 angel stories in the book is the story of my first angelic experience. Since then I have walked, talked and celebrated with angels on a daily basis and they have helped me all the way. I hope that, whether you read this book through or dip into it by opening a page and reading the story there, you will be switched on by the angel energy so that you too can connect with their help, guidance and inspiration. For those of you who are already living with awareness of angels, the energy of the stories within this book will further enhance your connection.

The angelic realm consists of angels, archangels and others with different roles. I have been blessed to be able to connect with angels, archangels, powers (which include the angels of birth and death and the lords of karma), thrones (who are in charge of the planets and stars including Lady Gaia), cherubim and seraphim (who sing the frequency of creation round the Godhead). I share some of these stories in this book.

The unicorns are fully of the angelic kingdom and we include some stories about these illuminated white ascended horses. Their energy and light is very pure and gentle and it is wonderful that they are returning to Earth now to help us for the first time since the fall of Atlantis.

Elementals are also part of the angelic kingdom and many people now connect with them. These little but powerful ones have also become part of my daily life.

The planet is in transition as we rise from the fourth to the fifth dimensional. This means that everyone must deal with their unresolved issues. Angels are always ready to help us, but we must ask. The stories I have chosen demonstrate how much assistance, healing and guidance is available from angels.

I do hope that you enjoy this book and that it enables you to feel and benefit from the presence of angels.

ABOUT THE DIANA COOPER SCHOOL

THE DIANA COOPER SCHOOL was formed in 2003. Since then it has grown into an organization with over 700 teachers around the world. We are a not-for-profit organization with a vision:

> *"To empower people to spread the light of angels, ascension and the sacred mysteries of the universe"*

And our mission:

> *"We are dedicated to supporting the creation of the new golden age on the planet. All our activities will align with this purpose."*

Our teacher-training programmes and workshops are based on Diana's many amazing books. As the consciousness of the planet rises we want to ensure that we can support as many people as possible to move into the new golden age with the wisdom and understanding they need to become fifth-dimensional beings.

Our teaching programmes need to expand to support this. All the royalties from the book will go to the School. These funds will enable us to truly make a difference and allow us to reach many more people around the world.

Enjoy your journey through this wonderful book. Its many stories will bring inspiration, comfort and, most importantly, a deep universal "knowing" that we are all part of the divine plan and when we connect with the angels and wise ones miracles do happen.

If you want to find out more about the Diana Cooper School and its work, please visit our website *www.dianacooperschool.com*. We open our hearts and invite you to join us in our work. Together we will create a new golden age on Planet Earth.

> *Yours in divine service*
> *Namaste*
> *ELIZABETH ANN*
> *Principal, Diana Cooper School*

ACKNOWLEDGEMENTS

For the completion of this book we wish to give special thanks to the following people for their dedication, hard work and vision:

Karin Finnigan, Jillian Stott, Penny Wing, Karelena McKinlay, Barbara Howard, Carol Deakin and Rosalind Horswell.

We also wish to thank everyone who contributed stories. Your stories will inspire and uplift many people around the world.

NOTE: Stories which have been submitted by a Diana Cooper School Teacher have the initials DCS after the person's name.

PART I

True Angel Stories

Diana's Experiences

E ver since my first angel experience I have been in constant contact with the angels, elementals and unicorns. It has been a wonderful golden journey, though I have experienced many challenges, trials and dangers along the way. I have, however, emerged with a sense of trust, faith and gratitude. I know my angels are always with me and that they have helped me move from victimhood to mastery. I also know that even when I am challenged they are always there to carry me.

So, in the hope that it may fill you with the trust, faith and gratitude to enable you to become a master, I share a few of my stories in this chapter and include many more throughout the book.

~ My First Angel Visitation ~

My first awakening to angels was many years ago. It feels important that it should be the first of the angel stories in this book.

• • • • • •

In my rock-bottom state and with no spiritual experience, I called out to the universe for help. I said, "If there's anything out there, show me – and you've got one hour." Immediately a beautiful six-foot tall golden angel stood in front of me and pulled me out of my physical body. We flew together and it showed me many things. Finally we flew together over a hall full of people with rainbow auras and it told me I was on the platform. When it brought me back it was exactly one hour later.

After that experience I still felt hopeless and despairing at times, but now I knew that there were angels surrounding us, just waiting to help us.

~ A Sign from the Angels ~

It took me a long time to learn that the angels are constantly trying to remind us of their presence and give us signs all the time.

• • • • • •

This occurred some weeks after the angel first came to me. I felt rejected again and asked for a sign. I looked up and there were huge hands in the sky, cupped as if to hold me up. I could see them clearly and I knew it was a message from the angels to say that they were helping me, which gave me great comfort.

~ Earth Angels ~

When the signs they gave me did not lift me from my negative state the angels came in with some direct action.

••••••

The weeks went by and my life was slowly coming together, but still I worried about everything. One day I was sitting at the back of a hall listening to a speaker. I didn't know what she was talking about as I was consumed with anxiety! I asked the angels to please help me. At the end of the talk a stranger came to talk to me. He said, "I'm sorry to intrude on your thoughts but I couldn't help tuning in and the angels asked me to tell you everything is going to be all right."

Well! I thanked him but I continued to worry. A few days later I was looking in a shop window, standing in lashing rain that matched my mood. "I need help again," I murmured.

Once more a stranger came up to me and said, "I've been told to tell you that everything is going to be all right." The same words! And this time I did begin to believe.

~ Angels and Water – Bathwater ~

Water is a wonderful element, for it carries love and raises the frequency of everyone who is in it or touched by it.

••••••

I had just moved house and was starting a new phase of my life. I lay in the bath and asked for guidance about the classes I was running. To my astonishment an angelic voice replied like a golden thought directly into my mind. "We want you to tell people about angels."

I was horrified and replied that I didn't want to do that – people would think I was crazy. The angel then spoke the words I have never ever forgotten. "Who is doing your work? Is it your ego or your higher self?"

I agreed that I'd do it. I got out of the bath and sat on the bed and three angels stood in front of me and gave me information about the angelic realms.

~ Angels and My Book ~

When angels want something done and everyone is willing it happens quickly!

••••••

I sent my angel book to Findhorn Press (it was then called *A Little Light on Angels* but the title is now *New Light on Angels*). Thierry, the press's owner, phoned me and said they would like to publish the book. I said it would be great to get it out in time for Christmas, but he laughed and said that was impossible. I responded that if the angels wanted the book out by Christmas they would arrange it.

Half an hour later Thierry rang me back and said that they could get the book out in six weeks after all. Five weeks later the finished copy was in my hands!

~ An Angel in my Aura ~

When the angels use you to give a message to others, miracles can happen.

• • • • • •

My book *A Little Light on Angels* had just been published and I was invited to appear on Richard and Judy's morning TV show. As I was about to go on air they asked if they could take my aura photograph.

I asked my angel to step into the photograph and to everyone's surprise my angel and guide both impressed themselves onto the aura photograph. You could see the round head of the angel, a gold bar reaching to my guide and rays of golden light pouring through the picture.

As a result the programme received 114,000 calls ... I was asked to return the following day because so many people wanted to talk about their angel experiences – experiences that they had never dared to speak of before! You can see this photograph on *www.dianacooper.com.*

~ Angels in the Night-time ~

When we fall asleep or wake up, we are more open to angel messages.

• • • • • •

Many years ago I went to Mount Shasta in California, as I had received guidance that I must attend the Wesak ceremony to talk about angels. The first evening in the hotel, I had a phone call from my publishers, Findhorn Press to tell me that they had arranged an interview with Dawn Fazende, the editor of the local newspaper the *Mount Shasta News.*

In the early hours I was woken by angels. They said that this was to be a very important meeting and gave me some specific things that I must say. I wrote down everything they said.

Arriving at the restaurant the next day I was full of curiosity about what would happen. Immediately an extraordinary thing happened. Dawn and I shook hands – and couldn't let go. There was huge power pulsing between us. I thought, "My goodness, this is some powerful lady," and I learned afterwards that she had thought the same about me. Our lunch lasted all afternoon.

It did turn out to be an immensely important meeting: Dawn was instrumental in arranging for me to speak at the Wesak ceremony the following year. As ever I was awed and grateful to the beings of light.

~ My First Talk: to 2000 People ~

If you are feeling nervous ask the angels for help.

• • • • • •

My *Angel Inspiration* book was flying out of the shops. People were buying multiple copies. This gave me confidence. I was to talk to a huge audience at the Wesak Conference. I'd had no experience of speaking to so many people before this, and so could not understand why I felt as calm as a still summer's day, even when the time came for me to make my presentation. As I made the long journey to the platform I felt the wings of my angel enfolding me and holding me. It was magical. I relaxed totally as the angels spoke through me. Later my guide Kumeka told me I had had a seventh-dimensional experience on that stage.

~ Michael on the Road Home ~

One of the greatest energies you can have is faith. On this night I trusted Archangel Michael to assist me.

. . . . . .

I'd spent the evening with friends and when I came to leave the roads were covered with sheets of ice. My friends suggested I stay the night, but I wanted to get home so I put my faith in Archangel Michael.

I said to him, "Please, please Michael, the conditions are very bad. I need extra protection to get home safely." An extraordinary thing happened – it was as if a bright blue light had been switched on in front of the car. It shone all over the road in front of me and to either side and stayed there until I reached the main road. Michael showed me his light to comfort me.

~ Luggage ~

Archangel Michael is very special. He protects and looks after everything – including luggage!

. . . . . .

My case was being transferred from plane to plane, so I asked Archangel Michael to look after it and make sure it made it to the right plane. As I waited at Heathrow case after case appeared but there was no sign of mine. I was anxious about it and mentally said to him, "I asked you to look after my case."

Clear as a bell he replied patiently, "And I did so. It is coming."

Sure enough, a few minutes later my case appeared.

~ Angels Find My Dream House ~

Write down exactly what you want before you ask the angels.

. . . . . .

I have always loved the sea and wanted to live about twenty minutes away from it but within reach of a motorway to the airports and London. When I decided to move I wrote this dream down together with a description of my ideal house. I looked at a map and found that Bournemouth met my criteria.

I mentioned this to an acquaintance and she phoned a friend of hers who lived in Bournemouth. Within half an hour her friend, Dee, phoned me to say that I was welcome to stay with her and she would drive me round to look at houses for sale. I was so grateful.

I found one house that fulfilled everything on my wish list and we went to look at it. It was perfect but I decided that it was too big and too expensive and – not without difficulty – I let it go. I knew that letting go of something if it is not for the highest good was very important.

At four o'clock in the morning I was woken by a voice saying, "Diana, that is your house." When I went down to breakfast, Dee came rushing into the room. She said, "Diana, an angel woke me at four o'clock and said, 'Tell Diana that is her house'!"

So even though it was the only house I'd looked at and I could not afford it I bought it. I love it.

~ Make Living in My Dream Home Possible ~

Here is what happened next.

• • • • • • •

When I moved in to my new house I had £2,000 left in my bank account and no other reserves. On the first day there, bills for a total of £10,000 came in. I stood in the kitchen and said aloud, "Angels, if you want me to live in this house bring me the money to cover these invoices this week. If it doesn't come I'll put the house back on the market again." I meant it. The full amount arrived that week.

~ Metatron's Room ~

Dedicate a special place to a particular angel and that angel will look after it.

• • • • • • •

I have a beautiful room in my home that I decided to make into the Metatron room. I wanted to paint the walls pale orange and the alcove, where my altar is, deep orange. I bought the paint and felt very pleased. But as I walked into the room I had doubts. "Oh dear," I said to myself, "I hope I got the right colours." Loud and clear came the voice of Metatron: "You did. I chose them!" I love that room – when the sun shines in the orange walls look so warm and welcoming.

~ The Song of Fairies and Elementals ~

A melodious high-pitched hum is the key to the elemental kingdom.

• • • • • • •

As I walked through the forest, a lovely fairy came and sat on my shoulder and started to sing. It was simply beautiful: high and sweet, like no earthly singing. I was overwhelmed with joy – and imagine how I felt next, when hundreds of fairies and other elementals joined in and sang too. It was a melodious high-pitched hum and I later learned that this is the sound of the key to the elemental kingdom. There is a fuller version of this story in my book *The Keys to the Universe*.

~ A Thousand Angels ~

There are a thousand petals at the crown chakra signifying a thousand lessons to learn here!

• • • • • • •

One day as I was visualizing the many-petalled lotus at my crown chakra, I was reminded of my stay at spiritual leader Amma's ashram in Kerala, India. I used to get up early to hear the swamis singing the thousand names of God. It took over an hour and was thrilling to listen to.

As I remembered this, I felt the thousand petals turning into tier upon tier of angels above my head. I mentally asked them to sing the thousand names of God. They did not sing them one at a time as I'd expected, but all together, and repeated it seven times. It felt like a sonic boom of energy into the top of my head. Wow! Angel energy is awe-inspiring.

~ Angels "om" ~

You can om and ask the angels to om with you. They will send their vibration to you – even if you can't feel it it is there.

• • • • • •

On one occasion the angels asked me to om into my crown chakra and indicated that they would sing with me. I started to om while I focused on my crown and they accompanied me with the most beautiful chanting. They opened my chakra up so much that I later felt as if my head had been split open. I know it opened my crown centre to a new level that enabled more light to flow through me.

~ Golden Wings ~

Sometimes a vision or experience comes out of the blue and is really breathtaking in its glory.

• • • • • •

In a quiet part of my local forest where there are no major paths, I stood silently, looking at the beautiful trees. Suddenly I felt wings bursting from my shoulders. They were pure gold and I could feel that they were huge – they had a thirty-metre span. They radiated such light that I was sure everyone in the forest would see. I stood there in awe and rapture.

Then I thought I must use this energy, so I directed the energy of the wings in various ways to embrace people in need. Finally I directed them at Syria and visualized them embracing and bringing peace to the people there. The experience faded but the impression of those wings lasted for over an hour. It was so special that I could not bring myself to tell anyone for several days.

~ Gobolino ~

Goblins are fifth-dimensional, heart-centred elementals who are extremely wise. They dedicate their lives to helping the planet.

• • • • • •

I tell stories of my goblin friend in other books. I still smile when I think of him teaching me so simply about oneness.

When he jumped out of a tree and walked along a forest path with me I asked him about his relationships with other elementals and humans. If I'd expected him to tell me that fairies had an easier task or that other elementals were lazy I was much mistaken. His reply to everything was, "We are the same but different."

How stunningly simple! This applies to all cultures, religions, countries, races and anyone in another skin who is reflecting a different aspect of the divine. I carry his words in my heart always.

~ A Goblin's Sense of Fun ~

Elementals and all high-frequency beings have a great sense of fun and they love it when you laugh.

• • • • • •

I was walking by a lake in Africa with Gobolino, my goblin friend from the story above, who has a mischievous yet innocent sense of humour. When we saw a big waterbird sitting on a post in the lake, fast asleep with its head under its wing, he nudged me to make the sound of the elementals. I must say I was curious and so I made their high melodious hum. I was amazed when the bird jerked out of its sleep and looked around in astonishment!

~ Archangel Gabriel's Persistence ~

When the angels want you to do something, they will arrange it, so go with the flow!

• • • • • •

I received a call from Paivi, the organizer of a spiritual fair in Finland, asking me to talk at the fair, but I was booked already on that date. They were disappointed and I distinctly remember Paivi's words, "But that's not right. I know you are meant to come."

As I went for a walk that morning Archangel Gabriel kept saying to me, "You are to go to Finland." In the end I said in exasperation, "OK, if you want me to go, please cancel the event and I will go to Finland."

When I got home there was a message to say that the original event I'd been booked for had been postponed! So I was able to go to Finland to talk at Paivi's event.

~ Angels and Elementals Sing My Name ~

You choose your name to carry the vibration of the essence of your soul journey. Then you telepathically impart it to your parents, often before you are born. Every time your name is sounded with love and joy it enables you to feel the wonder of being you. When it is sung with love, especially by the other realms, you are truly blessed.

• • • • • •

It was one of those days. Someone had said a very nasty thing and I felt upset and low. The following morning it was still churning over inside me so I decided to go for a walk in my local woods. It was a beautiful morning and I said aloud, "Nature, please take these negative feelings and transmute them." I became aware of a fairy sitting on my shoulder. Then lots of elementals surrounded me and sang my name with great love and caring. Then angels joined them. A unicorn added its light. Heaven was pouring waves and waves of love into me as they all sang my name over and over. They gave me a message: "Forgive the person you were then and rejoice in who you are now." Two hours later I could still feel love in my heart and did not even remember what the upset had been about.

~ Helping Children to the Light ~

When you look at or visualize an Orb around you, the energy of it is absorbed into your aura.

• • • • • •

As I walked out in nature, breathing into the bright-pink Orb of Archangel Chamuel and Mother Mary around me, an elf ran towards me surrounded by six small children. I realized they were lost souls who had not passed over. When they saw the light of Mary and Archangel Chamuel round me, the children ran towards me, except one, who ran away instead. I knelt down and handed them one by one into the light and their mothers collected them.

I particularly remember the radiant, joyful look on the face of one little fair-haired boy of about two dressed in a sailor suit as he saw his mother. I walked on, wondering about the child who had run away. Almost immediately the elf reappeared, holding him firmly by the arm and reassuring him. This time as the child saw the light he too ran to me and was collected by his mother and father.

~ Healing from Trees ~

When you bless and appreciate trees, flowers and other aspects of nature, it responds and helps you in ways you may never even realize.

• • • • • •

I was in the woods when I suddenly had a thought about a baby dying and the family's grief. I didn't know where this thought had come from, but I had a sense that I was picking up the emotions of a local family. The sense of grief grew stronger and stronger and I asked for help. The grief felt unbearable for a minute. Then it lifted.

My guide Kumeka told me that I had picked up on the loss of a local family whose baby had died, and then the feelings of loss for every baby and child I had lost in my past lives had come back to me. The trees had taken it from me. After this intense, almost unbearable feeling of grief had lifted, I felt indescribably free and with deep gratitude thanked the trees for transmuting my grief.

~ Meeting Pan ~

Pan is a mighty ninth-dimensional master in charge of nature. He and Archangel Purlimiek work together to help the nature kingdom.

• • • • • •

I was walking through my local forest when I became aware of a huge being standing among the trees. I telepathically asked him who he was and he replied, "Pan."

I really did not know what to say, so I tried just to beam gratitude for all he did. I was also very aware of all the things humans had done to the natural world. I stood, sending him gratitude, until eventually he withdrew, leaving me with a deep sense of peace.

~ Angelic Protection for Flying ~

Many people are concerned about flying – angels can give us confidence and reassurance, as this story illustrates.

......

I was on holiday in Thailand and from the beach we could see planes from the local airport taking off and landing. I was intrigued to see that the photographs I took showed dozens of guardian-angel Orbs and some of Archangel Gabriel's angels around the planes. The guardian angels were so prominent that I knew their charges – the passengers – must have been nervous.

This was why their angels stayed close and held the energy, helping them to feel safe. If only people realized how much support and assistance we have when we are flying. Nervous flyers would feel so much better!

~ Animals' Angel and My Dog ~

Worrying about people – or animals – you care about sends them negative energy. Instead ask the angels to surround them with light.

......

My beautiful little dog Venus was due to be spayed. As I took her for a good long walk before driving her to the vet, I asked Archangel Fhelyai (the archangel who looks after animals) to look after her. I heard him say, "I will be with her. All will be well." It was a huge relief to hear this and I really was able to trust that the operation would go well, as indeed it did.

~ Healing Your Relationship With Your Father ~

If you connect with the angels they will use their energy to heal or change others through you – without you even knowing.

Anita, my bookkeeper, was a lovely, bright bubbly person. One day she came to lunch with me before going to visit her father. This is the email she sent me a few days later.

......

Whether you realized it or not there was more than lunch going on between us! If you remember I was on my way to my father's from your house.

It was forty years to the day since he left home without any explanation. I have spent many hours working on my inner child clearing hurt, anger, sadness etc. While we were having lunch the angels were sending healing through you to me to finally clear, release, let go and forgive the entire episode. When I saw my dad that day I felt detached and un-irritated, which was unusual. There was no anger, just acceptance and understanding. I didn't realize what had happened until the following morning. Spirit are so good at planning things.

So this is a huge thank you for the healing and a little thank you for lunch.

— *ANITA*

CHAPTER 2

Guardian Angels

Everyone has a guardian angel, who is with you from birth and who holds the divine blueprint of your life. No matter what you do your guardian angel loves you unconditionally and is with you all the time. They constantly whisper to you to do what is for your highest good and try to guide you. I have seen many photographs showing the Orbs of guardian angels, right by someone's ear making suggestions to them.

They encourage you to make the best choices, arrange for you to meet people who you need to come across and comfort and help you in any way they can. Because you have free will your guardian angel cannot save you from an experience from which you must learn. They will, however, save you from danger or death if it is not your time.

~ Meeting My Guardian Angel ~

I love this story from Karin, which illustrates that your guardian angel loves you however bad you feel.

• • • • • •

Although I was a reiki master and healer, and always knew I was psychic, I didn't feel any connection with angels until I decided to train in the Transform Your Life Programme with Elizabeth Ann Morris.

She asked if I wanted to meet my guardian angel and took me through a guided meditation. I was terrified! I really believed angels wouldn't want to know me. I felt very deeply that I wasn't lovable and they wouldn't come.

However, this amazing teacher brought angels of healing into my heart and I felt it! I had a strong physical sense of my breathing calming, of light of some kind engulfing me, and of the pain in my heart lessening.

The name "Harold" came into my mind. I saw the most beautiful being, and what was most amazing was that love for me in his eyes. My life changed in that moment. I realized that love was there if I wanted it. All I had to do was close my eyes and ask Harold to come.

— *KARIN FINEGAN DCS*

~ Cocooned by an Angel ~

Your guardian angel holds your hand and supports you whenever you are most in need.

••••••

My partner and I were thrilled when I became pregnant, but at eleven weeks I started spotting and had backache. I went to bed while my partner phoned the doctor. I closed my eyes and saw myself on a hospital trolley being wheeled through some doors. I kept telling myself to keep calm and everything would be OK.

The room seemed to go "soft" and I felt surrounded by physical warmth and love. All fear left me and I was calm and safe as if I was held in a cocoon of gentleness. I knew that whatever was to happen I would not be alone.

I went for a check-up and was kept in overnight. I dreamed I saw the outline of a foetus highlighted in electric blue light but the foetus separated from me and I woke up. I miscarried. I was very upset but somehow I knew I was still held in that cocoon of calm, peace and love.

The next morning I was taken on a trolley through those doors I had seen in my mind's eye. An inner calm stayed with me for days afterwards. I'm sure the presence was my guardian angel helping me through a challenging time.

— **KAREN SPRING-STOCKER**

~ Guardian Angel Diversion ~

This girl was blessed when her guardian angel protected her. Angels work in a million ways to keep us safe even from our own mistakes.

••••••

I was in my early twenties, on my way home, worse for wear after a late night out and I missed my train stop. I stupidly accepted a lift from a stranger. All was fine until I tried to get out and then I realized I was not safe.

Suddenly both the driver and I were drawn to the sound of someone walking towards the car. A man with a trilby hat was approaching. The street lamp seemed to shine down on him. I managed to get out of the car and home safely.

The next day two things struck me. Although the "man" had seemed to be approaching the car, he never got there or walked past. I went back to the spot and saw that there was no street lamp there. I can only conclude that my guardian angel caused the diversion to keep me safe. I send thanks for this.

— **ANON**

~ Guardian Angel and My Life Mission ~

If you ask for something that is for your highest good, your guardian angel will step in and make sure it happens.

••••••

I found an advert for Diana's ascension teaching course. I was so excited I called the number straight away and Diana said she was sorry but the course was full. I asked my guardian angel to make sure a place came up if it was for my highest good. Two days later I had a call to say there was now a place if I wanted it. I thanked Eleanor, my guardian angel, for her help and haven't looked back since!

— *ELOISE BENNETT DCS*

~ Angels Watching Over Me ~

Our guardian angels watch over us all the time and it is such a wonderful, comforting feeling when we sense them.

• • • • • •

It has been only a few years since I discovered angels. I was always looking for physical signs like feathers, but eventually realized that I needed to have more faith.

One day I was sleeping in my bedroom, which also contains my shrine. I felt someone else in the room and sensed a large shape sitting on the table nearby. I forgot all about this and went about my business.

A day later when I was tidying up my bed I found two white feathers on my blanket. They were so pure white in colour that I knew that they had been left by my angels.

— *MELODY CHOPHLA*

~ Walking with My Guardian Angel in the Swiss Alps ~

Your guardian angels will give you an indication when there is danger so that you can take avoiding action.

• • • • • •

I went hiking alone in the Swiss Alps. The routes are well laid out and easy to follow. Every day I asked my guardian angel to look after me and let me know if it was unsafe. My "gut" reaction – my angels – always lets me know.

One day I was on a route that led between two mountains into a valley. My gut started reacting and I felt afraid. The feeling intensified and after lunch I went back down the mountain.

Some days later I followed another route into the valley and there was a plateau with a derelict mine. I have no idea what danger may have lay ahead but I had to listen to my guardian angel.

— *EL GLEESON DCS*

~ Angel Comforts Patient ~

When someone has a fever they are often able to see beyond the veil into the spiritual realms, as in this story.

• • • • • •

I had believed in angels since I was a child, but was put off by being told that I must not talk about them as some of them might be evil. Some years ago, on night duty at the hospital where I was a nurse, I had a patient with a very high fever. I cooled him with wet towels, then stood at the foot of his bed and watched how he was. Suddenly he lifted his hand and said, "There is my angel." I could not see an angel. I shuddered a little because of my childhood memories, but realized that the patient was deeply comforted by this angelic presence.

— *MONA LISE DAMKJÆR*

~ The Comfort of Knowing My
Guardian Angel is with Me ~

In the following story Sharon shares how her guardian angel saved her from an accident.

· · · · · ·

I know my guardian angel is with me and on several occasions this has definitely prevented me from coming to serious harm. Once, as I was driving at 2.30 a.m., he told me to approach the traffic lights with caution even though they were green – just as a car sped through the red light. He prevented a serious car accident.

— *SHARON*

~ Saved From a Robber ~

Sharon, from the previous story, and how her guardian angel also saved her from being robbed.

· · · · · ·

I was in Spain when my guardian angel warned me to be careful and on my guard with a man sitting close by at a little beach bar. I found out later that this man was a robber. Luckily I was prepared: after my angel warned me, I'd taken all my money, cards and keys out of my handbag and put them safely in my pockets and given my son some of my things to look after. The robber got nothing from me. It is so comforting to know my angel is always with me.

— *SHARON*

~ Saved by My Guardian Angel ~

Your guardian angel will save you if it is not right for you to get hurt or die.

· · · · · ·

I have believed in my guardian angels since I was a little child. I've always recognized their interventions for my safety and well-being, and on one important day my guardian angel saved my life.

As I walked to work I was listening to music. I came to a junction and looked both ways before stepping out. I saw a car coming straight at me at speed – too late for me to react! In my mind I saw myself being hit by the car, thrown into the air and landing way down the road.

However, as the car approached I felt myself being pushed back onto the pavement. I recognized that this amazing force was my guardian angel, Geranum, who had pushed me back out of harm's way. I knew without the shadow of a doubt that my guardian angel saved my life.

I hope my story inspires others to find and work with their guardian angels.

— EL

~ *Angels Speak to Us Through Our Inner Voice* ~

Your inner voice is the whispering of your guardian angel.

∙∙∙∙∙∙

I was at home on my own when I started to feel nauseous. An inner voice told me to call my brother. The voice was insistent. When my brother answered the voice told me to say I was having a stroke, but I was unable to speak and my brother was about to hang up when I finally managed to shout my name. By the time he arrived at my house I had collapsed.

Afterwards he said that if I had called ten minutes later, he would already have left for work. For me it was a miracle from my guardian angel.

— *VIVIEN BARBOTEAU*

~ *Help with My Visa* ~

If I am in any sort of trouble the first thing I do is to ask the angels for help.

∙∙∙∙∙∙

We were on our way to Egypt for 11.11 and I needed an entry visa and was given one at Heathrow airport. I placed it carefully in my waistbag and zipped it up. In Cairo we stood in a queue to hand in our visas and to my horror, when I reached for mine it was missing. I searched my waistbag twice and looked in my handbag even though I knew I hadn't put it in there. There was no sign of it. "Oh help, angels. I really need help with this," I whispered. Then I added aloud to no one in particular, "I've lost my visa!" A woman standing behind me spoke up. "Oh, I was sent two by mistake," she said. "Here, you can have my spare one."

— *DIANA COOPER*

~ *Angels Help Find the Perfect Dress* ~

Angels love ceremonies and weddings, of course, are very special.

∙∙∙∙∙∙

My only child, Simon, was getting married and it was imperative that I looked nice on his special day. I spent many weeks looking for an outfit, but had no luck and began to panic. Simon said, "Mum, why don't you ask your angels to help?" So I asked them.

My friend mentioned that she knew of a shop that might suit. As I entered I saw an ice-blue dress with silver accessories. I loved it and it fitted me perfectly.

When I arrived home my neighbour asked to see my purchase. Lifting up the dress, she remarked, "What a lovely logo on the back." I looked and was amazed. Woven into the fabric was a pair of angel wings. Printed on the label were the words "Theme Angel". I realized the soft drapes of the dress resembled folded wings.

My son married in a church filled with over seventy angel statues and mouldings. We were surrounded and blessed by their presence during this sacred ceremony!

— *SUSAN VENUS*

~ Guardian Angels' Names ~

Angels take messages to and from God. Your guardian angel has a name, which is a vibration that helps you to connect. Knowing your angel's name helps personalize the relationship.

· · · · · ·

I have always believed in angels and quite regularly talk to my angel. Sometimes it is a simple "Good morning", or it can be a long conversation if something is troubling me. One night lying in bed I asked my angel for his name. As I settled into sleep I heard a voice say "Nicolas". I was surprised and got out of bed and checked the directory in the back of my Bible for that name. It described Nicolas as being a deacon, so I looked that up and it said "Messenger of God".

— *ANON*

~ The Wonder of My Guardian Angel ~

Here is a mesmerizing story of miracles and magic with a guardian angel.

· · · · · ·

My parents divorced when I was two, leaving my mom to raise two kids alone. I was a daydreamer with vast imagination. I believed in miracles and they happened almost daily in my young life. I could sense and hear my guardian angel. However, I needed to be the man of the house. I gave up my childhood and stopped daydreaming.

Fast forward and now I am twenty-two years old and working as a bartender. I met a regular who seemed familiar. I asked him what he wanted to drink, and he laughed and said "You'll learn." No matter what I asked him, he always answered "You'll learn."

He told me a story about a child who used to have an imagination, but gave it up to take care of his mother. He told me how this child had grown up and forgotten all he knew; shunned his power and forgot what his life purpose was.

The boy was visited by his guardian angel when he was in his twenties. The angel showed him miracles beyond human belief, restored the young man's faith and then saved the young man's life. He concluded that once these things had come to pass the angel left the man, because it was time to save another soul from a life of sadness.

All this time I was using drugs and partying all night. I had hit my lowest low when he showed up. He said "At this rate you have two weeks to live. You need to choose. Live or die, make the choice." He disappeared ... and that was the last time I saw him.

I chose life.

Years later I remembered the story and it hit me like a ton of bricks! Surely this was my guardian angel in the flesh. He came into my life, did all he said he would do, saved my life and then disappeared. I was amazed! Was this my guardian angel? I'll leave it to you to make your own call.

— *KEITH LEON*

~ Guardian Angels Communicate with Each Other ~

Miracles happen when your guardian angel talks to someone else's. However it is important to recognize that angels never condone driving too fast!

••••••

My husband and I were taking our son to Gatwick Airport. My husband was driving fast because we were fearful that our son would miss his flight. We didn't notice that we had entered a 50-mile-per-hour speed zone until we saw a sign saying UNMARKED POLICE CARS IN THIS AREA – and, yes, next thing I knew we were being pulled over. I asked our guardian angels to talk to the guardian angel of the police officer to ask them to be lenient, explain our mistake and let us go on our way.

My husband went to talk to the officer, and miraculously, got back in the car almost immediately. He had been let off with a warning. My son caught his flight and arrived safely.

— *ANGELA INWARD*

~ The First Time I Felt the Love of My Guardian Angel ~

If you are not meant to suffer your guardian angel will help you.

••••••

I had been married for six months and we had a lot of responsibility including a mortgage and bills to pay. I was in full-time employment during the day and was also working as a dancer at night.

One night my partner and I had had a row and I rushed out of our house in my pyjamas and jumped into my car.

It was raining heavily and as I raced down the road I took a corner too fast and felt myself losing control of the car. Suddenly it was as if the wheel had been taken from me and the car straightened up and all was fine. My heart pounded and I remember thinking, "I have a guardian angel who just saved me!"

— *ANGELA INWARD*

~ Learning from My Guardian Angel ~

Your guardian angel does look after you but you are expected to learn from what you do.

••••••

I enjoy adventurous pursuits and my guardian angel has always looked after me. When I was young my friends and I were playing at the edge of the forest when we decided to climb a high wall nearby. When we got to the top we saw a meadow.

I did not want to walk round the wall, and when I saw a rope hanging nearby I decided to swing down like Tarzan. As I caught the rope it snapped underneath my weight and I fell ten metres. My landing was gentle, though, and I knew that my guardian angel had caught me. I realized that although my angel saved me I needed to start taking responsibility for my actions.

— *MARTINA MARIA SERAPHINA KAMMERHOFER DCS*

~ Angels Calm the Elements ~

You can ask your angel to calm the weather – they can make your journey smoother.

* * * * * *

I travelled from Greece to Italy and back by ferry. On both journeys the sea was rough and most of our group felt seasick. We were about to make the same journey again and were afraid. I asked my guardian angel for a quiet journey.

Before our trip I checked the weather forecast: it indicated strong winds, but from the moment we boarded the boat until we arrived in Venice the sea was calm. No one felt seasick. It was the same on our return. I thanked my guardian angel wholeheartedly for his help.

— *DANIELA GABRIEL LEVENTOPOULOS*

CHAPTER 3

Angel Signs

Angels use many ways to remind us of their presence and to guide us. You can choose your own personal sign and ask the angels to herald their presence by using this. I love these examples that people have contributed. I hope this chapter inspires you to look for angelic messages in many different ways.

~ Trust the Signs ~

The angels constantly send us signs. Sometimes trusting is the difficult part.

· · · · · ·

Walking in the woods, I asked for a sign that a project was going forward. In that instant I saw a rainbow. I said, "But it has been raining, so you'd expect to see a rainbow anyway." The rainbow brightened as if a light had been turned on and then a second one appeared. That's more like it, I thought, but I would like something more definite. At that thought, pink clouds appeared in the tops of the trees in just one section of the woods. "Is that meant to be a sign?" I demanded, whereupon the pink clouds vanished and then reappeared in a different section of the woods. "Well, give me just one more sign to be certain," I pleaded. "Something like a white horse or a unicorn." At that I saw, with my third eye, a pure white stag. All deer are about trust so I laughed. The following morning, in the field by the woods there stood a pure white horse. I have never seen one there before or since.

DIANA COOPER

~ Angel Book ~

Sometimes our connection with angels is triggered by something someone says. There are also many books on angels that will enable you to learn how to forge your connection.

· · · · · ·

It was one of my lovely sisters who told me that we all have a guardian angel. I started to communicate with my personal angel. Sometimes I woke up in the middle of the night and saw movement in the room, and my sister would say that I seemed to have made contact.

I was in a bookstore one day and felt led to the spiritual section, where I found and bought Diana Cooper's book *A Little Light on Angels*.

From then on my life changed. The angels have helped me to heal my life and now I am starting to understand who I am.

— *SYLVIA STEIN*

~ *Angels at the Hairdressers* ~

I smile at the thought of the angels blessing Kari's hair when she washed it.

• • • • • •

I was at the hairdressers the other day and the hairdresser was so sweet and helpful. As my hair was dry, I asked her if she could recommend a good conditioner. She went over to the shelves and chose a pink bottle. I paid and went home; and imagine my enchantment and pleasure when I read the name on the bottle: "Angel Rinse!"

— *KARI NYGARD DCS*

~ *Heart-Shaped Pebbles* ~

Look for ways of setting signs that have significance for you.

• • • • • •

My angel group was discussing angel signs and I told them how they could set their own sign for the angels to communicate. One student set her sign as heart-shaped pebbles as she lives near a beach. A few weeks later she had a gift for me – a beautiful heart-shaped pebble.

She had been on the beach and asked the angels to help her find them for people who she loved. She opened her eyes and saw this pebble.

— *SUSIE*

~ *A Loving Heart in the Snow* ~

Automatic writing is a wonderful way to connect with the angels.

• • • • • •

I connect with angels using automatic writing – they send me messages, which I write down during my meditations. One winter we had heavy snow where I live in Germany and my husband discovered a bare spot on our otherwise snow-covered terrace in the shape of a "snow heart". My angel Samuel wrote that this was his loving sign for me and from then on he signed our correspondence with the words "Your loving 'snow heart' Samuel!" How fabulous was that!

— *CAROLINE*

~ *Snow Heart* ~

The angels will use any medium they can in which to leave messages.

• • • • • •

I was living in Lake Tahoe, Nevada and was going through a challenging and depressing time. One winter day I was slogging along in knee-deep pristine snow with my dog. I was alternately praying and crying, but my dog was having great fun in the snow.

As I stopped to pat him, I saw a perfect 18-inch heart "carved" out of the snow. I felt loved, protected and more peaceful than I had felt in days. There were no footprints around and I knew the angels were showing me that they were there for me.

My tears were now tears of joy. I fell to my knees, laughed, gave thanks and felt so blessed. In a second I was transformed, thanks to the message from the angels. I am still moved to tears when I recall the memory.

— *CATHERINE*

ANGEL CLOUDS

ANGEL CLOUDS form where an angel has rested in the sky. Condensation forms round their high frequency, leaving their impression for all to see. Keep looking up!

~ *Angel in the Sky* ~

The next two stories illustrate these angel clouds beautifully.

•••••••

I went down to Provence for the New Year. On New Year's Eve we sat under the trees in the village square drinking coffee. I picked up a leaf and wrote what I would like for the coming year – to bring love, light and hope to others through the angels and to practise harmlessness to all sentient beings.

Later we went for a walk into the mountains. I asked Beauty, my angel, to come with me and enjoy it. I looked up and there was a beautiful angel-shaped cloud above us. What a wonderful moment.

— *SUSIE COOPER*

~ *Angel Clouds* ~

I was out walking one day, feeling the weight of the world on my shoulders as I wrestled with some problems in my life. As I looked up at the sky I saw that there were some clouds shaped like an angel. I instantly felt better, knowing that I was being looked after.

— *MARGO GRUNDY DCS*

~ *Winged Pink Cloud* ~

Pink is the colour of love.

•••••••

The most significant way in which the angels show me their presence is through "angel clouds". They come as messages of reassurance and in answer to my questions, or prior to a dramatic life event. Sometimes they also appear on more ordinary days, just to let me know they are there.

After asking for help at a particularly difficult time, I saw a pink angel cloud with wings, about eighteen feet tall, above my house.

— *SUE*

~ A Healing Sunset ~

When you need healing or inspiration, remember to look up to the clouds to receive angelic messages.

••••••

A group of healers and I gave healing to a friend of ours who had cancer. The healing was powerful and we could feel the presence of angels. Afterwards when I went for a walk I felt very thankful, as I could still feel their presence.

I saw the most spectacular sunset! The sky changed to pink and one after the other the clouds changed shape until they all looked like angels. My heart called out "Thank you" and then all the clouds joined together into the shape of a big heart.

— *WENCHE MILAS*

~ A Joyful Sign ~

This is a reminder of the importance of dedicating some time each day to a spiritual practice.

••••••

When I was "introduced" to angels it was life-changing. I felt inspired about the future and could not wait to start my "new life" with the angels. Despite this I still needed to search for "evidence". I looked so hard for feathers that I would almost have plucked one out of a bird! I believed it would take several years before I was worthy enough for the angels to show themselves to me – and then one day I realized the meaning of those magic words: divine timing.

In my meditation room I had a special corner in which I kept a hanging curtain and a candle. One morning I came in to see that my curtain was bathed in light – my candle was burning by itself. It lit up the whole curtain! I was overjoyed; tears came to my eyes as I realized that this was my sign from the angels.

I was worthy after all – we all are!

Angel – THANK YOU, THANK YOU, and THANK YOU.

— *MARIET*

~ Angelic Om ~

Om (or ohm) is the sound of creation, sung by the seraphim round the Godhead. It is a sacred sound and it raises the frequency of everyone and everything when it is sung. It is used in meditation to raise consciousness and focus our concentration.

••••••

I had just come out of personal therapy feeling good about myself and was walking towards the Underground thinking, "I need to meditate or do something to keep myself 'centred', but I'm not quite sure if I'm doing it right."

I got on the tube and sitting in front of me was a boy with a huge O.H.M. written in felt tip on his hand. There was my answer. Thank you angels.

— *CAROLINE FRANKS*

~ A Removal Van with Meaning ~

The angels will draw your attention to words on hoardings, vans, in the newspaper, on a T-shirt, a book – anywhere – to answer your questions or inspire you. Keep looking!

● ● ● ● ● ●

I was sitting at traffic lights on a busy road near my home, contemplating life. I was worried and stressed, and asked for a sign that angels were with me. As I drove off I saw the lettering on a large removal van – it said WE WON'T LET YOU DOWN! I had to laugh – that was indeed a sign.

— *ANGELA CUMMISKEY DCS*

~ Ask and It Shall Be Given ~

What clearer sign than a little angel statue?

● ● ● ● ● ●

During a horrendously stressful period I prayed a lot that God would send an angel to take me away, as all I wanted was to end this life. At the time I worked as a reflexologist and on one occasion my last patient of the day was a lovely little boy. I noticed he was carrying a small parcel and when I looked at it I knew exactly what it was. He had brought me the angel I had prayed for that morning!

I laughed and knew the angels were working with me. I thanked the boy for his present. From then on, I found feathers everywhere. Some evenings I would feel someone stroking my head. Then a man came into my life and I knew he was sent to me by the angels as, on our first date, he stroked my head! We are now married and have been together for ten years.

— *COLLEEN KERR*

~ It's All in the Name ~

Susie was really determined to get the right message. The angels gave her an unmissable sign that she should train with our School.

● ● ● ● ● ●

I had been fascinated by angels for a long time. I had information about various angel training courses but couldn't decide which one to choose.

Driving home, I asked the angels to send me a sign. I was sitting at traffic lights as I did so and noticed that there was a shop on my right. As I continued towards home, a voice in my head said, "Remember that when you ask for a sign you need to be aware that the answer can come in a variety of ways!" I started to think, "What have I just seen as I sat at those lights?" I went back to the traffic lights.

I looked at the shop properly and its name, written in golden letters, was "Coopers". As a centrepiece, it had a golden lectern in the shape of an angel! It was such a clear message that I immediately booked my place on the DCS training course. The angels continued to support me, including helping to find the course fees. Angels continue to support me to this day.

— *SUSAN RUDD DCS*

~ A Pair of Angels ~

This is a poignant story of angels expressing sympathy for a couple separated by an illness.

· · · · · ·

My wife was admitted to a psychiatric hospital suffering from advanced vascular dementia. It came on very suddenly and she deteriorated very quickly and was barely functioning. At home we have a mirror in our entrance hall with two terracotta angels on either side. I came home from work one day and found one of the angels on the floor, broken.

The strange thing is that the screw and the hole in the back of the angelic wing were both still intact, so neither could have caused the angel to fall and break.

— *ANON*

~ Angel from a Father ~

And here is a wonderful story to remind us of oneness.

· · · · · ·

Two years ago I was made redundant and I saw in it an opportunity to work as a healer. My father (who was a vicar) and I used to joke about his angels and my angels, although we both know really that they are one and the same.

One day he said, "I have something for you" and gave me the most beautiful blanket with an image of an angel with its wings outspread. My parents had bought the blanket in Jerusalem many years ago.

He told me, "Here's one of my angels to work with your angels." I use this blanket in my healing room.

— *SARAH*

~ Always with Me ~

Angels remind us of their presence in many ways. It is especially beautiful when they leave an impression of their special fragrance.

· · · · · ·

Angels are always giving me hints and reminders of their presence. Sometimes it is an inexplicable fragrance, or a book will drop off the shelf in front of me, or lights flicker: many, many little ways – I often think they have quite a sense of humour. I know though that they are always looking out for my best interest.

— *ALICIA*

ANGEL FEATHERS

ANGELS OFTEN LEAVE a little white feather to let people know that they are near. You can find them anywhere: in sealed cars, sitting on a doorstep, in a gale when everything else is getting blown away … Sometimes the angels bring lots of feathers, if that is what you need.

~ Exercise Class ~

When we know the angels are with us and supporting us it gives us strength and energy to continue.

......

I came home from work in the snow, cleared it from the driveway and dragged myself, exhausted, to my regular exercise class. I was lying on the floor concentrating on lifting my tired legs up and down as the instructor counted 19, 20 … I saw, to my amazement, something swirling upwards in the air just above my feet. A tiny feather!! Wow, talk about being blessed. That gave me energy and my legs felt fine again.

— *KARI NYGARD DCS*

~ A Timely Feather ~

I smiled when I read this story.

......

Brian, my nephew, and his wife were watching TV and a lady was talking about angels. Brian is a macho man. He stated, "The angel lady on TV made sense, until she mentioned they leave you feathers – now that's rubbish!"

As he said it, a feather floated down between him and his wife. He exclaimed, "I BELIEVE, I BELIEVE."

— *MARGARET GRUNDY DCS*

~ How Did That Get There? ~

Sometimes the angels just want to remind you they are there.

......

A weird thing happened one day. I got up, dressed and drove to work, ate breakfast in the canteen and then went to the bathroom. To my surprise, caught in my zipper was a white feather. I couldn't believe it – it had not been there when I got dressed. There was just no logical explanation for it being there. I have always believed in God and angels and knew that this was a sign.

— *ROZ JORDAN*

~ White Feathers in Unlikely Places ~

I have had this experience too, where a little white feather seems to be stuck in an impossible place or windy conditions, determined to attract your attention.

......

As I was walking on the beach trying to find a quiet space to contemplate my life, I looked down and saw a white feather that seemed to be stuck to the path.

Even more exciting was when, today, I got in the car to take a short journey. I looked up and saw a small white feather on the side mirror. It had been raining but, rather than washing the feather away, the rainwater seemed to be holding it to the mirror. Definite signs!

— *HILARY ALEXANDER*

~ Not to Worry ~

Here is an example of a feather from an angel taking someone's worry away. This allows the new to come in.

· · · · · ·

I always feel that angels are with me, and if I'm having a sad time or feeling a bit down I talk to them and ask for signs that they are near. Last week I was coming out of the bank, a bit stressed and worried about money, and as I looked up a little white feather dropped onto my shoulder and I knew that I was being looked after and not to worry.

— *ELIZABETH FINEGAN*

~ A Special Encounter ~

Angels choose their timing carefully when they are placing feathers.

· · · · · ·

Diana Cooper and her friend came into my shop and bought some jewellery. After she left I felt a sudden warmth around me and I had the best day's trading in weeks. I decided to look at her website and was fascinated.

When I got home I found a white feather that had not been there before. It was so strange – I'd just watched the clip on Diana's website about white feathers.

— *COLIN CARTER*

~ Always There ~

Angels are with us all the time, even when we're doing the most mundane tasks.

· · · · · ·

My sixteen-year-old had had a party just before Christmas. After all the guests had left I started clearing away and I was sweeping the floor when I noticed a white feather floating in the air. I realized that the angels were there for the youngsters and me. I felt pleased and blessed and said thank you to them.

— *KARI NYGARD DCS*

~ Floating Feather of Joy ~

Sometimes you just cannot miss the fact that the angels are drawing your attention to their message and the wonderful feeling they bring you.

· · · · · ·

I was trying to write a difficult and heartfelt letter: I had decided to turn down a job offer. As I struggled to find the right words I became aware of a flickering white light above my left shoulder. I turned and saw the tiniest of white feathers.

There were sensations of pure joy sweeping up and down my body. The feather floated upwards until it reached the ceiling and vanished. My eyes welled up and tears began to flow.

— *DAVID MILLS*

~ Laptop Feather ~

Yes, the angels help us with our computers too!

• • • • • •

I found a little feather under my laptop station. How it got there I don't know – but maybe the angels do! Just a little sign from them to let me know they are around.

— *KARALENA MACKINLAY DCS*

~ Car Park Feather ~

Look wherever you go, for the angels may be trying to tell you they are there.

• • • • • •

One evening I was going out for a Chinese takeaway. When I pulled into the car park and came to a stop, to my surprise there was a large white feather on the ground in front of my car. I picked it up and had such a warm fuzzy feeling. I knew this was a sign from the angels.

— *ANON*

~ Angels in a Bookshop ~

I love this story, which demonstrates how tirelessly the angels will work to draw our attention to something or to offer proof.

• • • • • •

I was walking round a bookshop when a book fell from a shelf and landed at my feet. It was *A Little Light on Angels*. I purchased the book. Shortly afterwards my husband and I attended an evening with Diana Cooper.

On the way back I asked my husband what he thought. He said it was interesting but would be more convinced if a white feather appeared in a place where you would not usually see one.

Next morning he walked into our kitchen to find the most beautiful white feather lying in the middle of the floor. He's now convinced!

— *GLYNIS*

~ A Feather for Courage ~

We have all had to do or say something that takes courage. The angels will help us.

• • • • • •

My friend and I wanted to change our lives, and thought a new business would be a good idea. After careful thought, though, my husband and I realized it wouldn't work. I was worried about how my friend would feel, so I bought her some flowers and went to visit her. I wondered how to begin. Then, floating down from nowhere came a huge, fluffy, white feather. That was my cue! The angels were saying: "Now!" I blurted out that I had changed my mind. She understood and said it was absolutely fine. There is absolutely nowhere that feather could have come from, other than the angels!

— *WENDY STANLEY DCS*

~ Cough Medicine ~

It is no surprise that they gave Truda a little white feather to tell her she had the right medicine!

⁕ ⁕ ⁕ ⁕ ⁕ ⁕

Truda was going to visit her friend Heather but before she left home they talked on the phone and Truda said that her husband Terry had a cough. Heather told her to get a particular cough medicine and added jokingly, "I'm not going to let you into my flat until you've got it." So Truda went to the shops and found the right brand. As she walked out of the chemist a little white feather landed on her hand.

— *TOLD TO DIANA COOPER*

~ You Are Not Alone ~

We are never alone but sometimes it takes a nudge from the angels to remind us!

⁕ ⁕ ⁕ ⁕ ⁕ ⁕

I was given an angel pin by a friend. The card accompanying it said "Hang in there." I was going through difficult times but this made me realize that I do have support, even if sometimes I feel I am doing everything by myself. Later on my way home a little white feather floated down from the sky; I said "Thank you." I now know for sure that I'm not alone: the angels, as well as my friends, are there for me.

— *ANON*

~ Archangel Metatron's Feather ~

It is not just our angels who give us feathers but archangels and unicorns too. I was delighted to receive this feather from Archangel Metatron.

⁕ ⁕ ⁕ ⁕ ⁕ ⁕

We had private access to the Luxor pyramid on the evening of 10 November 2011 in preparation for 11.11. We did a powerful meditation to fill the temple with light and chanted, toned, sang and prayed.

At the end I walked in silence through the temple and mentally asked Metatron, had we done enough? Instantly a white feather fell down in front of me like a stone. It landed by my foot and everyone around saw it. I knew Metatron was telling me we had raised the energy and done well.

— *DIANA COOPER*

~ A Ring of Feathers ~

Sometimes one feather is not enough to give us the nudge we need.

⁕ ⁕ ⁕ ⁕ ⁕ ⁕

I was having a stressful time at my job, which I had wanted to leave for some time. The decision was difficult as I had a good wage and pension, but I was unhappy. As I walked to work I was deep in thought about this dilemma when I found myself standing in a ring of white feathers, large and small.

I felt completely at ease and knew that I must leave my job and do what I had always wanted to do – holistic therapies. This was a sign from the angels. I went in to work and typed my resignation. It was the best decision I've ever made and it was thanks to the angels.

— *ESTHER*

~ *Feathers and Your Angel's Name* ~

Cool angels!

* * * * * *

I have always believed in angels and felt protected and helped by them, but have never experienced anything physically "real" from them. The morning after attending an angel workshop, I was walking to work and what should come falling toward my head, but a small white feather. I caught it as it fell and heard my angel's name. Pretty cool.

— *DARREN*

~ *A Rain of Feathers* ~

And sometimes a rain of feathers falls!

* * * * * *

Before leaving for the school where the workshop I was running was to be held, I connected with angels and said a prayer. As I stepped out of my front door several white feathers were scattered over me, although there were no birds to be seen in the vicinity.

— *MARJETKA NOVAK DCS*

~ *White Feathers* ~

If you know the angels have used a bird to bring feathers to you, thank and bless the bird.

* * * * * *

Recently I have been a bit low while waiting and hoping for a new romance. On my front lawn there were so many white feathers. I felt truly blessed by this message. Thank you angels.

— *ALISON BENSTEAD*

~ *A Sisterly Message* ~

Here the angels send feathers twice for comfort and reassurance.

* * * * * *

My sister Frances died after a hard-fought battle with cancer. She had a husband and two young children. All the family went up to stay with them the day before the funeral.

The house was full and chaotic and I needed to find a quiet place. I went to the bathroom to be alone and found my other sister already in there. We had a quiet chat and talked about our feelings. She told me that the day before she was feeling sad when she noticed a tiny white feather in front of her. She felt this was a message from Frances to say "I'm OK." As she was telling me this another tiny white feather gently floated down!

— *ANON*

~ Surrounded by White Feathers ~

When we are in need, the angels will do all they can to remind us of their presence.

• • • • • •

Driving home from work one day with a million things on my mind, I felt stressed and unsupported. A friend told me that she had found a white feather and that she knew the angels were with her.

As I parked and got out of my car I thought to myself, "How come I've yet to see a white feather? Everyone else sees them!" I glanced back at the car – and couldn't believe my eyes. I had driven into a huge circle of white feathers. They were lying all round my car, although there wasn't a bird to be seen! Even stranger, I looked again and they had disappeared.

— *KARIN FINEGAN DCS*

~ Comfort and Support ~

The angels will always find a way to reassure and comfort you when you are in distress.

• • • • • •

It was the eve of the inquest into my father's death and I was dreading it. My siblings came over to comfort me and make sure I was coping. I went into the bathroom and the toilet lid was down. I lifted it up to find a long feather in the bottom of the bowl. The window was closed – how did the feather get there? I raced downstairs to ask if anyone had put a feather down the toilet. The answer was a resounding no! I just knew it was put there by the angels to assure me that all would be well.

The day of the inquest, although emotional, went better than I'd expected. Thank you angels.

— *ZOE LOUISE HODGKINSON*

~ Proof of Angels ~

Ask and they will give you proof!

• • • • • •

As an angel teacher I taught students that white feathers are a sign that angels are around. I never usually felt the need to ask for proof of their existence; however one day I did, and asked for a sign. Next morning my husband said, "You had better come and see this." The back garden was full of white feathers; I had never seen so many before or since. Thank you angels!

— *BARBARA HOWARD DCS*

~ A Car Feather ~

The angels love to reassure us and it really helps if we just accept the message and relax.

••••••

I was leaving home for an important meeting and I was very anxious about it. When I got in my car to go, I saw a small white feather in the middle of the windscreen. I was so pleased as I knew then that this was a sign, to let me know that the meeting was going to go well.

— *ANON*

ANGELS AND RAINBOWS

RAINBOWS are a message of hope and promise from the universe. It is the energy of the leap of the heart as you see one that allows the angels to open new doors and arrange something good for you.

~ Rainbow Inspiration ~

When you see a rainbow you know angelic energy has placed it there.

••••••

While I was on holiday with my sister in London, the angels arranged an amazing excursion for me to Stonehenge, Glastonbury and Avebury. As we returned to London we hit peak-hour traffic but the angels provided a beautiful rainbow for us. It reminded us of their presence even in a busy city. It was one of my most wonderful holidays ever.

— *LILA NORVAL DCS*

~ A Double Rainbow – and a Double Sign ~

When angels give you a sign and then add a rainbow, you are doubly blessed.

••••••

I attended a "2012" teaching course. We were asked to go into the garden to select a stone and I found one with dark gray spots. As we meditated in a circle the stones were placed in the centre and at the end we picked up the stones to tune into the "love energies" they were now charged with. The dark spots on my stone had formed into the shape of an angel. Full of gratitude, I thanked the angels for the sign.

Then we saw the most powerful double rainbow. We thanked the angels for this beautiful vision and left the course with a feeling that something beautiful would happen in 2012.

— *WENCHE MILAS*

~ Triple Rainbow ~

Rainbows reflect the colours of the archangels and are used to radiate light and energy. They offer hope and promise.

I first spoke to my guardian angel after I had separated from my husband. Just before I went to court for the financial settlement, where my ex was contesting my keeping my home, I saw a very strong, bright triple rainbow over my home. I took this as a sign from the angels that I would keep my home. My ex agreed minutes before we went in to see the judge. The rainbow is now my spiritual sign. I have since seen an upside-down rainbow, which was to me a sign of hope for the future.

— *ALISON BENSTEAD*

~ Rainbows of All Sizes ~

The angels respond to a warm greeting with opening up a new golden opportunity.

∙∙∙∙∙∙∙

I was on a long drive for work when I noticed a tiny rainbow in the distance. I said "Hello angels" and then turned a corner. To my amazement, the tiny rainbow had grown into a full, double rainbow! Its colours were so strong against the dark sky, it was breathtaking. I pulled over as soon as I could to admire the rainbow even more. I thanked the angels for their wonderful message and carried their light with me for the rest of the day.

— *CHERYL*

~ Seven Rainbows of Love ~

Seven is a spiritual number: when you see seven of anything it is a lucky sign.

∙∙∙∙∙∙∙

I was driving home to Scotland with my daughter after a trip to see family. After a really difficult and challenging five years, we felt like we were finally coming home to start a new life. We felt happy as we talked about the future. Then we saw seven rainbows! The angels were letting us know that everything would be all right. They were right – life is getting better for us. We will always remember that day and we thank the angels for their beautiful message.

— *SEONAD*

~ Rainbow Magic ~

Angels fly because they take things lightly.

∙∙∙∙∙∙∙

I used to talk to angels. I could hear their comments and also their advice. It was such a privilege. One day, there was a group of angels round me so I asked them "Do you never laugh or smile? Are you all always so serious?"

One said, "Not always. Yes we do ..." Another one said, "Yes, we do smile and laugh, yes ..."

At the end of the day my husband and I went outside to see the sunset. Suddenly, he pointed to the sky and said, "Look, a rainbow." It was the most perfect rainbow I have ever seen. For me it is clear: each time an angel smiles, the sky shows it as a rainbow. I am so grateful for this.

— *BEATRIZ BOYSEN*

ANGELS WORKING THROUGH NAMES AND NUMBERS

THE ANCIENTS recognized that every number works on a frequency that affects people, situations and events. This is why the date of your birth has such an impact on your life. Because each letter is connected to a number, your name also has a vibration, which calls your soul mission forward when it is spoken.

Naturally the angels use numbers to give you messages or draw things to your attention. Master numbers are particularly significant and the energy is enhanced if they are tripled.

- 11 is about taking mastery of your life, for then it is time to take responsibility for all the situations and relationships in your life and change them if you wish to.
- 22 is the master builder. Build on a solid foundation to co-create the life you want. Hold your vision and ask the angels to help you manifest it.
- 33 is the number of the Christ consciousness, so if you see this number make sure you work with the Christ light of unconditional love.
- 44 is the number of Golden Atlantis. Bring the energy of that era into your life and live as they did in the fifth dimension.
- 55 is Metatron's vibration, so attune to him and rise above worldly attitudes, working for higher enlightenment.
- 66 reminds you that you are a cosmic being and can influence the heavens.
- 77 is the vibration of Heaven, so connect with the angelic realms.
- 88 is the vibration of your I AM Presence or Monad, so be who you truly are.
- 99 means you have mastered the lessons of Earth.

~ Number Plates ~

111 is about taking responsibility and accepting the opportunity to begin again, a level higher.

••••••

I've noticed that when I'm driving I constantly see the number 111 on car number plates. For me it is a confirmation and a sign that angels are with me.

— *GILLIAN WEBSTER*

~ Angels at the Bank ~

1133 means moving to a higher level and acting with love, so for this lady it was an opening to abundance consciousness.

••••••

As I was paying a bill at the bank I noticed the price was a special number – 1133. It was a special message from the angels. I said, "Thank you for being with me, angels, even as I pay my bills." This was an eye-opener that let me pay with pleasure!

— *KARI NYGARD DCS*

~ A Solid Foundation ~

22 reminds you to build a strong foundation. This may be for a business or relationship – or whatever you are creating.

· · · · · ·

For the last few years the angels have been communicating with me through numbers. I constantly see 22 or 22:22, as well as 11:11. Whenever I look at a digital clock it seems to be a double number.

Recently I met someone with whom I sensed a strong soul connection, so I asked the angels for help in opening our hearts in love and compassion and in helping me find a way to initiate a conversation. Just then a white feather floated down.

I got on the bus, looked out the window and saw two number 22 buses and a beautiful rainbow in the sky! I took this as a sign that the angels are with me and doing what they can to help.

— *VEEVEE*

~ Angelic Numbers ~

When we understand and pay attention to numbers we can be truly inspired, as this story illustrates.

· · · · · ·

Just before Christmas, I popped into the post office to buy stamps. I took my queue ticket and was delighted when I saw the number:111. I felt blessed by the angels' presence.

On Christmas Day I woke up and looked at the alarm clock and it was 11.22. That was special for me and brought a big smile to my face.

— *KARI NYGARD DCS*

~ Numbers Can Guide Our Destiny ~

Trust the guidance and take action!

· · · · · ·

I woke up from a vivid dream with the numbers 882 in my head. The definition of 882 was "As one door is closing another door is opening. Trust your intuition to maintain steady abundance at this time."

This made perfect sense as I was looking for additional ways to support myself financially.

Acting on my intuition I rented my beauty-salon space to another therapist. When it was time for me to let go of my business she took over the lease. It always amazes me how everything works out perfectly when we trust in angelic guidance.

— *JILL WEBSTER DCS*

~ *The Power of Three* ~

The angels often present opportunities to us three times.

······

I saw an advert for an angel workshop but didn't go. A few months later I saw another one advertised; again I didn't go. Then I saw an advert for a Diana Cooper workshop and knew I didn't want to miss another opportunity. I am so happy that I attended; it has become such a great passion for me, and the love I feel for and receive from angels is amazing.

— *MARGO GRUNDY DCS*

~ *Special Meaning* ~

777 is a very spiritual number.

······

I feel like I'm in my very own *Celestine Prophecy*! I have been asking the angels for help with building up my business and one day I found myself in a shop that I don't often go in. The owner started telling me about lots of networking opportunities. I left the shop and saw a car approaching with 777 on the number plate. Then I saw another one with the same number. In my numerology bible the number 777 means "Congratulations, you are on a roll. Keep up the good work. Expect more miracles to occur."

I asked for confirmation (I trust when I get a message three times that they mean business!). As I drove home another car approached with the number plate 777.

The angels whispered, "End the struggle and dance with life." ...Wheeee!

— *JILL WEBSTER DCS*

~ *Archangel Gabriel's Confirmation* ~

Angels use technology to let you know if something is right. Here Archangel Gabriel rings the phone three times. Three is a spiritual number.

······

I went up Mount Shasta with a group from the Diana Cooper School. The leader asked me to facilitate a chant to bring in Archangel Gabriel, but the energy in that particular place felt wrong, so I declined.

Then guilt set in! Was I letting the group down? Even worse, was I letting down Archangel Gabriel?

We travelled further up the mountain. When we stopped I realized that this was the perfect place to connect with Archangel Gabriel. As I did so, my phone gave three rings. It had been completely dead since we arrived! I knew it was Archangel Gabriel agreeing that this was where I must make the invocations.

We all experienced the most beautiful and profound energy. When I finished the phone gave three more rings and I knew it was Archangel Gabriel thanking me for my work.

— *ROSEMARY STEPHENSON DCS*

ANGEL NAMES

~ Archangel Michael Comes Through ~

However challenging things have been Michael is always prepared to help us change.

．．．．．．

The magic of Archangel Michael helps me and I am glad. Every February I have a trip that I dread – a very difficult client group have to be pleased. This year I decided to take my Archangel Michael cards along to give me courage.

As the plane landed I started noticing the numbers 11, 111 1101 ... wherever I looked. Archangel Michael appeared, surrounded by lots of blue colour. This was my cue. I picked my card and it said GOD IS IN CHARGE. I almost cried with gratitude. My client could not find a single fault with the event.

Three Blue Cheers to Archangel Michael!

— *SMITA RAGHANI*

~ Repeated Signs ~

Always look at the signs on vehicles. There may just be a message for you!

．．．．．．

Birinder is a good friend of mine. She wanted to see me and said to the angels, "Remind me to call Diana as I keep forgetting!"

Next day she saw a van parked outside her house with the sign D COOPER on it. The following week she saw three vans in a row with the same name on them. She got the message! That evening she phoned me and left a message saying, "When are you in Yorkshire? I'd like to see you."

I phoned back and said, "I'm coming up tomorrow!" We were able to meet for dinner and had a wonderful evening together. Thanks angels.

— *DIANA COOPER*

~ The Written Word ~

The answer is in the name!

．．．．．．

One day I was feeling a bit low so went out for a walk with my dogs. As we walked round the block I saw a paperback book lying on the pavement. I picked it up and saw that the title of the book was *Angel*.

— *PENNY WING DCS*

~ Gabriel Helps ~

Look out for the name of the person who helps you. It is often a sign – the angels will always endeavour to send the right person.

．．．．．．

My husband and I had to go to the garage to sort out some paperwork with regards to our car loan; I was concerned that we would not get the result we wanted so I asked the angels for help. When we reached the garage the assistant walked up to us and I noticed his name badge said GABRIEL – it goes without saying that he was really helpful and all ended well.

— *PENNY WING DCS*

~ Michael ~

The great protector angel, Michael, sends his namesakes flying to bless you with angel protection.

The angels have given me many signs to reassure me that they are always there to help guide and protect us. I don't enjoy flying and the last time I had to, I asked my guardian angel to hold my hand. I also asked Archangel Michael to protect everyone on the plane and mentally asked if Michael was with us. At that moment the flight attendant offered me a drink. I turned to look at him and my eyes were drawn to his name-tag: it said MICHAEL!

— *SYLVIA STEIN*

~ Ask and There Will Be a Sign ~

Whatever your intentions or fears, if you think about angels or even just the word "angel", they will do their best to light you up and help you.

• • • • • •

I ask the angels for protection when I am travelling, particularly when I have to fly. As I took my seat for a short flight I sent up a little prayer to the angels, and when I sat down I noticed that the lady beside me was reading a book called *Angels*.

— *KARI NYGARD DCS*

~ The Name of an Angel ~

If you ask for a sign the angels will send you an "angel" in some form!

• • • • • •

It was a quiet day in the café I owned and I was worried about business. I said to the angels, "Please send me a sign that this will get better." Later a lovely woman came in and ordered lunch. She had been before and returned because there was nothing like it in town. The food and customer service were great, she said, and she loved the décor.

I remember thinking how wonderful and thanked the angels for sending her to me. I asked her name and she said it was Angel! What a wonderful sign.

— *KARIN FINEGAN DCS*

CHAPTER 4

Angel Wake-Up Calls

The year 2012 marked the end of a 260,000-year cosmic era and new high-frequency energies started to come into our planet. It is the end of the old and the start of a new spiritual way of being. Many who have been psychically asleep have started to wake up to an understanding of the angelic worlds beyond our physical one, some gently and others in a more dramatic way. The angels also send us experiences to wake us if we are sleepwalking into the wrong relationship, job or pathway.

~ Your Life Will Never Be the Same Again ~

Here is a story about the most beautiful way one man met the angels and woke up to the angelic worlds.

······

It was a beautiful spring morning. I awoke from my sleep and heard a gentle voice say, "Jason, your life will never be the same again." I looked round and saw stars of silver around my room. I was in shock; I hadn't expected anything like this to happen – but I sensed sadness and joy at the same time.

As I was eating breakfast I saw a transparent being. The more I looked the more clearly I saw that this being was beautiful as the colours of the sun's rays. Then it vanished.

Little did I know I was to see many things from the heavenly realm – and to this day I continue to see wonderful beings. From that day my spiritual awareness has grown so much that now I simply accept it.

— *JASON LAMBE*

~ Wonderful Vision ~

Moments such as these truly are life-changing.

······

I will share a moment that changed my life. One day in 2007, I was woken in the early hours of the morning. There beside my bed were two angels holding hands and smiling. I was in tears looking at these amazing beings that emanated so much love. They presented themselves in angelic golden sparkly lights. It is a moment that has changed my life for ever.

— *ANON*

~ A Stroke ~

Our souls sometimes agree to a health challenge as a wake-up call.

• • • • • •

There had been many attempts to wake me up and this was my final call. I had a stroke in 2008 and was severely paralyzed. I called in Archangel Michael and Archangel Raphael to stay with me through this ordeal.

I called my husband to come quickly with an ambulance. I got to the hospital in time for the doctors to administer the TPA drug that removed all the paralysis. The nurses and doctors call me the Miracle Lady blessed by God.

Until then I was a workaholic and never put myself first. The doctors said that I would be unable to return to my previous job. This was my wake-up call to start doing what I came here to do.

— *DEB HAACK*

~ A Little Light on Angels ~

The angels can connect to you through a book.

• • • • • •

I attended an evening workshop facilitated by a friend. One of the attendees had with her a book that radiated such energy. It was *A Little Light on Angels* by Diana Cooper.

I bought it and as I read it, it was like a window had opened and sunlight poured in. It was a revelation!

My husband read the book and felt the same. We thanked the angels and welcomed them into our life. The next morning, under our bed was a mass of little white feathers. We were overjoyed. The angels were truly with us. I collected up the feathers and I still have them in a little pouch.

That was the beginning of a most wonderful journey.

— *CAROL DEAKIN DCS*

~ Call to Awakening ~

Occasionally the angels come in themselves to wake us up.

• • • • • •

I received an angelic wake-up call. My life was predictable and safe and I knew there was something missing. In the early hours of one morning, I slipped into an altered state of awareness. I felt myself rising towards Heaven, with two angels either side of me. I remained unquestioning, feeling safe and unconditionally loved. I found myself standing with my two companions in a beautiful hall, surrounded by wonderful paintings covering the walls and ceilings.

Nothing was spoken in this place; yet I understood everything I was meant to understand. My shining companions impressed upon me that this was a holding place where great beauty originated. It was crafted by heavenly hearts and "hands" and waited for a suitable channel into the world. They told me I would be given something from this sacred place.

I was shown a super-fast flash of the way that my life was about to unfold and evolve. When I awoke I knew that life had to change and starting on that day, I turned my life around.

— *DIANE HALL*

~ Get Up and Write ~

Listening to and acting on our intuitive guidance can open new doors.

••••••

I began to meditate but the answers to my questions still weren't entirely clear. Then I heard a voice in my head saying, "Get up and write" and so I did. It felt like the most natural thing in the world to do.

Once we are fortunate enough to be guided so lovingly, all we have to do is hear the call and begin to walk the path that has been lovingly prepared for us. All love and gratitude to the heavenly beings and divine, angelic messengers who inspire all earthly treasures ...

— *DIANE HALL*

~ The Beginning ~

Being attuned to reiki often starts people on their spiritual journey.

••••••

Reiki started my spiritual journey. The day I took my reiki master attunement my daughter came to my house to ask my reiki master if she knew any angel teachers as she wanted to attend an angel workshop. "Yes," she replied, "There is a woman called Mildred Ryan who's a great angel teacher." Talk about a divine plan – I had met Mildred and still had her number.

I telephoned Mildred and asked for information about angel workshops for my daughter. I was going to Dublin the next weekend and Mildred said she would meet us and give me information. That was in March.

Don't ask how it happened but in September I found myself in Dublin starting the DCS angel and ascension teacher-training course. The angels and Mildred did a great job in recruiting us. It is one of the best things they ever did.

— *SUE WALKER DCS*

~ Time to Wake Up ~

There are many avatars in the world that carry a high degree of light and dedicate their lives in service.

••••••

In one of Diana Cooper's books on angels I read about the avatar Mother Meera and decided to visit her. The night before my visit I could not sleep and decided not to go. Then I heard an angel voice calling "Krystyna." The voice carried so much love that I knew I had to see Mother Meera. I believe the angels called me and guided me to attend.

— *KRYSTYNA*

~ Angel Before My Eyes ~

When you are in a higher frequency, such as in a meditation or a led visualiza-tion, you may open up enough to see angels and other beings.

. . . . . .

A friend was giving a talk about angels at a festival. One lady was fascinated as this was the first time she had attended something like it. She found herself lis-tening to the talk about angels and ascension. She asked how angels could be "for her" and my friend invited her to join in a meditation. When it finished, the lady said, "WOW! I closed my eyes and did the breathing as you told us. Then a very large angel was right there before my eyes!"

— *ANON*

~ Reading a Book ~

Many people now are having gentle wake-up calls.

. . . . . .

It was Diana who gave me my wake-up call. Her books made so much sense to me and there was a huge amount that I knew already. Having read it, it just blew me away because here were my truth and beliefs being confirmed in her writings. I am no longer confused or feel weird. It's all perfect!

— *TONI BALE*

~ Relax and Enjoy Life ~

Angels will sometimes take us off our route and give us a scare in order to wake us up to the fact that we are racing through life and missing the point of the journey.

. . . . . .

One weekend I was driving to work and missed a turning, finding myself on a country road. I was driving fast, went round a corner and there was a large lorry coming towards me!

I managed to do some "cadence" braking but the road was wet and muddy and I had to pull over onto a grassy bank.

Amazingly I hadn't turned the car on its roof and the lorry passed me. I was un-harmed but shaken. I said a big THANK YOU to my guardian angel and Archangel Michael for his protection.

— *ANGELA INWARD*

~ A Human Angel Changes My Life ~

Sometimes we have to go to rock bottom before the angels can send someone to touch us and wake us.

. . . . . .

My husband left me three years ago. My children were devastated. He moved in with his girlfriend, then things got worse and he stopped paying me support for the children. I cried for days.

I found meditation, angels and wonderful people. I read Diana's wonderful book *Light Up Your Life* and it gave me inspiration. At a meditation I attended, there was a being sitting on the floor next to me, who rested his head on my knees. I felt he was an angel and he gave me so much strength and security. He showed me that all will be OK. I still have this impression and carry it with me even when things are difficult. It truly comforts me to know that I am lovingly supported by angels.

— *CAROLINE CAMERON*

~ *Leaving* ~

Angels can give us courage to change what seem like impossible situations.

• • • • • •

A lovely lady came to my angel workshop. She was quiet and did not say a lot during the day but was profoundly affected by meeting her guardian angel. She felt such deep love that she was in tears. A few months later I found out that she had gone home, packed her bags and left an abusive relationship. She said she had never felt so much love before and realized that angels truly loved her unconditionally. Later she met a loving partner and they have been together since.

— *ANON*

CHAPTER 5

Angelic Help

Angels are around us all the time, whether or not you can see or feel them. The more you ask them to help you or others the more angels are near you.

You can always help a place, person or situation by sending angels and miraculous things can happen. Angels can never interfere in what may be a person's lesson, however – in these cases the energy you sent will be used to assist someone else. Prayers, requests or energy sent to angels are never wasted.

~ Tuning in to Angels ~

There are many different ways in which angels connect with us. We may see them, hear them, feel them, smell their essence, or know that they are there. Learn to start trusting your own unique connection, as this story demonstrates.

* * * * * *

When I first started my conscious spiritual journey, I spent a lot of time "trying to see" angels and wise beings. I attended workshops on aura reading and all manner of things, but all to no avail. I just could not see angels. Naturally, like many others, I thought I had failed, but I kept trying.

Then one day I attended a workshop with my sister, who was totally new to all the angelic concepts. She was able to see angels instantly, without trying!

I was despondent. I sat down and then a miracle – a voice in my head said "Elizabeth Ann, why don't you just listen and pay attention to us; you can hear us, you can feel us, and you know we are there – what more do you need?"

This has been one of my most precious lessons. As soon as I allowed my angels to connect with me in their own unique way I have blossomed in wisdom and confidence. Now I always say to people to stay fully open to the messages of angels – honour your own unique connection and let them guide, support, and inspire you.

— *ELIZABETH ANN DCS*

~ Trusting Your Intuition ~

Learning to trust your own intuition is so important. When we listen to it and act on it our pathway can truly expand, as this example illustrates.

Many people ask how I started working with and teaching about angels. I certainly had no conscious thought about doing it; I had never read a book about angels, but had read a book called *A Little Light on the Spiritual Laws* by Diana. I loved that book, so when my reiki teacher said Diana was coming to Glasgow in 2001 to give a talk I agreed to go.

During the workshop Diana mentioned that her guide Kumeka had told her that she needed to start training other people to teach about angels. Was anyone interested in becoming a teacher? My hand went up instantly. I didn't know why and my friends were puzzled too. They said, "We didn't know you were interested in teaching about angels," and I replied, "Neither did I!"

I never thought I would have any chance of attending the teacher-training as there would be so many other people with more experience. However I was on the very first teaching programme and am now proud to be Principal of the Diana Cooper School.

Needless to say my intuition is my best friend and I never doubt it.

— *ELIZABETH ANN DCS*

~ Help with Paperwork ~

This simple example illustrates how angels will help with anything, however seemingly mundane.

• • • • • •

One day I had a lot of office work ahead of me. I was not in the mood and was thinking about how it was too much and I didn't like doing it. I remembered to call in the angels. I asked them, "Please help me to do this office work with joy and lightness." I started my work and suddenly doing it felt quite easy .

At the end of my day I was proud of the results and the amount of work I had done. Thank you to the angels!

— *CORNELIA MOHR DCS*

~ Angels Help with Concert Ticket ~

When we hold our vision the angels will find a way for us.

• • • • • •

After reading *Angel Answers* I started talking to my angels and asking for help. Each time I spoke to them, I felt such a feeling of love.

On one occasion I failed to book tickets to watch my daughter sing at a Christmas concert at a cathedral. The concert was sold out but I decided to go and try anyway. The woman in front of me in the queue handed her ticket in and said, "I have two spare tickets that I shall not use, perhaps someone else can." I asked for one of the tickets and saw my little girl sing.

I was so happy and could feel the love of the angels almost like "fizzing" inside me. I thanked them. When I told my daughter she smiled and said thank you too.

— *DONNA POOLE*

~ Angelic Travel Assistance ~

Put your faith in the angels and miraculous things happen all the time.

● ● ● ● ● ●

Checking in for a flight from Johannesburg to Cape Town, I discovered that the airline did not have a booking in my name. It turned out that instead of booking a return trip, I had mistakenly booked two flights from Cape Town to Johannesburg!

It was a long weekend and all the flights were overbooked. I was in tears as I had to get to Cape Town to do a workshop. I left the enquiries desk and asked the angels to please, please assist me as I was desperate.

I remembered the Hindu god Ganesha, who removes obstacles, and asked him to remove those in my pathway. As I did this, the lady at the enquiries desk went on a break and I took a chance and presented my ticket again. The new lady gave me a ticket, and what's more it was a window seat, which I always ask for. The lady sitting next to me told me her sister hadn't been able to get on the flight as it was overbooked by twenty people. That is when I realized that we have such a support system out there and we just need to ask.

— *CAROL DE VASCONCELOS DCS*

~ Ongoing Help ~

If the intention is right the angels will find a way to help us.

● ● ● ● ● ●

I milked cows for a living but with the introduction of the new E.U. farming regulations I found myself unemployed. Having just qualified as an angel and ascension teacher I was told to go to the social service offices in Waterford.

Can you imagine the reaction to someone asking for, and getting, funding to start their own business running angel workshops and teaching reiki? Well with the help of Liam Murphy and the angels that is exactly what happened! My insurance was paid for and I obtained funding for ongoing training with the DCS. Angels both human and etheric have always been there to help me spread the light.

— *SUE WALKER DCS*

~ Angels Help Find the Perfect Venue ~

Just ask!

● ● ● ● ● ●

Once I became a master teacher with the DCS, I wanted to find the perfect venue for my first course. My angels guided me to go to St Non's Retreat Centre in St David's and I made an appointment to visit. They took my booking but could not accommodate me for the fifth weekend as it was Palm Sunday.

I told the nun that I would hand it over to the angels to find me the perfect space for that weekend. Just then the doorbell rang and she went to answer it. Another nun appeared, radiating an amazing light. She continued with my booking and said, "It just isn't right that you have to go elsewhere for your final weekend. The energy won't be right!" Then she added, "You leave it to me. I will find a way for you all to stay here." And she did and we had a wonderful time!

— *ELOISE BENNETT DCS*

~ Angels of Happiness and Joy ~

For anyone who runs classes or workshops or is part of a group, here is a wonderful story about calling in the angels to change the atmosphere.

• • • • • •

I was conducting a reiki course. On the first day the group seemed rather depressed and were not talking much. Next morning during meditation, I asked the angels to enter and help everyone feel joy and happiness in their hearts. I also asked for a happy atmosphere to prevail in the group. When we concluded the meditation the atmosphere had changed drastically and was much lighter and happier.

— *MARJETKA NOVAK DCS*

~ A Crashed Computer ~

Yes there are computer angels! Much of our technology is downloaded to us from Sirius, so call on the angels of Sirius for this kind of help. It is also a good idea to bless your computer when you use it and send light down the internet. When you raise the frequency of the World Wide Web you help everyone.

• • • • • •

A few months ago, my computer crashed. Unfortunately I had no back-up. I tried to fix it but to no avail and called an expert. A day before he was due, I asked my students to conduct a group prayer to save my lost data.

Together we asked the angels to repair the computer. By the time the expert came everything was completely all right – as if nothing had happened. I am indebted to my students and the angels.

— *MARJETKA NOVAK DCS*

~ A Passport Angel ~

If you ask the angels they will keep you calm and smooth your path while you take the necessary action.

• • • • • •

A friend, Adela, was preparing to travel to Spain with her two children. The flight was at 6.00 p.m., so at 12.30 she checked the passports and only then discovered that her three-year-old daughter's passport had expired. She had less than six hours to get a new passport and travel to the airport, and a passport application usually takes at least ten days.

She immediately called in the angels to help. She rushed out to get new photos taken, filled in the forms, got them signed then drove to the passport office.

They had the passport by 3.45 p.m. They arrived in time to check in. Adela and her husband both recall how calm they were through all of this.

The angelic intervention continues. A security officer noticed her with the buggy, luggage and small children and moved her to the front of the queue. Adela is so grateful for the heavenly help.

— *CATHERINE MCMAHON DCS*

~ Safe Home ~

This is a heart-warming story of a stranger sending angels to help a sick person.

• • • • • •

I was told this story by Ann. She was on holiday in the Canary Islands with her mother Una when Una became very ill and was hospitalized for three weeks. Ann was convinced her mother was going to die. All she wanted was to get her mother home to Ireland before she made her transition. After several arguments with the insurance company, they allowed her to travel to Dublin by air ambulance.

Before they left, Ann met a woman and told her her story. The woman said she would send angels to guide her and her mother safely home. Ann thanked her but did not believe in angels. As they approached Dublin airport Ann looked at her mother and saw that she was smiling. Later, in the hospital, Ann asked, "Were you delighted to get back to Dublin?"

Una replied, "Did you see all those angels at the airport?" Ann truly believes that the angels travelled with them that day and her mother was privileged to see them.

— *CATHERINE MCMAHON DCS*

~ Held Steady by an Angel ~

I am sure we would all have more courage to try things if we were absolutely certain the angels were with us, holding us and protecting us from harm.

• • • • • •

My husband bought me a new bike and, not having ridden for a number of years, I was shaky to say the least. I fell off twice but after a short while I made progress and was able to stay on the bike for a few minutes!

I pedalled down a country lane and started to gain speed. Heading for a barbed-wire fence at speed, I knew I was losing control but I couldn't stop. Within a couple of inches of the fence I stopped. I was completely stationary and sitting securely on the bike! I am certain I was stopped and held steady by an angel. Every time I walk past the spot, I stop, smile and give grateful thanks to my angels.

— *EVELYN*

~ A Fifth-Dimensional Experience ~

In moments of exhaustion or despair we are open to the spiritual worlds and that is often when we have unforgettable experiences.

• • • • • •

I was booked to sing at a concert at the top of a 2,000-metre mountain. To get there involved a four-and-a-half-hour climb and I struggled with the exertion. My legs shook and I felt fear. I managed it though and had a great night performing. I felt so connected with the sky, birds and the other mountains.

The next morning as I started to descend, I felt my legs shaking again. Someone was with me, so I didn't understand why I felt so anxious. At that time I was reading a book about the fifth dimension and I thought about that and wondered what could help me. I suddenly collapsed. I couldn't breathe properly. I asked my friend to fetch water from a stream. As I waited I called my mother and she said that she would call the angels and the Christ to help me.

I felt as if I was being lifted up, and saw Jesus in front of me. I was smiling and feeling "high" and people approaching from the other direction looked strangely at me. I walked down the mountain step by step and when we finally reached the car, we drove to the doctor just to be checked over.

That night in bed I asked myself, "What was that about today?" I was so at peace. I remembered thinking: "If I lived in the fifth dimension today, then I don't want it to stop ever again!"

— *JO-ANN SERINA ANDRE*

~ The Angels Sound the Horn ~

Hold the intention and call on the angels.

● ● ● ● ● ●

I was in the back of my parked car, with my daughter sleeping on my lap. I didn't want to wake her but I couldn't move. I couldn't use the phone or read, let alone sound the horn to attract my son's attention.

I was really uncomfortable, so I sent out a very strong thought, "Please angels if you are here send Erasmo down here!!" After a short while I saw him running down the steps towards me.

He said, "I heard the horn." I answered, "Well I really wanted to push it but I couldn't move a thing!" I was honestly impressed.

— *CINZIA TAFFURI*

~ Angels and Presents ~

Buying presents is much easier when you ask the angels to help you.

● ● ● ● ● ●

During a training course a few of us went looking for ceremonial dress. The angels had told me before the trip that a crystal was waiting for me but I didn't know where this crystal would be. I noticed a shop sign saying ISIS. I knew Isis was a connection to Golden Atlantis so I went into the shop. I saw a beautiful clear quartz crystal ball that had an amazing energy and I decided to buy it.

At that moment my friend came over and said, "I would have liked that beautiful crystal ball too." As I waited to pay I noticed a turquoise crystal ball. I got the message that this was the crystal that was waiting for me so bought it and gave the other one to my friend!

— *ALEJA DANIELA FISCHER DCS*

~ *Synchronicity* ~

Angelic guidance is always there – but we often don't get the message until it's repeated. Then we must pay attention to it!

......

I had been working part-time teaching about angels, but came to the realization that it was my passion and my true career. I knew in my heart that I must leave my other job, but little niggling doubts made me cling on.

I used to pick angel cards every day, and for seven consecutive days I picked the teaching and learning card. OK, I thought – but still did nothing. Then one morning I decided to pick two cards and guess what? The teaching and learning card came out twice. There were two copies of this card in the deck! I had had these cards for five years and had never noticed this before. I have no explanation as to why I had two cards the same – however I understood the message!

I handed in my notice that month and since then I have truly lived my passion through working with angels. When they want you to see something they will do the impossible to ensure that you pay attention.

— *ELIZABETH ANN DCS*

~ *Manifesting the Perfect Home* ~

Remember to ask the angels to help you manifest what you need. If it is for your highest good they will be delighted to assist, as this story illustrates.

......

I needed a home for my son Kingsley, our cat Jasper and myself. I told the angels exactly what I wanted. Most importantly it had to be a price I could afford, but for a while this seemed to be impossible. I put my faith in the angels and kept telling them what we needed. Then the perfect house became available: light, airy, in a lovely road away from traffic and I could see the treetops from my bedroom. More importantly, I could afford it and we all felt at home immediately.

— *CHRISTINE MARSHALL*

~ *Guardian Angel* ~

This story is a delightful reminder that our guardian angel is always beside us ready and willing to support us.

......

I was totally absorbed in playing my DS game when I heard three distinct knocks. I went to the front door and then the back door, but no one was there. This puzzled me so when I was writing to my guardian angel, Joachim, later in the day I asked him if someone had been trying to attract my attention. He replied, "It was me. I want you to know that I am here with you. You sometimes think I am out of reach when I am not." This response made me realize he really is beside me even when I'm not thinking about him! It's amazing, comforting and reassuring to know this – not only for me but for everyone in the world.

— *ANON*

ANGELS ANSWERS PRAYERS

EVERY PRAYER we offer is heard by the angels and taken to God. If a prayer is for the highest good, the time is right and it comes from your heart it will be answered. If it is a cry from the depth of your soul the angels will also respond. Always remember the power of prayer. It does not matter if you pray to God or to the angels.

~ *Sabbatical* ~

When we ask clearly for what we want or need the impossible becomes possible.

······

Early one morning I woke as the moon was sinking behind the branches of the tree outside my window. I spoke with the angels about my husband Paul, who was exhausted by his travelling and worn down and demoralized by work issues.

He wanted to stop and had told me he needed a sabbatical. I asked the angels to help and guide him for his highest good. The next morning there was a little white feather on his pillow.

The first morning of the new term the Head of School asked for a chat and offered him early retirement with a deal that amounted to nearly a year's sabbatical! Eighteen months later he has started a new job teaching in an art school in Paris.

— *SUSIE COOPER*

~ *Home Sweet Home* ~

The following story illustrates how to write down your vision so that the angels know you are very clear about what you want.

······

I was living with my five children in Edinburgh, having moved there after my husband died. I was desperate to head back to the country! I needed the peace and quiet of a rural area.

I wrote a wish list – a pretty, rural location, a cottage or farmhouse, with outbuildings so that I could work and teach from my home, a beautiful garden, special energy to work with nature and a close-knit community nearby. Every day I asked the angels to help me. I put my house on the market and prayed for it to sell quickly and within six weeks I had a buyer. I then saw the perfect place. The price suited my budget; however other people were interested in it too.

I asked my angels to help. I imagined angels surrounding the cottage and garden and looking after it for me. Every day I visualized myself living in it and working from the cottage. I put my bid in and pictured myself winning and all the angels rejoicing! I was overjoyed when I heard that I was the proud owner of Ugston Mill. Not only had I got my wonderful new home, I had also done a good deal, which left me spare money to convert it to the healing centre I had visualized. The angels did an amazing job. I was so grateful to them!

— *JILLY GREIG DCS*

~ A Child Makes a Wish ~

Angels love the purity and innocence of children; they listen with total trust and understanding.

••••••

A little girl I know told me with delight that she had asked the angels to help her get into Nightingale House when she moved school. "And they did," she told me, her face beaming with delight. "But I know if it wasn't right for me they would not make it happen." I was bowled over by her understanding and faith.

— *AS TOLD TO DIANA COOPER*

~ Praying to the Angels for Peace ~

The angels respond to prayers for the highest good of the community.

••••••

An organization decided to protest against our local town council's decision to build a mosque in Dudley. When I heard that an opposition group planned to hold a peaceful protest against them at the same time I was really worried.

I prayed to the angels that the day be as peaceful as possible. I am sure others prayed too for the whole place felt otherworldly that day. Before, during and after the event, Dudley council announced their disappointment that the town should bear the brunt of the fear of others and also affirmed that our community is multicultural and indivisible.

We can all live in peace, and I am so grateful to the angels for illuminating this fact and protecting our community that day.

— *JEEVAN*

~ Angelic Help with a House Sale ~

The angels answer a prayer for a friend. When a prayer is selfless it has added energy.

••••••

A friend had been having problems trying to sell her house and was working very hard to avoid repossession. I'd heard that you can ask the angels for help, so I asked them to help her sell her property. The very next morning she called me to say that, after eighteen months on the market, her house had been sold. I am so excited! It proves there really are angels.

— *VALERIE CRAIG*

~ A Happy Retirement ~

Here is another example of someone praying for someone else's highest good.

••••••

My mum lived in an area that had changed a lot in the ten years since she moved there and was becoming rough. Though she was isolated, she was resistant to moving, as she is eighty years old. I asked the angels for help as I was concerned. I persuaded her, although she was reluctant, to apply for a flat in a sheltered-housing complex. She was offered a flat at the complex that was exactly what she wanted. It was two doors away from her best friend and she had her own front door! Furthermore, the day she signed for the flat I discovered she had been offered the very last one.

The move went without a hitch. She is so happy in her new home. She has a new lease of life and has even joined the t'ai chi club. Thanks to the angels, my mum can be happy in her late years.

— *ANDREA BENN*

~ Supported and Composed ~

When we ask for help for others our prayer forms a link to them, like a bridge of light, which allows the angels to assist.

• • • • • •

I attended a memorial service for a friend who had died suddenly. Her niece was trying to deliver a reading but was very upset and crying. It was obvious she wasn't going to be able to get through it. I silently asked the angels to support her and within seconds she regained her composure and delivered a beautiful reading. We are so blessed to have angels in our midst.

— *EVELYN*

~ Taking Care of Everything ~

When we let go of worry and control and trust the angels to take care of things, they really work on our behalf.

• • • • • •

My husband's son, Dave, who had already found and worked with his guardian angel at this point, emigrated to New Zealand with his partner, Tracy, in 2004. When they arrived in Queenstown, they emailed us to say that they had arrived safely, they were settling into their accommodation and we were not to worry as the angels were out job-hunting.

The angels found Dave a job that utilizes his degree expertise. They really looked after Dave, helping him to progress with his job, and now he has a good career that he loves.

— *JILLIAN STOTT DCS*

~ A Broken Boiler ~

When we ask for help it does not always arrive in the way we expect, but the angels always ensure it works out well.

• • • • • •

My central heating boiler broke down and I wondered how I would pay for another one. I work at a healing centre and as we opened that day I told my friend, who asked the angels for help. Half an hour later, I was in the middle of giving an angelic healing when we heard banging and crashing. A refuse lorry had reversed into a big wall, which had fallen onto and demolished my car.

But it all ended well: I was able to buy a new car and a new boiler with the insurance money I received – and no one was hurt!
— *ANNE FEARON*

~ Court Date ~

This prayer came from a still quiet centre, which rendered it very powerful.

* * * * * *

I had been battling with an unpleasant court case for a year. Each time we went to court, the case was postponed and I had to take yet another day off work. I was frustrated that none of the legal people seemed to understand my position.

On this occasion, though, rather than getting frustrated I sat in meditative silence asking the angels to conclude the case with a verdict that would be fair to all. My case was concluded that day, with a verdict that was most favourable to me.
— *ANONYMOUS*

~ Angels Restored My Confidence ~

Here is another example of prayer that comes from a quiet still place being answered and confirmed.

* * * * * *

Teaching was natural for me and I never gave it a second thought, but one day I was asked to demonstrate my craft to groups in various countries. For some reason I had a fear of doing it. My hands shook and I felt stressed. People couldn't understand – I was usually so outgoing and confident. I continued, hoping that I would conquer my fear, but it became worse and I reluctantly decided to stop.

A lady in New Zealand asked me if I would be their "demonstrator" for their annual conference. Without hesitation I said yes.

On the morning of the conference I got up early to ask for help. I sat quietly on a bench and said, "If anyone's listening to me, I need help and I need it now, because in two hours' time, I am going to be on a stage in front of many people."

I became aware of a golden rod of light above my head. I pulled it down through my body and feet. I was in a bubble of stillness. I remember thinking about reiki and angels.

As I was introduced to the conference audience my first thought was "Any minute now I will begin to shake!", but my hands were still. I began to enjoy it so much, I made the audience laugh.

A miracle had occurred and I knew it. I have been touched by angels.
— *MAISIE*

~ Lost in Italy ~

When we ask the angels calmly they will always send help in some way.

* * * * * *

I was visiting Italy on a touring holiday with my mother. We flew into Naples, collected our hire car and travelled towards the heel of Italy. It was a wonderful sunny day. We parked the car and wandered round, but when we decided to head back to the car, neither of us could remember where the car park was. We didn't recognize anything and a mild panic began to set in. No one spoke English and there didn't seem to be anyone around who could help.

I felt inspired to say to my mother, "Why don't you ask your guardian angel to help us find the car park." She tuned in and asked.

Within a few moments a tall, dark and handsome Italian with sparkling eyes appeared. In perfect English he asked if he could help us. He knew the place we wanted and helped us back to the car.

— *JACQUELINE MARY PIPER DCS*

~ Trip to Findhorn ~

However scary the challenge, if we relax and trust the angels, they will find a way to help.

• • • • • •

In June 2008 I planned to visit Findhorn via public transport. It was a long and potentially stressful journey but a kind bus driver said he would take a detour to enable me to get an earlier connection.

He dropped me off at the spot where I was to wait for the connecting bus. As I watched the bus disappear, I realized I had left my handbag on the bus containing my money, phone –everything!

I called the angels for help. Another bus arrived and I told the driver my story. He suggested I rang the depot but I reminded him that I had no phone and no money. He said he would be back in an hour and a half – with or without the bag.

I had no option but to wait. Another bus appeared and to my amazement it was the original bus with its kind driver. He'd noticed my bag on the seat and done a detour to return it. I could not believe it! I hugged and thanked him. What a lesson in trust for me. Thank you, wonderful angels.

— *ROSEMARY*

~ Trusting Messages ~

In the following story the writer's prayer was answered. It is a reminder to trust.

• • • • • •

There were quite recently two natural disasters in Indonesia: a tsunami followed by a volcanic eruption. When I hear of disasters like that I always try to give a moment to prayer for the people and families affected.

My sister, her partner and daughter had gone to Bali for a holiday. I had to face the idea that they might be hurt. I prayed to the angels for news; I emailed and phoned to no avail.

I asked for a sign and three days later I "saw" as in a vision a calm beach, with shallow pale-blue water. I stopped to listen and see again. There was nobody on the beach but it was calm, warm and beautiful. There was no fear and nothing bad had happened.

That was my answer – my family were safe! My lesson is to trust these messages and be grateful for my connection. Messages like these are an extraordinary reminder of our heavenly home.

— *STEPHANIE DUCKWORTH PORRAS*

~ Prayers Answered in Church ~

The angels know what we need, not what we want!

••••••

At a very difficult time in my life I found peace by attending church and praying to God. One day I had my head down, praying, and when I looked up I got a fright – there was a man in the seat in front of me. He had turned so he was facing me.

He had just come out of a treatment centre for alcoholics and needed money to stay in a hostel that night.

I gave him five euros so that he wouldn't have enough to get drunk. I put my purse back and when I looked up again there was nobody there! I stormed out of the church cursing God, saying out loud that I wasn't an alcoholic.

Within a month I was in a treatment centre.

I haven't had a drink in six years. I take a day at a time and I know I am at that place in myself that I was so far away from before.

— *MAURA*

~ Thinking of You ~

We are all linked telepathically together in an ocean of love.

••••••

I had a phone call from my best friend's wife, letting me know that Brian had one month to live. I spoke with him on the telephone and said I would ring him again. I decided to send him a card that simply said "Thinking of you." Next day I prayed for the angels to take him and told him to close his eyes and ask the angels the same thing. I did not want him to be in any more pain. On the following Friday I wrote what I had done on my card and sent it. On Sunday afternoon my friend's wife phoned to say that Brian had passed away on Friday. I thanked the angels for answering my request.

— *MARY*

~ Healers at Accidents ~

The angels are aware of the whole picture and make sure everyone is in the right place at the right time.

••••••

My husband and I were walking through our town in Greece to get our shopping. As we approached a small road we saw a car turn in and a motorbike coming towards it. The car driver didn't see the biker until it was too late and the biker tried to swerve but skidded. The biker hit his head on the bumper. He didn't have a helmet on, which is quite normal for Greece.

I called to the angels for help for the driver and bike rider. Amazingly the biker, although he initially struggled to stand up, was perfectly OK! I asked the angels to help bring calm and peace to the situation, as the biker was very angry with the car driver!! Once we knew they were both OK, we walked away and I said to my husband, "This is the second time we've witnessed an accident. Why are we here when accidents happen?"

My husband said, "It's because we had to be here with our healing energies and your angel energy to make sure everyone was kept safe and well." I said thank you to my angels for their help and support at all times!

— *JANIS ATTWOOD DCS*

~ Angels and My House Sale ~

If you ask the angels and the time is right for you to move, they will find a way to help you sell your home.

. . . . . .

My house in Portugal had been on the market for four years. My husband had passed away in June 2010 and I badly wanted to go back to the Netherlands.

I registered with nine estate agents. It was a bad time to sell – no offers! I decided to ask the angels to help. That Friday afternoon a man came to my house. He was an estate agent looking at the house for a client. He was very pleased with the house.

I asked how he knew my house was for sale. I lived up on a hill and he told me that he'd met an old man with a walking stick at the bottom of the hill. He asked the man if he knew if there were any houses for sale in this area and the man directed him to mine. I know everyone who lives on the road and there is no old man with a walking stick! The house was sold quickly and I was able to move back to the Netherlands.

— *ALIDA WIJENBERG*

~ All You Have to Do Is Ask ~

It really is so simple. Ask and have faith and the angels will ensure it all works out.

. . . . . .

After a busy week, I accidentally left my house keys locked up at work on the Friday night. I rang the landlord to get a spare set and he arranged for one to be left in his letterbox at Clifton Terrace, one of the steepest and longest hill roads in Christchurch, New Zealand.

It was the company Christmas dinner that night so I did not have much time. I took the bus to the foot of Clifton Terrace. As I walked up the long, steep hill I felt hungry and shaky and I asked the angels to send someone to give me a lift. Then a car pulled up and the woman driver offered me a lift. I silently thanked the angels.

Walking down that hill with the key was like floating on a pink, fluffy cloud – I felt so loved! All I had had to do was ask!

— *LEESA ELLIS DCS*

SAVED BY TRAFFIC ANGELS

WE HURTLE along roads at great speeds and in busy traffic. Our angels work incredibly hard to ensure that we arrive safely. Always remember to ask Archangel Michael for protection before you set out on your journey.

~ Wrapped in Cotton Wool ~

Even in the most dangerous and dire circumstances, angels whisper to us and help us survive.

• • • • • •

I was driving down a country road with a friend when a car travelling towards me lost control and hit us head on at around 70mph.

In the instants when I realized what was about to happen, a voice told me to relax and close my eyes. Then we collided. I heard a loud bang and expected to go through the windshield. The opposite happened.

I felt as though I was wrapped in cotton wool: everything happened in slow motion and I felt totally safe. It was a violent impact though: my glasses ended up in the car boot and there was a circular crack on the windscreen caused by my head.

I sustained no head or facial injuries. I just had some cuts and bruises and was discharged from hospital the next day.

The occupants of the car travelling behind had thought from the look of the crash that no one could have survived it.

I know I was being looked after that night. Before this I did not know about angels, but now I fully appreciate, respect, trust and accept the job that they do and try to thank them every day

— *ALFIE HENWOOD*

~ Safe Journey Thanks to My Angels ~

Here we see again how angels look after us on the motorway.

• • • • • •

I was driving along a busy motorway and I had a feeling that I should slow down, but I was keen to get home so ignored it. Suddenly I felt pressure pushing up from UNDER the accelerator, forcing me to touch my brake and take my foot off the pedal. That second a big lorry skidded and slid across the road in front of me. I now had time to brake and stop but I would have been crushed under the lorry if I had not felt that pressure under the pedal. I thank my angels every day.

— *LESLEY SORRIDIMI*

~ Angels Watch Over Me on the Road ~

Angels make miracles happen.

• • • • • •

I was travelling on the M40 to London one Sunday morning to attend a course. It was a beautiful sunny day and I was looking forward to the workshop. Suddenly there was a loud bang. I remember looking in my rear-view mirror but seeing no traffic anywhere. As the motorway turned to the right and I turned the steering wheel, the car became impossible to control. I hit the central reservation at speed, gripping the steering wheel and calling loudly to the angels, "I am not ready to go yet, I still have important work to do, I need help NOW please!"

Despite hitting the central reservation, spinning on the carriageway, hitting the hard shoulder bank and coming to a halt facing the wrong way, I was shocked but unscathed. My tyre had blown, my car was a mess – but the angels had saved me, for which I am and will always be very, very grateful.

— *JILLIAN STOTT DCS*

~ Snowstorm Angels ~

Always ask the angels for protection, especially in hazardous driving conditions!

• • • • • •

My fifteen-year-old granddaughter and I had driven for three hours to attend an angel course. We had a great day but as we left a snowstorm descended, so I asked the angels to protect us and get us home safely.

We also needed to refuel so I turned off to a service station. Due to the snowstorm I misjudged where I was going and turned too far into one lane. There was a lorry next to us and we could easily have ended up under it, but instead my granddaughter and I both felt our car being pushed out of the way into the correct lane.

My granddaughter said, "What was that?" to which I cheerfully but shakily replied, "The angels pushed us out of the way." Without blinking she went back to reading as if nothing had happened. These incidents make me aware of all the assistance our angels give us when we ask.

— *ELAINE*

~ Guided to Safety ~

Another gripping story of a miracle in action!

• • • • • •

My friend was travelling to work on the motorway and as she got closer to her turn-off she saw that the cars in front were slowing down.

Suddenly a car cut across in front of her and she thought she was going to crash, so she called out for help and then closed her eyes, waiting for the impact. Instead the car stopped and when she opened her eyes she found herself on the side of the road, safe and sound.

Her angel had cleared the road and guided her hands to drive to safety. When she reached work, she told me what had happened and that she couldn't understand it. I explained what the angels had done. They had intervened in her life as it wasn't her time to pass over. She is now a very strong believer in angels.

— *JANIS ATWOOD DCS*

~ Angelic Hands Take the Wheel ~

It is extraordinary to think that the angels can take over and do what is impossible for humans to do!

● ● ● ● ● ●

Driving from London to Birmingham some years ago I asked the angels to keep me safe. When I reached my turn-off I felt very nervous; it was the morning rush hour and I had never been to Birmingham before.

I looked up at the signposts and wondered if this was the correct junction. I took my eyes off the road for a moment and when I flicked my eyes back down I was horrified to see that the traffic in front of me was stopping and I was surrounded by huge lorries. I stood on the brakes but could not stop as fast as the lorry in front, so I steeled myself for the crunch of metal against metal. At that moment the steering wheel was "taken out" of my hands and my car was steered from side to side until it came to a stop an inch from the lorry in front of me.

— *ANNA KNIGHT*

~ Angel Diversion ~

Another miracle on the roads thanks to the angels.

● ● ● ● ● ●

I was driving on the M6 on my way home from a wedding when a car hurtled across from the southbound carriageway and landed on top of the cars in front of me. Then a second car did the same thing.

All I could see and hear were brakes and brake lights and lots of cars behind me. I thought, "This is it! How do I get out of this one?" Calling on the angels to help me, I braked and put my head down, waiting for the impact.

Suddenly something made me look up and a gap opened up in front of me. I weaved between the cars and managed to get off the hard shoulder and onto the slip road of the M6. When I stopped I was in total shock.

It was only when I looked back that I saw how lucky I had been. There was a massive pile-up, with many fatalities and injuries. I cried and thanked all the angels for guiding me out of the maze.

— *ROSEMARY STEPHENSON DCS*

~ Protecting Car Engine ~

You can always ask the angels to look after your car.

● ● ● ● ● ●

I took my car to be serviced, knowing that it was overdue. The mechanic started to drain the oil and said that the service was very overdue and there was hardly any oil left in the engine.

He proceeded to lecture me on what could have happened and how expensive a new engine would have been.

As he finished talking, I was thinking, "Thank you angels for protecting my car and giving me the time to get the service done," when suddenly as confirmation a little white feather blew out from under the car, wafted across the garage floor and drifted out of the doorway.

— *SUSAN RUDD, DCS*

~ Engine Stops Itself ~

Angels will always intervene if it is not our time to pass over. The following story is an example of this.

•••••••

I was in the car with my aunt and uncle and we were travelling at approximately 70mph when a large deer suddenly stepped out in front of us. Amzingly, the engine cut out on its own and the car slowed down rapidly.

We were lucky enough to only hit the back end of the deer –if we had hit it full on it could have gone through the windscreen and we could all have been killed. We knew our guides and angels were there for us.

— *SAM LITTLE*

~ My Lifesaver ~

Here is a story of an angel physically moving someone out of danger.

•••••••

Once I got out of my car on a busy road, totally preoccupied and not watching the traffic. I was about to cross the street when, all of a sudden, I was physically thrown back against my car by a force that came from nowhere. At the same moment a car hurtled by. If I had not been pushed out of harm's way I would have been hit and injured or even killed. I was deeply relieved. I smiled and promptly thanked my guardian angel. My lifesaver!

— *ALICIA*

~ Angels Save Family from Danger ~

I shivered when I read this story.

•••••••

I will never forget the day my children were in danger. They were in my sister's car when it started to roll towards the edge of a steep ravine. As soon as I called in the angels the car stopped. I saw the angels holding the rear of the car so that it could not slip off the mountain until the wheels were firmly on the ground again. Everyone was amazed but I knew how it happened!

— *DANIELA SORAYA SHANTI MARCINNO DCS*

~ Protected and Helped to Feel Safe ~

Angels protect us from danger and find many ways of helping us

•••••••

The day after a hurricane alert I was leading a bike trail through a forest in Minnesota. There had been terrible storms but I'd checked the route and bikes in advance and everything was fine. When I started the trail my gear-shifter broke

– I had not even touched it. I stopped to check and, as I did, a huge mature tree fell across the path in front of me. The angels protected me.

— *JEEVAN*

~ *My Sister Looked After Me* ~

Our loved ones in spirit are always with the angels.

· · · · · ·

I was on my way to teach a spiritual group with a friend when my neighbour rang to say that my house alarm had gone off and I made my way home. On the way I had to cross a large roundabout, which was particularly busy as it was rush hour.

At my exit I indicated to turn off, but the car continued round the roundabout as if someone else was steering it. As I looked over my shoulder I saw a red car head towards me and then swerve. I looked at the driver, who had his hand over his mouth as if he couldn't believe that he'd missed me!

I reached home, turned off the alarm and resumed my journey. My friend and I discussed how lucky we had been. The red car would have hit her side and could have killed her. Just then the Michael Jackson song 'I'll Be There' came on the radio and we both burst into tears. We knew we had been protected.

The following day I called my phone provider and was put on hold. I was thinking about the incident the night before. I asked the angels who had saved our lives so that I could thank them personally.

When the assistant at the phone provider came back on the line he said, "Sorry to keep you waiting Sarah." I replied, "Sorry, what did you say?" and he said, "Sorry – I meant Nicola, I don't know where that name came from!" I do – Sarah, my sister, is in spirit and there was my answer. She was my guardian angel that night and for that I am truly grateful.

— *NICOLA FARMER*

WARNED BY ANGELS

IF IT IS NOT YOUR TIME to die or to experience an accident your guardian angel will find a way of saving you. I have heard stories of angelic beings literally lifting people out from a dangerous situation. There are some amazing stories in this chapter, stories in which angels have warned individuals or helped them to take avoiding action.

~ *Fire Hazard* ~

Here are a couple of remarkable examples of angels saving people's lives by warning them about the imminent danger of fire.

· · · · · ·

When my sister and I were young and lived in South Africa we shared a room. One extremely cold winter night we had put a heater between our beds. Early the next morning something woke me and I saw a figure in a white robe with long golden hair next to my bed. I noticed that my eiderdown had fallen on the floor against the heater and had started burning. I got out of bed and moved it away. At the time I had no idea that I had seen an angel.

Years later I related the story to my sister. I thought she had been asleep at the time, but she had also seen the angel. Had it not woken me, both our beds would have caught alight! We were saved by that angel.

— *CARON*

~ *Hand on Her Shoulder* ~

And here her angel literally shook her awake to save her from danger.

• • • • • •

My niece was pregnant and went to bed one night leaving a small candle lit beside her. Although she was on her own she woke during the night with the feeling of someone – or something – shaking her shoulder and she realized that the duvet was on fire. Thankfully it had just started burning and she was able to deal with it, but if she had not woken when she did it would have been an inferno.

She believes it was an angel who woke her and saved her and her unborn baby.

— *ANNE CONNOLLY DCS*

~ *Averting Accidents* ~

I sometimes wonder if, without our angels, we would ever arrive safely at our destinations!

• • • • • •

I first came across the work of angels years ago when travelling along a coastal road. It was almost winter; the sun was low and the sunlight shone straight into my eyes. I suddenly saw a figure in the road but, as I pulled out to pass him, he disappeared. I looked to my left and there was a cyclist in the road dressed in beige. He was totally hidden from me by the sunlight and I would have hit him had I not pulled out to overtake my disappearing angel friend.

— *ALISON BENSTEAD*

~ *Driving Advice* ~

When you hear an angel voice you obey without question!

• • • • • •

A few weeks ago I was on my way to visit my mother, travelling alone in the car at about 50mph.

Suddenly I heard a voice very clearly telling me to pull into the inside lane and slow down. As I did so I could see that in front of me there was mayhem; many cars had crashed into each other. If I'd been on the outside lane travelling at the speed I was doing I would have also ploughed into them. That voice from my angels saved me.

— *GLYNNIS*

~ Listening to My Angel ~

Often the quiet voice in our head is the guidance of our guardian angel. Listening to this can save our life, as this story illustrates.

••••••

I had been out shopping and my route home involved driving across a very busy roundabout to get onto the motorway. As I approached the roundabout, the traffic lights changed to red and I stopped. As the lights turned to green, I sat still with my foot over the brake. Something or someone told me to stay where I was.

I sat at those green lights for what seemed like ages but was in fact probably only seconds. The driver behind me tooted to move me on and as he did so, a giant articulated lorry appeared at very high speed and roared through the red light to my right.

Had I not listened to my angel that day, I would most definitely have been killed, as I would have pulled out straight into his path. To this day, I cannot explain it, other than to guess that this was my guardian angel.

— *ANON*

~ Falling Bricks ~

Here is another story that makes me realize just how important it is to develop our connection with our angels.

••••••

I was driving with my newborn baby strapped into a car seat in the rear. I passed a very large truck loaded full of bricks, going very slowly. As I stopped at the next traffic lights, the truck came up beside me to my left.

I then heard a very loud voice in my head shouting at me to just go through the red traffic light and that I would be safe. The voice continued to shout and I realized that I had to listen, so I drove through.

As I looked back in my rear-view mirror I saw that all the bricks on the truck had fallen over into the lane where my car had stopped at the traffic lights.

I was really shaken and knew that my guardian angel had warned me of this impending disaster. I now always listen to the voice that speaks to me.

— *TRACEY*

~ Put on Your Glasses ~

Sometimes the voice of the angel is so clear that we just have to take action.

••••••

One day I was driving home. It was just starting to get dark. I normally wear glasses for driving but on this occasion I didn't put them on. As I drove along a voice said, "Put on your glasses." So I did. About ten seconds later a car came rapidly towards me on my side of the road after overtaking on a bend.

If I hadn't had my glasses on I would not have been able to judge the distance and been able to pull over to the side just in time.

— *ANON*

~ *Warning of Danger* ~

This story is a reminder of the importance of protecting yourself and your car when you are driving.

······

When I get into my car I always ask for a rainbow of protection and that angels will look after me and my passengers.

One night I picked up my partner and his friend. It was a few yards to a round-about we had to cross so I was going slowly. As I reached the roundabout a loud voice in my head said "Wait!" I looked at my partner but knew he hadn't said it. I shrugged it off and as I couldn't see anything I started to drive onto the round-about. Again the loud voice said "Wait!" So I did.

My partner asked what was wrong: what was I waiting for? At that moment a red car zoomed past us, straight through the roundabout, without slowing down. If we'd been on that roundabout there would have been a major collision.

I know it was my guardian angel looking out for me, and I thank her every day.

— *KARIN FINEGAN DCS*

~ *A Kick to Slow Me Down* ~

Here someone is warned in a physical way and her reaction saves her.

······

When I travel I always ask Archangel Michael to look after me. He sends me a blue flash of light and I know that I have his protection. Once when I was driving I got a sharp, physical kick in the ribs from him that made me slow down. Had I not done so, I would have been crowded off the road. I felt very blessed and I thanked him many times.

If we learn to see, then we see. If we learn to listen, then we can hear. I see them and hear the angels and am very grateful for their patience and patronage.

— *CARINA*

~ *Slow Down* ~

Our angels constantly look after us when we are driving and it can be a lifesaver to listen.

······

A few years ago I was driving on the motorway with my husband and my baby daughter. I was going fast on the outside lane when a voice in my head said, "Slow down." I did so just as a lorry appeared from the inside lane in front of us and went right through the centre of the motorway.

Fortunately that part of the motorway had grass in the middle, so the lorry slowed and didn't end up on the other side of the road. The driver managed to right the lorry and eventually drove away.

If I had kept at the speed I was going we would have been in a horrible acci-dent. I don't know if it was my guide or angel but I am so glad I listened.

— *CLAIRE SHEARMAN*

~ Find Out the Hard Way ~

Very often we wish we had listened to our angelic guidance when we realize that it truly was for our highest good.

......

My friend Christine and I were walking home. We passed our neighbour's new dog, who was sitting leashed in front of their house.

Christine ran over to pet him. She kept calling me over but I hesitated.

I clearly heard a voice saying "Stay where you are! Don't go over to the dog!" It repeated it three times. Christine kept calling though, so I went over – and the dog bit my ear!

I thought, "If I had only taken notice of the warning!"

From then on I promised to trust my intuition and my angels – I realized that the voice had been my guardian angel trying to protect me. I am grateful to my angels. It was a lesson I will never forget.

Thank you my dear angels!

— *CAROLINE*

~ Rain on the Way ~

Angels help you all the time. They smooth your life and make it flow more comfortably in all kinds of ways.

......

I was driving home and as I reached my house it was drizzling. I put the car away and was about to shut the garage door when I heard, "Hurry up. We're waiting for you," in a rather exasperated voice. I shut the door quickly and hurried up the garden path. As I entered the house, there was a sudden tropical downpour. A second earlier and I would have been drenched.

I walked to the window to watch it, saying "Thank you."

— *MARY*

ANGEL GUIDANCE

THE ANGELS CONSTANTLY whisper guidance to you. We usually think this is our own thoughts and sometimes call it our intuition, but it is usually their voice in your ear. The angels try to find ways to help you to move in the right direction and make the best choices. However, if you do not hear and respond they will nudge you in another way.

~ Emotional Cards ~

If you find it hard to connect with the angels it can often help enormously if you use angel cards, unicorn cards or Orb cards for guidance.

......

One day I was upset and emotional and I could not connect with the angels. I asked out loud for them to connect with me, as I needed their help.

I walked into the room where I keep my angel cards and one of the card boxes was on the floor, which was strange, as I always leave them neat and tidy. I took this as a sign and opened the box and shuffled the cards.

As I did this two dropped out my hand and onto the floor. I read them and, thank you, angels; they contained the perfect information to help my situation.

I know now that if I am ever too emotional to connect with the angels in my usual way then I can use a set of cards for guidance.

— *MARGARET MERRISON DCS*

~ Round in Circles ~

It is very interesting that, after we ask the angels for help, we notice possibilities that must in fact have been available before.

· · · · · ·

I was in a car going to an angel day in Leeds. We did not know the city well, so we used our satellite navigation.

It found the area for us but couldn't find the right street. I asked Archangel Michael to show us the way and we immediately saw a left-hand turn we hadn't noticed before, and found our destination in plenty of time. We thanked Michael for helping us.

— *KAREN SINGLETON DCS*

~ Prompted to Take Action ~

If you are tuned in to angel feathers the angels will use them to make sure you see one and that you are prompted to take the action that will be for your highest good – even if you think you cannot afford it.

· · · · · ·

Over the last few years white feathers have manifested more than once to prompt me to take certain actions. At a seminar in London the trainer talked about the benefits of attending a week-long training course.

I glanced down at the floor and spotted a white feather. "How did you get in here?" I thought and decided it must be a sign from my angels. Although I wanted to attend this course, the cost was substantial and I was hesitant.

I approached the booking clerk and explained my predicament. I mentioned the white feather and she smiled. She often saw white feathers and, like me, interpreted these as messages from her angels.

I took out my debit card to pay – and was suddenly paralyzed with fear at the thought of my dad's reaction – "throwing away" a huge sum of money on a training course. I asked for divine assistance: "Angels, if I am supposed to go on this course, please give me a sign." I opened my eyes and instinctively turned my head. I saw the tiniest of white feathers float across a woman's shoulder.

It was the reassurance I needed; I paid my deposit. Angels have helped me through many difficult times and continue to lovingly encourage me.

— *DAVID MILLS*

~ Angel Picture ~

Angels work in different ways. Sometimes they give us an urge to do something. At other times they offer us unmistakeable signs or even a push to guide us or make us take action.

······

I painted a picture of the local church in Altea, Spain, where I lived. When I finished, I hung it on the wall.

One day I happened to look at it and saw the perfect outline of an angel. I hadn't painted it! It was too perfect – I couldn't even have contemplated painting such a beautiful face.

I went onto an angel website to find out more. It said I was to ask my guardian angel to make itself known to me. I asked, "Please prove to me that you are there and that you are trying to tell me something." With that the night light went off and all I could see was a misty haze and flickering stars. I said out loud, "Thank you. I know now you are there."

I had the urge to go to my doctor for a check-up, and when I did I found that I had the early stages of breast cancer. I really do believe my angel was telling me to go. I would never have bothered if it hadn't been for that picture and the night light. Since then I always thank them when they help me.

— *MARIE ORR*

~ It's All in the Cards ~

Listen to the guidance in the cards and then take action.

······

For Christmas, Mum bought me some angel cards. I loved them right away. I picked the same card on three different occasions: WORKSHOPS AND SEMI-NARS. The message was urging me to either teach or attend a workshop to enhance my spiritual growth.

I asked my angels to show me what they meant. Mum found a Diana Cooper teacher-training course running in my home town in the UK in the coming weeks. We were both very excited, and signed up for the course straight away.

— *SUSAN*

~ Angels Find a Way ~

If you are seeking angel guidance, whether you can hear them or not they will find a way of bringing it to you.

······

We had a very dear friend who has been battling cancer. I was reading a book about visualizations, and it contained some to use to heal the disease.

It was as if someone was whispering in my ear that I should point out that chapter to our friend. Something urged me to get out my angel cards and the card that came out was BRILLIANT IDEA. I had no hesitation in letting her know.

Her husband said I was the second person that day to recommend that book to her. Amazing! Thank you so much angels for guiding me to pass this on to a very dear friend.

— *ANON*

~ *Angels There for Me* ~

When we ask for help, the angels will find a way to impress on someone else to help us.

• • • • • •

I read an angel card every morning, and I ask the angels to help me, watch over and protect me.

I had flu and developed an ache in my right hip. My doctor did an X-ray and the results showed an inflammation in my hip.

I attend yoga classes and told my teacher about my hip and my teacher decided to devise a class especially for me. I felt quite emotional about it. Afterwards as I walked to the car a white feather floated down. I feel that this was the angels telling me that they will always be there, not to worry about my hip as they will watch me and protect me always.

— *LUISA*

~ *Egypt Mystery Solved* ~

What better sign to guide you to go to Egypt than a pyramid!

• • • • • •

It was my third day of an angel teaching course. We went on a ten-minute walk in nature, asking the angels to answer a question during our walk.

I asked if I was meant to be part of the group going to Egypt with the Diana Cooper School. The angels guided me down a slope where I found some amazing crystallized rocks.

I started picking up the stones and a voice inside me guided me to look for a triangular stone to create the tip of a pyramid. It didn't take long; the crystal was there waiting.

At the end of our day I took the crystallized pieces of stone with me and formed the pyramid at the entrance of my house to remind me of the angel's message and to make sure that I would definitely be present at the 11:11 meeting in Egypt. I thank the angels for their ongoing guidance.

— *THALIA*

~ *Simple Advice from out of the Blue* ~

Just remember to ask your angels.

• • • • • •

I was pondering a business challenge when out of the blue I received an email from a wonderful angel teacher in South Africa, with a list of workshops she was running.

At the end of her email, she had signed off with "P.S. remember ... Ask your angels." And that's exactly what I did, and it worked! It's really that simple, and I know that my days will be filled with love, joy, magic and miracles. Thank you.

— *KIM*

~ *Don't Take That Journey* ~

Angels often guide us through technology. If an email refuses to send or something will not open, ask the angels if they are trying to tell you something.

• • • • • •

I was about to book a coach journey to London on the internet. I ordered the ticket and punched in my card number. The confirmation screen gave the wrong issue number so I corrected it. Back came the confirmation screen with another wrong number – odd. I re-entered the number again only to see another wrong number.

"OK, angels, if you don't want me to go on this coach you need to be clearer," I thought and started again. The site asked my name and offered a drop-down menu.

I clicked the drop-down arrow and there were only three options. The first contained my mother's two Christian names; the second my maternal grandmother's Christian name; and the third was the two Christian names of my maternal grandfather. The angels really had been clearer this time.

Needless to say I chose not to make the journey.

— *ANNA KNIGHT*

~ *A Sign* ~

When it is really important for you to take a particular path the angels make sure you get the message in a way that you will accept and understand.

• • • • • •

When a friend and I were looking at developing our spiritual side, we felt drawn to undertake angel training. On the internet we found the Diana Cooper School and a teacher in Scotland so we wouldn't have to travel far. However, when we added in hotel and travel costs it would cost too much.

I called my friend Jean and was telling her about it when she shrieked at me that a huge white feather had fallen down in front of her face. We knew we had to do it and not to worry about the money – the angels would help us find a way.

— *MAIRI BECKETT DCS*

~ *Angels Find the Venue* ~

I am hopeless at directions. Asking the angels for help is normally the first thing I do.

• • • • • •

I was going to a Lightworkers' lunch and arrived at the hotel exactly on time, only to discover that it was the wrong venue. I made some calls and discovered that the venue had changed. I was given cursory directions to the new hotel.

Were the angels telling me not to go or was this a different challenge? I drove in the direction given and was caught in heavy traffic. I was about to give up and go home when I did what I should have done before. I said, "Angels, if it is right for me to go to this lunch, take me to the hotel."

I aimed for a less crowded road, looped round a roundabout to go home and there in front of me was the venue! Clearly I was meant to go and indeed I really enjoyed myself.

— *DIANA COOPER*

~ A Trail of White Feathers ~

Angels guide the way.

· · · · · ·

I was on a walk in Malvern with Diana Cooper and because we were busy chatting we strayed off the path. We got a little disorientated as to how to get back on track, so we decided to look for white feathers. It was amazing: first one appeared, and then another and another until we were safely back on track.

— *LESLEY SORRIDIMI*

~ Wise Words ~

Unexpected things happen at the most surprising moments to move our lives on.

· · · · · ·

I was at a disco with my boyfriend but as he was chatting to friends I was dancing alone. Another boy came up to me and started dancing. He unexpectedly kissed me – just as my boyfriend looked over!

At that moment I heard a voice in my ear saying, "This will have a consequence," but there was no one there. I think it was advice from my angel and it did have a consequence – my boyfriend finished with me, but I realized later that this was a good thing because I knew deep down that I did not love him.

— *CLAUDIA POSCHL*

~ Show Me the Way ~

When you ask to be shown the way, whether metaphorically or literally, the angels will unfailingly tell you.

· · · · · ·

I have asked angels for help for many years. Once I was feeling unsure of which direction to take and I knew that my desperation was making it impossible to listen to my intuition, so I asked the angels to help me.

I stated which way I intended to go and asked for a sign. Nothing happened. I stood up and looked out of my window and watched as a pure white feather came floating down. It then sat on the branch immediately in front of me at eye level and only when I said, "Thank you" did it float away. I cannot explain the feeling I had – it was great!

—*LESLEY SORRIDIMI*

~ Directions ~

When they can the angels will offer a sign to guide you, as in this story.

✦ ✦ ✦ ✦ ✦ ✦

I wasn't sure which road to take to avoid roadworks. I was short of time so I asked my angels for help. A car changed lanes and moved in front of mine; I noticed that its license plate ended in LOW. So I took guidance from that and took the 'low' road. No roadworks! I got to my destination in time. If in doubt always ask your angels – they'll keep you right.

— *KARALENA MACKINLAY DCS.*

~ Decision-Making ~

Here is one way to connect with the angels for help with a quick decision.

✦ ✦ ✦ ✦ ✦ ✦

I was at a dance competition and felt conflicted about competing. The dance standard was lower than the competitive standard I was accustomed to, so competing felt like cheating. My partner was upset when I suggested quitting, though.

I wrote to my guardian angel. Before I even turned the page to receive the answer I had a response, "Just go for it."

I had planned to dedicate my dance to a special person called Precious. Shortly afterwards I saw a waitress wearing a name-tag with the name Precious on it. I knew I had to dance and went on to enjoy myself.

— *ANON*

ANGELS GIVE CONFIRMATION

MOST OF US need positive feedback to tell us that we are on the right track. The angels have many ways of telling us that we are doing fine and that they are with us.

~ Song on Radio ~

Trust the angels and they will remind you they are with you.

✦ ✦ ✦ ✦ ✦ ✦

My husband Ian, youngest daughter Vicki and I were returning from a day out to see my mother-in-law. It started snowing very heavily and the car was swerving all over the road.

I always ask Archangel Michael to protect our vehicle and all the other vehicles, so I was confident we would be OK. Ian wasn't so sure, but Vicki was so confident she fell asleep!

Halfway home the snow had eased. Ian switched on the radio and Robbie Williams was belting out 'Angels'. Just another reminder that all we have to do is ask – the angels are always with us.

— *ROSA*

~ A Coin Dropped ~

When you are doing something for the first time it takes courage.

· · · · · ·

I am learning to be a medium and was waiting to go on the platform for the first time. I asked for the angels' protection and help. Around me there were empty chairs and no one else around apart from a friend of mine, who I was talking to.

As we chatted I heard a coin jingle. I looked around and found the coin on the floor by one of the chairs. I was so excited – I have found feathers and the odd coin before and given thanks to my angels – but to actually hear this one dropping was fantastic. Needless to say, my experience on the platform went well.

— *BELINDA*

~ Chimney Smoke Angel ~

When you ask the angels to confirm they have heard you, expect the unexpected.

· · · · · ·

It was a two-hour drive to commence part 2 of the Diana Cooper School Angel teacher-training. I asked the angels to protect me, make my journey safe and allow me to arrive for my training relaxed.

I then asked for a sign so that I knew they had heard me. Almost immediately smoke started coming from the chimney of the factory ahead of me. Then it formed a side view of an angel, complete with wings and a halo. The image was unmistakeable. It was amazing.

— *PAULINE GOW DCS*

~ Fluttering ~

When the angels are present the air sometimes flutters as they move their wings.

· · · · · ·

I was preparing for my first angel workshop. Several times I had disturbances in my vision, or a little fluttering movement. I thought something was wrong with my eyes and ignored it.

During the workshop my participants each felt fluttering beside them as well as around the room. Then I realized that these flutterings were angels. The flutterings next to people were their guardian angels and the others were angels that had come in to help me. I knew they were there to give me confidence and tell me that this is part of my life path.

— *MARGARET MERRISON DCS*

~ A Sign ~

Sometimes you just have to do it regardless of cost. Then the angels find some way of bringing you the money.

· · · · · ·

I wanted to train as an angel teacher. I felt so drawn to doing this – however, I had just committed to an expensive holiday and knew that I could not afford to do both. I remember looking up to the sky and saying, "If you want me to do this you will have to provide the money!"

Later that day I received a call asking me to do some work I had not been expecting. It came to almost the exact cost of the training.

I knew I was being divinely guided.

— *ANON*

~ Earth Angel ~

And angels remind you that you are doing the right thing.

· · · · · ·

A couple of fellow teachers and I regularly met for meditation and healing sessions aimed at helping the planet. I was driving to meet them. On the way a van pulled in front of me. It was a gardening firm's van and on its side it said EARTH ANGELS.

— *MAIRI BECKETT DCS*

~ Reassurance on a Long Journey Home ~

The angels find ways of giving you messages that are meaningful to you even though they may mean nothing to anyone else.

· · · · · ·

The relationship between my daughter and her partner broke down and she wanted to come back to South Africa with my granddaughter. I went over to assist them.

We worried that her ex-partner might not permit my granddaughter to leave the UK, so I wrote a letter to my angel asking him to bring all three of us safely home. Despite some difficulties we managed to board our flight.

When the captain came over the intercom to introduce himself I recognized him. Our grandfathers were brothers! I also knew that he was one of the airline's senior pilots. I knew then that my angel was with us and that my daughter was making the right move.

— *ANON*

~ Amazing Confirmation ~

Trust your instinct.

· · · · · ·

When I first saw a white feather I didn't know much about them. Acting on instinct I asked a colleague, Mandy, who told me white feathers were signs from my guardian angel.

Mandy suggested I contact an angel specialist called Babs.

When she had said this, Mandy turned to me and said, "David – look on the floor." To my disbelief, sitting on the carpet between us was a little white feather. I knew then that I had to call Babs. This was such amazing confirmation!

— *DAVID MILLS*

~ Flickering Lights ~

The angels are always there listening to our conversations, ready to tell us when they agree.

······

I was in a restaurant with Diana Cooper talking about this book. We had already lost one draft due to computer problems. I said that I'd make sure always to keep a copy from now on. At that moment the lights in the restaurant flickered. Diana agreed and said she would be sure to keep a copy too. The lights flickered again and we looked at each other and laughed. We had both received angelic confirmation of our idea to keep copies!

— *KARIN FINEGAN DCS*

~ Feathers for Confirmation ~

As soon as you become aware of the significance of feathers the angels will bring them to you.

······

Just over a year ago I invited angels into my life and asked that I live in light and peace. Within two weeks my life changed drastically.

I was working as a chef and was in the kitchen with another chef, Dave, a down-to-earth Geordie. He suddenly cried out – a large blowtorch had fallen into the deep-fat fryer. We both thought we were going to die, but eventually Dave managed to retrieve the blowtorch, much to our relief. I reflected on how brave he had been. At the same moment I got a feather and I gave it to him.

Later as we left work and got into our cars, he sounded his horn and waved. He said, "I just got into my car and this landed on the passenger seat!" He held up a perfect white feather. "So what does that mean?"

I said, "Your angel is just saying hello." Dave said, "Well, I'm going to keep it right here." We both drove away with huge smiles. It was a magic moment.

— *KARRIE WALKER*

~ Golden Hands ~

The angels have magical ways of telling you to keep on keeping on!

······

I became an energy healer working with magnified healing and reiki and was a professional teacher.

I had taken my accounts to my accountant. I wasn't earning a liveable income and, feeling rather stressed, I said to my accountant, "Well, I haven't had a particularly good year on one level but very fulfilling on the other, perhaps I should give up!" As I said that I heard a loud buzzing in my left ear. The accountant stared at my hands and said, "Don't ever give up – your hands just turned to GOLD!"

I decided to keep going, knowing that the angelic realm was supporting me. I have continued to keep the faith.

— *ROWENA BEAUMONT*

~ Pink Roses ~

An unforgettable story.

· · · · · ·

A lady called Mags came to see me. Her son had been killed, leaving behind his wife and three small children. Two years later she was still in shock and could not understand why God had allowed her son to die.

The sessions were difficult – her grief was raw. I asked the angels to guide and inspire me and led Mags on a guided visualization with the angels. I asked her to allow her heart to feel the energy of her son. Then he stepped forward and placed two pink roses into her heart centre. After the visualization Mags sat up and began to cry. Every birthday, Christmas, anniversary, Father's Day and Easter she always went to the spot where he'd died and placed two pink roses.

This was truly a message, through the angels, from her son.

— *MARIEL FORDE CLARKE DCS*

~ Heart Shape ~

As we've seen above with the snow shapes, angels can make shapes in different materials to confirm we are doing the right thing.

· · · · · ·

Last year I hosted a workshop entitled *Opening up to Higher Love with the Angels*. A wonderful thing happened to one of the participants: when she went home she did a release exercise to manifest the qualities she wanted to attract in love.

When she was finished a perfect heart shape had appeared in the vibhuti (holy ash) she had been using.

— *ANNABELLA ONTONG DCS*

~ Kate's Bar in Crete ~

I feel this story is reminding us to ask for confirmation from the angels before we take a big step.

· · · · · ·

My partner Pete and I moved to Crete in 2009. We had planned to semi-retire and pick up odd jobs. However we realized that we needed more to occupy our days. Then we saw a bar for sale near our village. The owner admitted that he had let the bar become run down, but we decided to go for it and with some trepidation started on the legalities.

Just before signing the contract, I asked the angels for confirmation that we were doing the right thing. As we stepped into the elevator to the solicitor's office to sign the papers, there was a white feather lying on the floor. It was just the assurance we needed.

We are now in our second year at the bar and have turned it round, so thank you angels. Angels are with you wherever and whenever you need their help and assurance.

— *JANICE ATTWOOD DCS*

~ *Authentic Self* ~

Sometimes in order to be ourselves we need the green light of confirmation.

‧ ‧ ‧ ‧ ‧ ‧

The angels guided me to share my story so I posted a blog invite out to all my contacts. I had the misguided belief that it wasn't OK to be my creative self, but at the same time I knew that if I was to teach others about being their authentic selves then I had to be willing to be seen for myself too. A friend read my work and sent me a lovely encouraging message. I took it as a green light from the angels to say "Go for it girl." I now have several people subscribed to my blog!

— *JILL WEBSTER DCS*

~ *A Very Personal Sign* ~

There is nothing more personal than your name. I smiled when I read this.

‧ ‧ ‧ ‧ ‧ ‧

I felt under a lot of pressure at work and had come up with some radical changes, but I wasn't sure that I was on the right track. I felt overwhelmed as I drove home.

I sent up a message – "Please send me a sign that I am on the right road." A car overtook and there on its number plate were my initials: KF…1UP. I laughed. Then another car pulled in and it too had my initials: KF…UOK.

My mood changed completely. Then another car pulled in front. It had the initials KF. The angels made sure I was on the right road!

I have noticed that when driving, cars with my initials often seem to come into view when I need to give myself a shake and stop brooding! It always makes me laugh.

— *KARIN FINEGAN DCS*

~ *A Full House* ~

When you have a vision, do all you can to help achieve it and call in the angels to help.

‧ ‧ ‧ ‧ ‧ ‧

I directed a play for children: *The Ugly Duckling*. I wrote and produced it. I felt a bit frazzled with it all until I realized one day that I could call in the angels to help me fill the theatre. What an opportunity! The same day, I got out of my car and on the floor, between my feet, was the most beautiful white feather! SO awesome to have the angels in accord! WOW! It still gives me shivers!

— *JULIE MUELLER*

~ *Confirmation in a Photograph* ~

The angels will find a way to tell you they have heard your cry for help.

‧ ‧ ‧ ‧ ‧ ‧

I have suffered from chronic pain for the last four years. One day I was crying with pain. I looked up towards the ceiling and said, "Where are all those angels who are supposed to be helping me?"

I put my hand down and it touched my camera, so I picked it up, looked through the lense and zoomed in on one of the sunflowers in a vase on my coffee table. Later on I looked at it and in the middle of the sunflower was a black E. My name is Eileen. I knew it was a response from the angels.

—*EILEEN REDMOND*

~ *Material Detox* ~

I laughed when I read this story.

. . . . . .

I am blessed to have experienced a material detox! The 'detox-ers' (or burglars) were fortunate to acquire electronic equipment, household items and my car. I asked for divine assistance and within a few days I was ready to replace my car.

I told the sales consultant, "For someone who knows little about cars, I am surprised that I have made such a quick decision." He replied, "Don't worry; you have made the right decision!"

As I sat down at his desk I thought to myself, "Angels I hope I'm doing the right thing!"

As he placed the contract in front of me, and a soft white feather landed on the dotted line of the document, I knew that this was the confirmation I needed. Feeling very blessed and with much gratitude I signed.

— *ANBIN DCS*

CHAPTER 6

Angels Comfort

Because angels come from the heart of God they radiate such compassion that they can heal and comfort humans who are in distress. In my books I tell stories of angels singing over people so that their grief disappears, or enfolding them in their wings or just touching them when they are sad. Angels can take our pain and bring us to peace and equilibrium in many ways. The following stories may help you.

~ Loving Advice ~

Here is a miraculous story of an angel appearing as a human and giving all the advice and comfort that was needed.

• • • • • •

I recently lost a very close friend and was struggling with my grief. We had a family holiday booked; it was the last thing I wanted but knew I had to go for my husband and young son.

We drove down to the beach. One of the fortune-tellers caught my eye and I felt that I wanted a reading. The reader took my hand. He had beautiful blue eyes, long blond hair and suntanned skin. He spoke about my friend and said that she was at peace. He spoke about my life and told me exactly what I needed to know.

My husband and son, who had wandered off, reappeared and said they'd been looking everywhere for me. I turned to thank the fortune-teller but he had gone. I asked people his name and when he would be back. They looked at me as if I was mad and said there wasn't anyone there. I saw him, my husband and son saw him – but he had vanished.

I truly believe he was an angel sent to comfort me.

— *MYRA*

~ Tender Love ~

This story shows how, in response to prayers, the angels can take away all those feelings of sadness, loneliness or negativity, for they have wondrous ways of helping us feel loved and comforted.

I have had several experiences of witnessing my angels' presence; I see many beautiful, opalescent sparks around me. When I feel lonely or sad I pray to the angels to remove the feelings. My prayers work and I wake up the next morning feeling lighter and mentally refreshed.

Once I asked the angels to let me feel them with me. Both of my hands were tenderly squeezed with such warmth and love and my body became warm all over. My angels are always there and your angels are there for you too and want to help you in any heavenly way they can.

— *MONICA OROSCO*

~ *Calmed by an Angel's Touch* ~

Loss or bereavement is obviously devastating but this story shares how angels have helped cope with the feelings.

•••••••

At my friend's funeral her husband asked me to say a few words. I was honoured to be asked but was really nervous. Just before the chaplain called my name I felt someone blow on the side of my neck and the nervousness was gone. I walked slowly to the pulpit and read out my words clearly and confidently.

I felt in awe, knowing that the feeling of a draught was a touch of confidence to say "You can do it" from an angel.

— *VIV BARBOTEAU*

~ *Comforting the Bereaved* ~

Just knowing that the angels are there can be a huge comfort.

•••••••

The end of 2007 brought sadness and confusion. I was forced to let go of things that had brought me joy: precious animals were killed; my voluntary massage work stopped; every mechanical thing in the house ground to a halt, including my car. I was tired and overwhelmed. I used angel cards for guidance and was shown that I needed to let go of some things if I was to follow my true path. Each day I asked Archangel Uriel for wisdom and understanding and Raphael for emotional healing.

I lay in my garden chair one moonlit night, upset and tearful. I felt the angels and tree spirits enfolding me with their love. I saw a cloud in the form of an angel pass across the moon, lighting her up in bright, luminous, silver light.

— *SUSIE COOPER*

~ *Peace and Calm* ~

It is not just being touched by an angel but how the angel touched the teller that makes this story so special.

•••••••

My mother had passed away and I was having a tough time coming to terms with it. One night I was awakened by someone touching my arm. Initially I was fright-ened, but then I realized it was my mom. She gave me the exact touch I had wanted to give her at her funeral before they closed the casket. The following morning I saw a white light with a yellow aura around it. It gave out a calming, peaceful feeling – it made me smile.

— *DONNA RUE*

~ *Comforting Sight* ~

If they want to comfort you and remind you of their loving presence the angels may leave you a little white feather.

. . . . . .

White feathers have continually manifested in my life, providing comfort when it is most needed. I recall climbing into my car one morning, still feeling distraught about having broken up with my girlfriend. On the windscreen in front of me was a large brilliant-white feather. I could not help but smile. This helped to put me in a much more positive frame of mind.

— *DAVID MILLS*

~ *Comforted in Grief* ~

Everyone finds comfort or proof in something different.

. . . . . .

At one of my angel workshops I was talking about angel signs and the appearance of white feathers. Later one of the ladies admitted that she didn't used to believe in white feathers.

Then, when her beautiful ginger cat died, she locked herself in the toilet and sat there in her grief. Out of nowhere a white feather floated down from above and she knew her cat was safe, which gave her comfort.

Then she chose a card from a goddess pack and got a picture of Yvonne (my name), holding a ginger cat. Now she is a believer in angels and has captured with her camera her own signs of angels in the clouds.

— *YVONNE*

~ *Angels Watching Over My Daughter* ~

I love to hear of children asking the angels for help and protection for I wish I had known of angels when I was younger.

. . . . . .

My fourteen year-old-daughter went on a school trip to France. Some of the boys bought firecrackers, replica guns, cigarettes and vodka. When the teachers discovered this, all the students were interrogated.

Many of the girls, including my daughter, started to cry. She went for a walk in the school gardens just as a thunderstorm began to rumble. She asked the angels to help her friends and to keep her safe.

Something made her stop and look up into the dark sky. She saw something circling round and round in the air, getting lower and lower. It was a beautiful perfect white feather. It landed in front of her.

The feather made her feel that the angels were indeed listening to her and watching over her. It helped her to get through a very difficult time.

— *MAI WORTH*

~ Comforting ~

In this story Dawn's third eye is opened and she describes the process of its opening.

• • • • • •

My grandson accidentally fell into my forehead (the third eye), giving me concussion. I believe that the concussion enabled my third eye to fully open.

The following year I had surgery to have a benign growth removed from my eyelid. During the "twilight sleep" used for my surgery I saw the image of my best friend. She smiled at me, letting me know the surgery would be fine. I felt comforted and knew I was being looked after by the angels.

— *DAWN*

~ Angels and a Distressed Mother and Child ~

Green is the colour of Archangel Raphael, the angel of healing.

• • • • • •

I took my son, Jack, for his annual check-up with the doctors. We were advised to get some blood taken to test for various allergies. I stood behind him as they took the blood, stroking his hair as he cried.

The moment the needle penetrated his arm, there was stillness in the room. Jack stopped crying and all was calm. His eyes turned an amazing green colour. We connected in love and protection and we knew the angels were with us.

It is a "knowing" I still have to this day. We are so blessed to be walking with the angels and to have chosen to be here on Earth at this very exciting time.

— *TARYN VAN DER MERWE*

~ An Angel Brings the Spirit of My Friend's Husband ~

The event I describe in the next story was one of my earliest connections with angels and it was a very special moment for me.

• • • • • •

On the hill near my house I found a clump of white violets in a secluded bank. The next day when a friend came to tea I just knew I had to take her to see them. I said I had something to show her, without telling her what the surprise was.

As soon as she saw them her face lit up. I was surprised to see a pure white angel with the spirit of a man standing by the clump of flowers, but I said nothing. Then my friend said a medium had told her that her late husband would be waiting for her where the white violets grow.

She was overjoyed and I could hardly believe that the angels had brought her husband there to meet her.

— *DIANA COOPER*

~ Comfort ~

When you know that the angels are with you there is a great sense of relief and comfort.

· · · · · ·

The people renting our house left suddenly with no warning and after seeing how they had left the house, my husband and I were pretty upset. As we returned home through the porch door there was a white feather sitting in the middle of the floor. What comfort.

— *PENNY WING DCS*

~ A Family's Special Angel ~

The following is a story about a brass angel that was found in an unexpected place and held special energy for this family.

· · · · · ·

Ryan, Andre and I had a holiday in Namibia. Andre found a gold/brass-coloured angel. It is beautiful and obviously very old.

Our little grandson, Kevin, was born five weeks prematurely. He became critically ill and Andre took the angel to the hospital. We passed the angel round and prayed. Kevin was operated on in the night. A week later he was discharged.

When each of our children got married we put the angel on the table where they signed the register.

During building work on our house we put the angel somewhere safe, but then we couldn't find it. Kevin's parents were getting married and Kevin was being christened at the same time.

I said to Andre, "We need the angel with us – it would be such a blessing for this special little family." Andre looked in a box at random and there it was!

When our son got married our angel went with us. The marriage officer said, "Ooo! Archangel Michael."

— *SANDRA*

~ Angelic Protection ~

Angels can leave an aroma to let you know their presence.

· · · · · ·

I had an unhappy childhood and spent a lot of time in my bedroom. Luckily we had some lovely neighbours, who I often visited. The stairway leading to their apartment had a unique smell that made me feel calm, loved and protected.

In my thirties I went to see my doctor about moles on my face and he advised me to have them removed. The night before my surgery, I felt very nervous. Instantly the aroma from my childhood returned and I felt calm, loved and protected! On my way to the clinic I felt anxious again, but then the aroma returned. I thanked the angels because I knew they were protecting me. I felt no pain and no cancer was found.

— *WENCHE MILAS*

~ Crystals for Reassurance ~

Crystals hold special energies and much wisdom. They come to you when you need them and disappear when they have completed their task.

••••••

One morning I was feeling a little sad because of personal circumstances. As I was tidying up I spotted something lying on the carpet. It was my blue goldstone crystal, which I hadn't touched or lifted from its dish for ages. This was a power-ful message for me as this kind of crystal reminds you that there is always light in the darkness. It certainly lifted my mood.

— *KARALENA MACKINLAY DCS.*

~ Happy and Thankful ~

This story is a reminder to ask the angels for help and guidance each day and to remember to thank them for what you have received.

••••••

The other day I went to the local massage therapist. We had a little chat and she told me about her experience with angels. Every day she asked them for guidance and help, especially in her work, and every evening she would thank them for their help.

She told me: "There are three hundred and sixty-five days in a year and thanks to the angels most of these days I feel happy."

—*CORNELIA MOHR DCS*

~ Something Extra ~

Always check for feathers!

••••••

I was really thrown when a relationship I was in finished unexpectedly. I hadn't seen it coming and was in shock. I knew I needed the angels' help, so I called them in to support me. Two days later I was at the supermarket checkout, still in a daze, when the lady at the checkout said while checking my eggs, "Look, you've got something extra – there's a feather here."

I knew the angels were letting me know they were there for me. This was so magical and special.

— *GILLIAN WEBSTER DCS*

~ White Light ~

Sometimes angel light comes in to give reassurance and to raise the energy.

••••••

I was going through a horrendous time at work and was on sick leave. During this period, my dear father passed away. One morning I could not sleep and went to make a cup of tea. In the living room was a portrait of myself as a child. A brilliant white light covered most of the portrait. I gazed for a while then went up to it – what would happen if I touched it? Would it stay or go away?

I touched it, expecting it to disappear, but it did not! I was amazed. I left the room and when I returned ... the bright light had gone!

I had never seen anything as beautiful as that. It has happened three times since. I believe my father is around reassuring me that everything will turn out OK, and that he will always be with me.

— *BERNICE*

~ A Pillar of Light ~

When you are in despair and cry out for help the angels always respond.

• • • • • •

I had just moved and was going through a divorce. My husband cut all the payments and I had no idea how I would pay for the moving costs, let alone living. My new relationship was falling apart. I was lying across my bed crying in despair. Then I felt a pillar of light coming through the roof onto my back and someone holding my hand reassuringly. I felt warmth, peace, strength, and positivity: all the qualities I needed.

I found new friends and connected to lovely people. I discovered Diana Cooper's books. Through Diana's CDs I met my guardian angel Zakkarie and he is helping to heal my heart.

— *CAROLINE CAMERON*

~ The Feather in the Dishwasher ~

Life on Earth can be a challenging experience, especially when we are growing spiritually and learning difficult lessons.

• • • • • •

During a time of despair I was home alone. I went into the kitchen and cleared the dishes from the dishwasher. Later when I opened the dishwasher there was a perfect white feather on the top shelf. It had not been there when I put away the clean dishes. The feather wasn't wet– it was dry and exquisite in its detail.

This was an affirmation that the angels were with me and it gave me great comfort. I still draw enormous comfort from the feather in the dishwasher and when I think of it I know that I am not alone.

— *JANICE*

~ Comfort on the Move ~

It is very frightening feeling lost and alone in a strange country, especially when you are young. Here is a reminder that when you read a book about angels it triggers you to accept their help.

• • • • • •

Aged nineteen I moved to Spain to learn Spanish and find work as an au pair. On the bus journey from Madrid to Salamanca I was extremely anxious and felt lost. I did not dare get off the bus as I understood nothing and was afraid to exit at the wrong place.

I was reading a book on spirit guides and guardian angels. As we drove into Salamanca, I saw the two spires of the cathedrals in full sunny radiance. Immediately I knew I was going to be fine – all anxiety left me. This is when I started to pray for angelic protection on a regular basis.

— *BRITTA*

ANGEL WINGS

ANGELS RADIATE LOVE from their hearts and this energy is often seen as wings. When they enfold you in this love energy it may feel as if they are wrapping their wings round you.

~ Angels Orchestrate Meeting ~

The angels, together with our guides, organize meetings and synchronicities.

• • • • • •

I had a friend who had not seen her father since she was a baby. As an adult she discovered that his family deliberately prevented her from meeting him. She felt very angry and sad.

She realized that I lived just a few miles away from her dad. The angels impressed on me that I should arrange a meeting for her with her father, in my home as it was neutral territory. They got on very well and it was a heart and soul healing for them both.

My friend's father died soon afterwards. Later she learned from her astrological chart that their souls were so entwined that she would not have fulfilled her destiny if she had had a close connection with him during her life.

— *DIANA COOPER*

~ Right Place at the Right Time ~

The angels find ways of making sure we are in the right place at the right time.

• • • • • •

I went for a 'flower' reading and the medium said to count the flowers that were open and closed and they would mean something to me. I asked my angels and they asked me to write in my diary the dates that matched up with the number of flowers I had. As one of the dates got nearer I fell ill with mumps. I was very unwell and was signed off work and in quarantine, so unable to visit my mum and dad.

My dad had been unwell and I had called him every day while I was ill. On the fifth day I felt better, but that day Mum phoned to say Dad had collapsed. He died just before I arrived at their house. I realized it was the day I'd marked in my diary from the flower reading. Then I felt angels around Mum and me, wrapping us up in their wings of love. If I had been at work, I wouldn't have been there to help Mum. Thank you angels for helping me to be in the right place at the right time.

— *JANIS ATWOOD DCS*

~ Enfolded by Angel Wings ~

Angels often guide us to contact enstranged family as this lovely story illustrates.

••••••

My parents split acrimoniously shortly before my birth and I didn't have any contact with my father or his family. When I married I had a strong feeling that I should connect with his family.

I found his mother and we arranged to meet. The meeting was emotional and as I looked into her eyes I felt that I had finally found an amazing love and kindred spirit.

I was devastated when she died shortly after. I felt such pain in my chest and cried. I felt a huge hug around me, as if I was being encircled in love. I was aware of the feeling of feathers; it was an angelic hug and it removed the pain. I know it was my guardian angel helping me.

— ANON

~ Giving Reassurance ~

The angels do not just comfort but also help with physical reality.

••••••

My mum passed away and as I was getting ready for her funeral I asked the angels to be with me, to support and protect me and to guide me through the day.

During the service I put my reading glasses away. There was another song to be sung and I needed to read the words, but I couldn't reach my handbag. As the song began each line came up clearly in my vision, as if there was a light shining on it, so that I was able to read and sing along.

As we stood round the grave I felt such peace, as if someone had put a cloak round my shoulders – an incredible experience. I thanked the angels for placing their wings round me. They stayed with me for the rest of the day.

— ELIZABETH C

~ Archangel Raphael's Wings ~

Archangel Raphael is the angel of both abundance and cosmic abundance. He enables you to have the qualities in your aura that attract what you need for the highest good.

••••••

In my early thirties, I was having a very tough time. My husband was very ill and couldn't work. I had three children under five years old and we had hardly any money. We had to pay the mortgage and I was despairing.

I was sitting in my bathroom, crying because everything felt so bleak, when I sensed a very big being in the room with me. It put its wings round me and I sensed the colour green. I felt comforted and knew I was not alone – I had help all along the way. Ever since then I have had a close connection to Archangel Raphael. We did get help and it all turned out well.

— ALEJA D FISCHER DCS

~ My Grandmother ~

Sometimes you are privileged to experience the angels when they come to collect the spirit of a loved one. They also enfold the bereaved with love.

· · · · · ·

I was very close to my grandmother and she was my rock. I couldn't imagine her not being there for me. She was always delighted to see me. After a mini-stroke she needed twenty-four-hour care for a while.

Then one day I arrived at her bedside just as she took her last breath. I sat with her and felt an angel shower me with love and wrap me in a blanket for comfort. The angels let me know they were taking care of my grandmother and that I needn't be upset. She looked so peaceful. I was privileged to be there at my grandmother's death as it was a very beautiful experience.

— *ROWENA BEAUMONT*

~ A Cloud of Angel Wings ~

Sometimes an angel rests in the sky above you and a cloud forms round it leaving a cloud angel wing!

· · · · · ·

At an Anzac Day sunset service, I just happened to look up and to my amazement there in the sky was the biggest pair of cloud angel's wings imaginable. I just gazed and gazed at this magnificent sight.

It was a special day anyway but that sight made it absolutely magical. I still feel so blessed to have seen the wings – I just had to write this.

— *ROBYN LEE*

~ Support for a Funeral ~

The angels enfold someone in their wings, like a blanket of comfort, at the perfect time.

· · · · · ·

My aunt's body was brought home on the eve of her funeral. Despite my intense emotionality, I was determined to keep my feelings in check.

I wanted to listen to the words of the pastor as he blessed her and sent her to the light. If I started crying, I would not have stopped. I asked my guardian angel and my unicorn to support and ground me and was aware of a strong energy enveloping me in a gentle blanket. I was completely comforted and able to mourn for my aunt and witness an important send-off ritual for her.

— *ANON*

~ Healing Wings Enfold Me ~

When angels enfold people they invariably feel that their hearts have been healed.

· · · · · ·

My first experience of seeing an angel was after I had a car accident. I was in a lot of neck and back pain and feeling miserable.

I was lying on my bed in pain when I became aware of a noise. As I looked up I saw the most beautiful angel flying towards me. At first I felt frightened but the fear vanished as the angel landed right beside me and placed her wings round me. I felt reassured and loved – as well as amazed that I had experienced such a visit.

— *SARAH*

~ Wellbeing and Contentment ~

This is an illustration of how, when the angels surround you, it brings a feeling of peace that may be inexplicable but is invaluable nonetheless.

* * * * * *

On holiday a few years ago I felt the presence of an angel beside me for the very first time. Although the experience was a little unnerving, it also gave me a feeling of being looked after and helped. My angel encounters are something that I can't really explain or understand properly (and that's OK!) but that continue to be a warm and reassuring part of my life.

— *AS, ABERDEEN*

~ Michael's Wings ~

It is the most wonderful experience to be wrapped in Archangel Michael's wings.

* * * * * *

I will never forget my first experience with Michael! It was during a daily meditation when I was training in Aura Soma. A pair of purest white angel wings wrapped themselves round me so tightly that I gasped for breath. The wings were several inches thick, and I could see a tall strong sword.

My instructor said I had been blessed with a "cuddle" from Archangel Michael and "the Big Will had blessed the Little Will."

There have been many similar events since then; I often feel feathery breezes against my arms as if I am being supported from behind by angelic wings.

— *WENDY*

~ Michael Brings Comfort ~

Call on Archangel Michael with pure intention and he will do whatever is necessary.

* * * * * *

I was giving a lady reiki healing. I didn't know it then, but she was in an awful relationship – as was I. I felt compelled to pick up a piece of rose quartz and placed it on her heart chakra. I asked Archangel Michael to guide and protect us both.

Then I saw a pair of massive wings enfold both of us and the couch. She started to cry gently – obviously a release. This was the most marvellous experience I have ever had. I could feel Michael's presence behind me, enveloping us both. I still get goose bumps thinking about it.

— *LESLEY MORGAN*

~ Archangel Michael's Wings of Protection ~

Once you have been touched by Archangel Michael you will never doubt again.

※ ※ ※ ※ ※ ※

I was working the platform and I heard a supreme being. Then giant wings of protection enveloped me and I knew Archangel Michael was present. A woman near me started crying because I was crying. I had said for years I work with the angels. However for the very first time I felt his powerful presence around me. After that night I never had doubts. I am overwhelmed even now as I write about it!

— *MONIQUE GUY*

~ Raphael's Healing Wings ~

Archangel Raphael's healing light is a beautiful emerald green colour and it's always a special feeling when you receive confirmation of his angelic support.

※ ※ ※ ※ ※ ※

While treating a reiki client I got a feeling that I should call on Archangel Raphael for his help. As I placed my hands on her head my client said, "Oh, these beautiful white wings have just wrapped around my head and I can see emerald green." Raphael heard my prayer.

— *ELOISE BENNETT DCS*

~ Angel on the Moors ~

Letty felt very connected to the Himalayas from a past life and elsewhere.

※ ※ ※ ※ ※ ※

A year after Letty's experience with the angel of the Himalayas (described in a later chapter), a friend drove her to Dartmoor, an area that she loved. Her friend got out of the car to go for a walk but Letty felt too unwell to accompany her. She felt so ill in fact that she could not keep her eyes open and decided to close them and take her thoughts to the Himalayas. As soon as she did this she felt herself leaving her body and she knew nothing else until she came back. When she did return she felt completely well.

When her friend came back from her walk she said she had at first felt compelled to keep away from the car, but when she was a little way away she had heard the sound of huge wings over the car and an angel flew away – in the direction of the Himalayas.

— *AS TOLD TO DIANA COOPER*

CHAPTER 7

Travel Angels

ANGELS ON AEROPLANES AND TRAINS

The following stories remind us that a thought sent to the angels can protect us from turbulence on a flight. I have done this myself many times and it does work. So here are stories that demonstrate different ways to ask.

~ Ask for a Safe Flight ~

There are always hundreds of angels around planes waiting to help.

• • • • • •

I was travelling to a Diana Cooper School reunion. Before flying, I asked the angels, as I always do, for a safe and speedy journey. I got on the plane and started reading a book. After a while we hit turbulence and the plane started shaking a lot. Smiling to myself, I calmly said inside my head, "We need a hundred more angels here please." Immediately the plane stopped shaking and the flight continued smoothly. Thank you angels!

— *KARI NYGARD DCS*

~ The Power of Thought ~

Send out the angels and all your own fear dissolves.

• • • • • •

On a flight to Mount Shasta I was getting anxious as we were encountering a lot of turbulence. Rather than worry I started to send out healing and asked the angels to look after us and calm the plane. The turbulence stopped and we had a peaceful flight.

— *MARGO GRUNDY DCS*

~ Angels Create Smooth Plane Journey ~

The angels work with the element of air to soothe turbulence.

• • • • • •

On a flight from Malaga to Bristol we were asked to keep our seatbelts on due to turbulence. The crew warned us that it was expected to get worse as we flew over the sea. My immediate response was to call on Archangel Gabriel for help. I visualized millions of angels supporting the plane and then went on calmly reading my book. It was no surprise to me that the turbulence stopped and we were able to relax and enjoy a smooth journey.

— *CHRISTINA*

~ *A Call to Archangel Michael* ~

Asking the angels to help really works.

・・・・・・

My niece had to fly to New York. She does not like flying at the best of times and was terrified when the pilot announced that there was turbulence and the plane started to shake. She remembered my advice to ask Archangel Michael for protection and asked him to hold the plane steady. The bumping stopped at once. The flight encountered turbulence twice more but each time she asked Archangel Michael for help and it stopped instantly. I got a call from her that night shouting, "It works, it really works, Michael helped me!"

— *SUZAN NEWMAN*

~ *The Plane is Coming* ~

All planes are accompanied by angels and they herald its arrival.

・・・・・・

I found it very reassuring the last time I travelled home to Dublin; when the plane came in for landing I saw five angels arrive and line up in a V formation. As the plane landed they moved closer together in their V shape. I was delighted to know they were already organized and would be with us on our journey.

— *ANN*

~ *A Difficult Train Journey* ~

An event may be inevitable, so that even the angels cannot change it, but if you have asked for protection they can help you to be unscathed or at least to escape with minimum harm.

・・・・・・

I always ask the angels to keep me safe while travelling. On a train journey near Edinburgh the window next to me exploded and shattered glass covered the carriage – but miraculously, none of it touched me. It had missed me completely. I thanked the angels for their protection.

— *KARI NYGARD DCS*

ANGELS ON THE ROAD

~ *Car Help* ~

Angels can use the power of your quiet connection with them to fix things.

・・・・・・

One morning I had an urgent appointment and was frustrated when my car would not start. My husband tried pushing the car down the hill where we live, but there was not a glimmer of life in the battery. My husband walked to a nearby garage for help, leaving me in the car.

I connected with my guardian angel and asked for help. I turned the ignition key and immediately the engine sprang into life.

Imagine the look on my husband's face as I pulled up at his side and told him to hop in – the angels had fixed it. We were both amazed and said a big thank you. As we were driving along, the radio started playing 'Angels' by Robbie Williams!

— *JENNIFER THOMAS*

~ Sending Help in the Snow ~

Even in seemingly impossible circumstances in the middle of nowhere, if you ask for help, the angels will send it. Trust!

• • • • • •

My son asked if I would drive him and his friends to a dance. Before I set out, I placed protection round the car. I drove carefully as the roads were very icy and we were using a narrow country lane. A car came towards us and I stopped to let it pass. I moved forward again but my car slid into a snow-filled ditch.

"Angels!" I called and immediately a car drove up. The driver had a rope, but was struggling to turn his car round to pull us out. Then another car arrived – a 4-wheel drive, better for pulling us out than the first car.

Everyone joined in and helped and finally the car was on the road again. I thanked them all for being "angels" and so helpful.

One of the boys remarked from the back seat, "This is what it is supposed to be like, everyone helping together, as one!"

— *KARI NYGARD DCS*

~ Safe and Sound with the Car through Angels' Help ~

If you ask the angels they can whisper to other people to do what is for your highest good.

• • • • • •

One morning doing the school run I slipped on black ice and crashed my car. The children were fine, but I was a little shaken to see the damage to my car. I immediately asked the angels for help.

The replacement-car company said I would be getting a small three-door car while mine was being repaired. With a two-month old baby and two older children, a small car like this was not practical, but unfortunately that was all I was insured for. However when the replacement car arrived it was a five-door one! I was surprised – but not as surprised and amazed as when I found a white feather resting underneath the handbrake.

The mechanic repairing my car replaced some rusty and dangerous parts that had been an accident waiting to happen! Had I not crashed the car this would have gone undetected and possibly caused a worse incident. Thank you angels!

— *SUSAN*

~ A Lesson in Clarity ~

I laughed when I read this story. The angels give us what we ask for – so we have to be very clear about what we want!

••••••

Years ago I asked the angels for a car parking space outside a shop in town. When I arrived at my destination, there was a lovely little space, just where I had asked. The problem was that I had a large estate car and the space was too small for it. I just had to thank the angels and find somewhere else to park after all.

Even though I now have a smaller car, I still ask the angels very specifically for a large parking space that I can easily get my car in and out of. It works!

— *MARGARET MERRISON DCS*

~ Tuning Out Stressful Noises ~

First ask the angels for help!

••••••

I was on my way to a Diana Cooper angel teacher-training course. Twenty minutes into my journey the car started to make a screeching noise.

The noise, which I thought might be from the fan belt, continued and I was getting very annoyed. As it was a teacher-training course I knew I needed to arrive relaxed and focussed. I asked the angels to help me – I explained the situation and why I needed a stress-free journey.

As soon as I asked the angels the noise stopped. I thanked them for making my journey stress-free and continued, feeling peaceful, relaxed and ready for my angel training.

— *PAULINE DCS*

~ Invisible Safe Hands ~

In times of terrible trouble and anxiety the angels do everything they can to smooth our path.

••••••

Over the past eighteen months my husband had been very sick. He needed constant assistance and I was very worried and exhausted. During my many trips to the hospital, it was as if my car was driven by invisible safe hands. I always found a parking space outside my home – usually it is almost impossible to park there!

When my husband's condition became serious I received an emergency call from the hospital. I got there safely just before my husband passed away. I was deeply touched and thankful to the angels who assisted me during those difficult months.

— *ERIKA BELLINI*

~ Angels Got Us Home ~

Angels may not prevent the inevitable but can help it happen at a better time!

••••••

We were on our way home from France in a camper van when a tyre burst. The other rear tyre was also about to burst but we only had one spare! We were unable to find a replacement so decided to try to get back to England. I asked the angels for their help and to get us safely onto English soil.

We made it to the UK. On our way home the tyre blew. The breakdown vehicle came and loaded the van onto the trailer and us into the cab.

On the motorway we saw a lorry with huge letters on the side saying ANGEL. My first reaction was "Wow what a coincidence," but then I had to laugh at myself – I'm always telling others there's no such things as coincidence!

— *WENDY OVERALL*

~ Locked Power Steering ~

When you travel, always ask Archangel Michael to protect your journey. As we saw in the story from the family travelling home from France with damaged tyres, he can arrange for the inevitable to at least be manageable.

••••••

My husband and I were returning from a holiday. Just as we were approaching home the steering on the car totally locked. Thankfully we were able to "glide" down to the house. I thanked Archangel Michael for keeping us safe.

— *BARBARA HOWARD DCS*

~ Damage Limitation ~

Here is a lovely example of angels protecting a man's car from damage.

••••••

After taking one of my angel workshops, one lady was very enthusiastic and told her husband about it. He wasn't convinced. However, he did accept the little angel she bought for his car to keep him safe.

Later he was reversing out of a car park when another car ran into the back of him. There was a huge bang, so he expected a lot of damage. There was – but it was all to the other car. His car barely had a scratch. He could hardly believe it: it seemed impossible. Back in his car something caught his eye – his little angel was cracked in two. He is now just as enthusiastic about angels as his wife!

— *ELIZABETH HARLEY DCS*

~ Traffic Angels ~

The angels help to take the stress out of driving in congested conditions.

••••••

On a recent visit to Johannesburg, I hired a car. I asked the angels to smooth my way and get me safely to my destination. Driving along the highway in a bad thunderstorm, I overshot my turn-off and had to turn round. Due to road erosion this was a difficult manouevre. After waiting for fifteen minutes with no break in the traffic, I said loudly, "Angels, I need to get into this traffic NOW please."

A bright yellow taxi drew up next to me. The driver looked at me and drove straight into the traffic and I realized this was my answer. I followed hot on his tail, and joined the traffic. I burst out laughing with a "Thank you angels, thank you thank you!". Soon I was home enjoying a cup of tea.

— *JENNY HART DCS*

~ Life-Saving Angels ~

Angels can pick you up and accelerate you out of danger, as the following two stories show.

* * * * * *

I was in Bristol on an English-language course. One evening, I started to cross the road and misjudged the speed of an approaching car. My only thought was, "Oh, this car is really fast – it will hit me." I suddenly started to move at a speed I hadn't known I possessed, and found myself on the other side of the road. The car just missed me. The friend I was with said, "I thought you were going to die!" I answered, "So did I!."

At the time I was completely calm. and the grace of the situation only hit me years later.

— *BRITTA*

~ Angels Save My Brother ~

Angels really do have the power to lift you and move you out of danger in a flash.

* * * * * *

My brother, who lives in Madrid, started to cross a road and was about two metres across when he found himself inexplicably back on the kerb, watching a speeding car go by.

— *BRITTA*

~ Car on Fire ~

Here Archangel Michael arranges for the fire to be discovered while the car is stationary. He can't prevent the fire, but he can limit its damage.

* * * * * *

While out driving, my husband and I noticed a smell of burning and thought that someone was having a bonfire. When my husband went into a shop, leaving me in the car, I thought I saw smoke coming from the bonnet but dismissed it, deciding that it was coming from the other cars' exhausts.

When he returned I mentioned seeing smoke. Then we saw flames coming from under the bonnet! Luckily he had a fire extinguisher and was able to put out the fire. Then he noticed a white feather on the engine!

The angels continued to help – the insurance company wanted to write off the car, but my husband appealed and they changed their minds and paid for the repairs. Thank you angels.

— *BARBARA HOWARD DCS*

~ *Angels Save My Life* ~

In extreme situations the angels will move matter to save your life.

● ● ● ● ● ●

While it was overtaking me, a rock the size of a small football spun up from the wheel of the lorry in front. It was heading straight for my face. I screamed and gasped in shock and horror, but in a split second the stone veered to the side, shattering my wing mirror. I know my guardian angel had a hand in saving my life that day and I am eternally grateful for the intervention.

— *BLENDA BRIGGS*

CHAPTER 8

Angels and Animals

Animals are ascending just as you are and the way you treat them affects both their spiritual journey and your ascension. Archangel Fhelyai is the angel of animals: ask him to help specific animals or animals in general. Fhelyai is bright yellow, which turns to pure white if he is focusing energy into a particular creature. One of Archangel Fhelyai's angels will always be there when an animal is passing over to support and comfort it. So too will one of Archangel Azriel's angels, who watch over all births and deaths.

ANGELS AND COWS

COWS arrived on Earth from Sirius in the time of Golden Atlantis to offer their milk, which was then the perfect frequency for humans, and to bring healing. They need our love and respect.

~ Recognizing the Divine Purpose in Difficult Experiences ~

Nothing happens by chance. Everything is orchestrated by the higher realms. Animals serve you by being in the right place at the right time.

∙ ∙ ∙ ∙ ∙ ∙

A long time ago my friend Sean lived and worked with the poor of Brazil. Sean hates all cruelty to animals, so this event upset him deeply. He had been driving for about eight hours and it was night. In Brazil, animals slept on the roads as they were warm, so drivers travelling in the dark had a code: one flash of the headlights meant nothing on the road ahead, two signalled cattle on the road.

Sean hadn't seen any vehicles for hours and so had no warning; before he knew what was happening, he had run straight into a cow. He was deeply upset as he had broken her leg. He had no way of putting her out of her misery so had to leave her.

Sean was still upset about this forty years later, and didn't know why it had happened; he had prayed for God to protect his journey and this appalling incident had come his way. I suggested that perhaps God or the angels had placed the cow in his path for a reason. He thought about it and said, "Oh my God – further on the road had collapsed into the ravine. I managed it fine as I was travelling slowly. If I had been doing the speed I'd been·going at [before hitting the cow] I would have had a terrible accident."

Angels help us in the most amazing ways, even if it takes years to understand exactly what they did.

— *EL GLEESON DCS*

ANGELS AND HORSES

HORSES came to Earth from Sirius to experience joy and freedom. They offered to serve us, intending to be ridden without saddle or bridle, but we tried to control them. Nevertheless, they still heal and help us.

~ Angels Saving Horses ~

When we look after and care for creatures who are vulnerable we receive "good karma" and positive things happen to us.

• • • • • •

It was raining one day and there were worms stranded in the yard outside my stables. I did not want my horses to stand on them, so I spent ten minutes moving all the worms to safety.

When I turned the horses into the field, a sudden sound spooked them and they ran down the drive towards the main road. I was terrified they would get hit and cause an accident, so I prayed quickly to the angels to save them in return for my moving the worms. The bottom gate suddenly shut with a great gust of wind, stopping the horses in their tracks. I put them in the field and returned to open the gate. A white feather was stuck on the gate latch.

— *REBECKA BLENNTOFT*

~ A Healing Home ~

When we ask for something with pure intention the angels will help us bring it about, as this lovely story illustrates.

• • • • • •

White feathers for me are a sure sign that the angels are with me. I had two very ill horses to care for. The stables I rented had deteriorated and I prayed to the angels that I would find a place of quiet and healing for them at an affordable cost.

While I was driving one day, my car lunged to the left and up the driveway of a large house. It was being renovated by a couple who were usually abroad, but by coincidence the husband was there that day. I asked if I could rent his stables and he said yes immediately as he wanted someone to keep an eye on the place.

It was quiet and surrounded by trees. When I moved my horses in, the field and stables were covered in white feathers. I found two cups in the tack room, with the word DIVINE written on them both in gold.

— *REBECKA BLENNTOFT*

~ Angels Comfort a Horse ~

When you work with the angels as Aleja does they will automatically help your animals as their loving resonance is transmitted through you to them.

······

We have a big horse, who used to be scared of going into the trailer. We had been training and working with her and she gradually became calmer about it.

The last time we'd had her in the trailer she came out with little white feathers clinging to her coat and around her feet. My daughter said: "Oh Mama, look, there are white feathers everywhere! The angels are here to help us." I knew that she was right – my, and my horse's, guardian angel was with her and calmed her down.
— *ALEJA DANIELA FISCHER DCS*

~ Unicorn and Rider ~

The angels will help you and your animals to do your best.

······

My daughter has a beautiful white horse that has healing powers and that I know will become a unicorn. They both love to jump and go to showjumping events. At their first event, we arrived late and things were getting hectic, although we all tried to stay calm. Then I noticed two little white feathers on the ground near the trailer. I showed them to my oldest daughter and explained that the angels were helping us.

We arrived at the jumping ground five minutes before her round. She warmed up her horse quickly and then her name was called. They won the competition. We thanked the angels for their help.
— *ALEJA DANIELA FISCHER DCS*

~ The Passing of Geanny ~

This story is a poignant reminder of the importance of talking to or otherwise connecting with your animal.

······

Geanny was a wonderful Haflinger, an Austrian horse breed. She was loving and gentle and particularly good with children. Eventually Geanny became ill and I know from my connecting with her that she'd accepted this was her time to go. We worked with Archangel Raphael, Mother Mary, Archangel Fhelyai and the Gold-Silver-Violet Flame to help her.

Geanny wanted to wait until my daughter was ready to accept it, but at first my daughter would not agree so I explained to her what Geanny had said. We all asked for higher guidance and I asked God if it really was time for Geanny to leave the planet. It was, so we called the vet, who agreed to help her pass that evening.

We held a wonderful ceremony for her. I called in many angels to do cleansing and releasing. Geanny was given a sedative by the vet and we lowered her gently to the ground. My daughter then stroked and cradled her head and I saw her soul leave her body.

The next day I contacted Geanny's soul and she told me that she was absolutely fine and happy. She thanked me for all we had done for her and for all our love. Geanny visits us often. Her physical time on Earth is over but I am sure she is great at whatever she does now.

— *ALEJA DANIELA FISCHER DCS*

ANGELS AND DOLPHINS

~ A Birthday Treat from the Dolphins ~

The angels work with the dolphins. They also work with the energy of sound.

• • • • • •

I had booked a boat trip to see the dolphins. It fell on my birthday: what a birthday treat! As we set off the sky was overcast, the sea choppy, and I feared that we wouldn't see any dolphins. I asked my angels to send dolphins to me and the whole tour group started singing loudly to the seas. The sailors laughed and said this had never happened before.

It worked! The wind calmed, a blue sky appeared and with a shout someone pointed out a dolphin swimming with its baby. It was a wonderful moment and I truly connected with the dolphins. I thanked my angels for their help in bringing them to me.

— *GILLIAN WEBSTER DCS*

~ The Angels Respond to Stillness ~

This is a profound illustration of being fully at one with the angels of nature and animals.

• • • • • •

Our usual dru yoga venue was unavailable, so instead we headed down to our nearby river to experience yoga in nature. We found a lovely spot on the river's edge. A local homeowner and her dog headed towards us, clearly concerned. We explained our purpose and she headed off.

The sun shone and the river rippled. In the field a mare and foal chased each other around in total joy. We could see a deer standing nearby.

We decided to do an observational meditation with our eyes open. I began my observation, taking in the varieties of bushes, trees and flowers.

As my eyes turned to the water I became aware that it had stopped flowing and became still. The mare and foal were gazing at us in total stillness. They were joined by the deer, standing completely still. Then a kingfisher appeared. Bees buzzed and the smell of freshly mown grass permeated the air.

Just when I was thinking that the world could not be more beautiful a white feather floated out of the sky and landed in the palm of my left hand.

When we finished the lady with the dog returned and told us to come back any time! It was a perfect end to a perfect moment.

— *MARION CRICHTON*

ANGELS AND BIRDS

ALL WINGED CREATURES bring messages from the angels. Birds come from Sirius. Some are third-dimensional and belong to a group soul, but those who are more evolved, like eagles, parrots and swans, have individualized and are fifth-dimensional. None of them are here to learn; they are all teaching us. The archangel in charge of birds is Archangel Bhokpy.

~ Angels as Robins ~

Birds are messengers for the angels and can bring great comfort.

......

I found it very difficult after Mum died. I had brought home flowers and bulbs from her garden and about six weeks later I thought I had better plant them. I was extremely upset, tears streaming down my face. My grief was horrible.

At that moment a robin landed on the fence just outside the door. He cocked his head to one side and looked at me with his bright little eyes. It was amazing and very lovely; he flew right up to me. I knew that he was sent to tell me that my mum was just fine where she was. I felt so much better. Angels come in many different guises.

— *SUE WALKER DCS*

~ Feathers … ~

Here is a very positive and beautiful way to look at the death of a bird that heralded a transition into something really good.

......

I woke up one day to find hundreds of white feathers in my garden. Then I found three more on my office step. I looked out of the window and saw another white feather coming down from the sky. I wondered what seeing all these feathers meant. Next morning as I went towards my office a flock of pigeons flew over my head. One of them fell at my feet. I picked it up and it died in my hands. I had to find out what it meant! I found a book on symbols, which said that birds and feathers are a symbol for: *something new coming into my life, Life Spirit, soul, the transition from a state or world to another.* Within a few days a new man came into my life; a spiritual healer.

— *WENCHE MILAS*

~ Messages from the Birds ~

This is a wonderful story of birds bringing the love of the angels to help a beloved father pass over and to comfort the bereaved.

......

My father, the kindest, most thoughtful person, passed away. It was a bitterly cold snap, with temperatures sinking to -6C. My father had adored birds and no matter where he was in the world he would feed them and tend to them.

I was sitting with family when the most incredible birdsong started outside – like a dawn chorus, only this was a freezing winter night. The following night the singing started again at exactly the same time and went on for two hours.

I believe this was a message from the angels to tell us that all was well and my father was happy. The angels still come to me as birds. The swallows, which my father loved, sweep over my head. There are robins and other birds in the garden who are so tame they almost speak to me.

— *SHARON*

~ A White Dove Bringing Peace ~

Doves bring love and peace from the angels. In this story, Elizabeth received their unmistakeable energy.

* * * * * *

As I walked home one day I was feeling incredibly sad and alone as my mother had recently died and, on top of this, I had suffered an accident at work. I looked up and there was a beautiful white dove, sitting on a ledge looking right at me. It was an unusual sight in the heart of the city. I felt love and peace float over me and my spirits lifted. I looked down and saw at my feet a perfect white feather. I knew the angels were with me that day.

— *ELIZABETH FINEGAN*

~ Blackbird's Song ~

This heart-warming story demonstrates so beautifully the loving connection be-tween birds and humans, especially when they are bringing a message from the angels.

* * * * * *

My mother was dying of cancer and we nursed her at home. Outside the window a beautiful blackbird sang his heart out every morning. Mum said it was her bird and would not let me close the window. She said, "I know I am alive when I can hear him." She thought it was an angel bringing her "late" husband to her. After she died a blackbird appeared in my garden every day, singing.

I moved house six years later and guess what? The blackbird followed me. It still sits outside the patio doors every day, singing its heart out. My family and I say, "That's Gag," our pet name for Mum. She's watching over us.

— *ISABELLA KELLY*

~ Angel of Birds ~

We can help birds by asking the angels to help them. It can save them so much distress.

* * * * * *

A baby bird came into our open patio area and couldn't find its way out, even though one side of the room was open. An adult bird even came in to try and show it the way, to no avail.

My husband and I tried to coax it out, as it was becoming distressed. It was there for hours until finally I clicked and asked the angels of birds to help. Within five minutes it found its way and flew out. I was so excited but also couldn't believe it had taken me so long to think to ask the angels for help!

— *TILLY*

~ Saving Little Bird ~

Birds are here to teach us and in this delightful and inspiring story the angels worked with the little bird to help Pauline to overcome her irrational fear of birds.

• • • • • •

I was working in my therapy room in my garden. On the way back to the house I saw my mum's cat at my back door. He had a bird in his mouth and he walked to my door and dropped it. It appeared lifeless.

I have a fear of birds, so I asked the angels to give me the courage I needed to touch the bird. I lifted it up and invoked the angels to help it recover. I took the bird in my hands and stroked its head to calm it. The bird was peaceful. Then I gave it an angelic healing. When I'd finished I took the bird back to my garden. It looked into my eyes then flew away. A small feather floated down in front of me. I saw this as a thank you from the angels.

— *PAULINE*

Anniversary ~

The spirits of our loved ones often visit on anniversaries and at times of celebration. Birds will often act as the messenger, as in this story.

• • • • • •

While visiting friends on a beautiful September day, I was standing by a stream in their garden watching the little birds flying about. I was enchanted by their beautiful singing. One of them came close enough for me to touch it.

Out of the blue, the song 'There's One More Angel in Heaven' came to my mind. That day was the anniversary of my daughter's passing. I was so moved and felt very privileged to have had that wonderful experience.

— *VIVIEN WHITEHEAD*

~ Confirmation That a Child Is Happy ~

The loss of a child is particularly devastating and often difficult to accept.

• • • • • •

A friend phoned me to tell me about the funeral of her three-year-old grand-daughter. As I answered the phone a greenfinch landed on the telephone wire outside my window. It had a brilliant gold streak of feathers, which shimmered and flashed pure gold in the sunlight.

I knew it was a message from the little girl to say she was all right in Heaven. As if to confirm it, as soon as we ended the phone call it flew away.

— *DIANA COOPER*

~ Flying Feathers ~

I love this story, for I believe the feather landing on Penny's heart was a thank you from the angels for her work with animal healing.

· · · · · ·

Travelling home on the train from an animal healing workshop, I saw something white fly in through the window. It swirled round and round and round and even though I tried to catch it I couldn't. After a few minutes it landed right on my chest; it was a small white feather!

— *PENNY WING DCS*

~ Margaret and Her Peahen ~

When you really want to help a bird, ask the angels to help and miracles happen.

· · · · · ·

I attended Margaret's class on painting ceramics. Going to her kitchen to wash my brushes, I noticed her pet peahen and was taken in by its tranquillity. Margaret said that the peahen was lonely and needed a mate. I told Margaret it was my mission to get a mate for the bird.

That Sunday afternoon as I lay in my garden, to my amazement I heard a peacock. There in my neighbour's garden was the most beautiful male peacock.

Wow, here was the peacock for Margaret! I tried to direct him to Margaret's house but he flew away. I asked Archangel Fhelyai to help me unite him with Margaret's peahen.

Margaret had an employee called Lucky who was very good at catching her geese, so I knew catching the peacock would not be a problem for her. It took just three minutes for me to direct him to the veranda, from where Lucky was able to catch him.

All my prayers had been answered by the angels.

— *LINDA SQUAIR DCS*

~ The Angels Help a Wood Pigeon ~

Birds are highly evolved and no animal can kill a bird without its permission.

· · · · · ·

I heard a dreadful squawking and rushed out to find that Jasper, the cat, had caught a wood pigeon as big as him. He had it by the neck and refused to let go. As soon as he saw me he ran off with it into the middle of the hedge. I couldn't see him but I could hear the bird flapping.

I thought I might have to bow to the inevitable but I said quickly, "Angels, is there any way I can help this bird?" Immediately the words came into my head, "Pick up the long pole that is in the vegetable patch and thrust it into the hedge."

I ran to do this and it must have shocked the cat into dropping the bird – to my amazement it flew unharmed out of the hedge and soared into the sky. I said a huge thank you to the angels.

— *DIANA COOPER*

~ Blessed by a Bird ~

What a wonderful blessing to ask for help in activating a portal and receiving it in such a magnificent way.

. . . . . .

I recently moved to a smaller house. I chose it because of the beautiful garden, which has amazing elemental energy and a portal.

I was not sure what to do to activate or connect with the portal, so I sat quietly one day and asked the angels to help me. Later that afternoon a large hawk flew into the centre of the portal. It had a smaller bird in its mouth. The hawk started plucking all the white feathers from its prey. Soon the centre of my portal was filled with white feathers. The bird then picked up its dinner and flew away, leaving a beautiful covering of feathers.

I realized later that the hawk was honouring and blessing my portal. I thanked the hawk, Archangel Purlimiek and Archangel Fhelyai for blessing my garden.

My garden is now a place of deep inspiration and connection to both angels and elemental energies.

— *ELIZABETH ANN DCS*

ANGELS AND CATS

CATS ORIGINATE from Orion and are healers. They are very psychic and look after the household. They help to raise the frequency of your home. Here are some wonderful true stories about angels and cats.

~ Extra Hands When You Need Them ~

This is such a sweet story.

. . . . . .

Our cat, Ginger, had been biting the tip of his tail and what a mission it was to bandage it! I had no one to help me hold Ginger down. I called on the angels, saying, "Angels, please help. If you cannot help, I will have to cut his tail short!"

What a miracle – my cat suddenly settled and lay still and calmn and I was able to bandage his tail without fuss. I thank the angels as who else could have given me such help? I now trust more and believe that the angels will come when I ask.

— *JENNY*

~ Finding Jasper ~

If an animal is lost or missing ask the angels to lead them home.

. . . . . .

I moved house with my big tabby cat Jasper and that morning he disappeared. For a whole day I kept going out into the street and the garden calling him, but there was no sign of him. Then I remembered the angels. I asked them to bring Jasper home and within five minutes he appeared and sat nonchalantly licking himself.

— *CHRISTINE*

~ Timble's Passing ~

At the very sad death of a pet the angels come to collect its spirit.

......

Timble was seventeen and a half when the vet discovered that he had a massive thyroid problem. I'd hoped he would die peacefully so we wouldn't have to put him to sleep. In the end though, we had little choice.

My daughter and I were with Timble and he lay across our knees. It was very peaceful. The vet gave the injection. After a few minutes I could feel a buzzing around my head and in my hand, and then Timble passed. We sat and cried.

The house feels empty – he has definitely left us! We are happy that his spirit is in a better place, though. What pleasure he gave us when he lived with us and how lucky we were!

— *RUTH PEACE*

~ Timble's Presence ~

This is a lovely sequel to the story above.

......

I asked the angels to show me a sign that Timble was with them. I was expecting a white feather. I lit some incense and watched the smoke change and shift, and suddenly it curled to my left and formed a cat's face! I wondered if I was seeing things, but it moved and changed – into a bigger cat face! What a surprise and how amazing!

— *RUTH PEACE*

~ The Right Time to Pass Over ~

It is always difficult to decide when to put a beloved pet to sleep. If you do so before it is the animal's time you earn karma in the form of your heart closing a little. But if you make your decision with integrity and hand your pet to the angels to take care of, they will ensure it passes well and you do not earn karma.

......

I had a beautiful tortoiseshell cat who was very special to me. She came to us when our son had a friend whose cat had just had kittens. My son kept asking for one but I told him we had a dog and that was enough!

One night, though, I had to pick up my son from his friend's house. A little bundle of fur was put in my hands. I fell in love with her and she came home with us. I formed a bond with the kitten, Dip – yes I know it is a strange name, but our dog was called Lucky – Lucky Dip!

When Dip was fifteen years a lump formed on her leg and the vet said it was cancerous. We knew that it was nearly time for her pass over – but when was the right time? I felt I was playing God with her life. I gave her lots of healing, but she was still in discomfort and I knew it was time to take her to the vet for the last time.

As we drove home, very upset, to my amazement a small white fluffy feather landed on the bonnet of our car. This was very special because the car was moving, which obviously created air currents around it, and yet the feather stayed there, as if glued to the bonnet, for a good five seconds before floating away. We took it as a sign that we had done the right thing and that Dip was safe, out of pain and being looked after by the angels. It gave us great comfort.

— *MARGARET MERRISON DCS*

~ Cat's Protection ~

Cats are wise, enlightened, relaxed beings from Orion but the angels still often have to help them!

· · · · · ·

Lucy likes to sleep outside. She is a peaceful cat and usually manages to avoid trouble. One spring though she kept appearing with torn ears and scratches. I was concerned as I could not persuade her to stay in at night.

I asked Archangel Michael to protect her. I asked him to place a cloak of invisibility round her that made her invisible just to her enemies. From that night on she got no more scratches. Simple, but effective!

— *ELIZABETH HARLEY DCS*

~ Cats and Butterflies ~

The angels will use animals to shift your mood if you ask them to.

· · · · · ·

I was feeling down. As I hung out the washing, next door's cat brushed round my legs. I stopped to fuss her and to my surprise on the end of her nose was a small white feather! I thanked her and the angels for cheering me up. Then a beautiful butterfly flew between the clothes. I was speechless! I felt full of love and happiness.

— *CHERYL*

ANGELS AND DOGS

DOGS ORIGINATE from Sirius. Domestic ones are learning to be faithful friends and companions and how you treat them hugely affects their ascension path. When you treat them as equals who have come to Earth to experience different things from you, your ascension light glows.

~ Venus Gets Lost ~

I always ask the angels to look after my dog Venus, especially if we are going into the forest. This is the story of the time I lost her.

· · · · · ·

My dog Venus knows our local forest intimately and I would not be concerned if she disappeared as I know she would find her way back. However, on this occasion I was visiting a friend and we were walking in woods that are very different from ours. Venus stayed close to me, which is unusual, until suddenly she was not there. My friend waited while I retraced our steps.

120

We called and whistled for some time but there was no response. I became alarmed, as dusk was falling. I would have to ask the angels to bring her back. I called in her guardian angel and Archangels Michael and Fhelyai and asked them to lead her to me.

No sooner had I asked than I heard her barking from the centre of the woods. I carried on shouting her name until a streak of white raced along the path towards me. I have never seen her look so relieved to see me, as indeed I was to see her.

— *DIANA COOPER*

~ Angels and Pets Passing Over ~

It is heartbreaking when your pet passes over but I hope this story brings some consolation.

• • • • • •

While I was visiting the vet with my dog, a couple in the waiting room were upset as their dog was there to be put to sleep. I asked the angels to help and I was given this vision. I saw the couple in the room. Their angels were standing beside them with arms round them. A pure white angel came forward and received the spirit of the little dog. The angels also removed the sadness from around the couple.

I felt privileged to see this and know without doubt that angels do exist. I do hope this can bring some hope to others.

— *ANON*

~ My Dog Is Brought by Angels to See Me ~

The angels bring the spirits of animals as well as humans to visit while you are separated.

• • • • • •

I do not like to leave my little dog Venus for we are very close. I was once unavoidably away in South Africa for two weeks, which was a long time to leave her. One night I was sitting in bed thinking about her and sending her love, asking her to be patient for my return.

Eventually I got off the bed to take some photographs out of the window and filmed many Orbs. One of the pictures contained an Orb of an angel carrying the spirit of Venus. Archangels Michael and Metatron were protecting her. The angels were bringing her to visit me while I was away. It was such a joy and comfort to me!

— *DIANA COOPER*

~ Juno and the Open Gate ~

Ask Archangel Michael and Archangel Fhelyai to protect and look after your dog.

• • • • • •

I share my life with Juno, a Labracollie (his mother is a collie and his dad a Labrador) pup. The angels guided him to me. He is gentle but has a fear of people as he had been badly beaten by his previous owner.

One day while working I received a text message from a friend in the same apartment building. Had I taken Juno away as he was not in the garden?

My friend also admitted he had left the gate open. I was worried – Juno was also afraid of traffic and our street was very busy. Another friend had taught me to say "I embrace all that comes my way," so I decided I would. A calmness came over me as I repeated it and I remembered that part of our garden was a wilderness and thought that Juno may be hiding there. As it turned out, he was!

As I thanked God and the angels I remembered asking the angels that morning to look after Juno until I returned. I now have total trust in the angels – they had done what I asked.

— *EL GLEESON DCS*

~ It's a Dog's Life ~

Sometimes it takes time for people to start to listen to the angels.

......

Mildred loves animals. She got her beloved dog from a farmer who kept his dogs chained outside. She decided to keep visiting him in the hope of pouring light into the situation. She constantly asked the angels to help.

One of the dogs died and, on her next visit, Mildred thought, "I do hope they haven't got another dog if they're just going to chain it up." But the old farmer announced, "We have a new dog. Do you want to see it?"

It was a German Shepherd puppy. To Mildred's delight it was not on a chain and was allowed inside. Even better, it was treated respectfully. "Guess what we have called her?" said the farmer. "Angel!" Mildred knew the angels were helping.

— *MILDRED RYAN, AS TOLD TO DIANA COOPER*

~ Telsa the Boxer ~

Animals are on an eternal journey to attain higher frequencies just as you are. They too reincarnate as often as needed, usually with the same people.

......

I was running a healing course in a monastery with my beautiful boxer dog, Telsa. Usually she stays by my side obediently, but she ran into the monastery, clearly knowing where she was going. Without a backward glance Telsa went straight to a guide – a lovely, wise spiritual man – and stayed at his side.

The guide told me that he knew my dog from a past life in the monastery and that when the Franciscans had built it they had a boxer dog. The guide showed me a picture in the guidebook of the dog with the monks.

— *ROSEMARY STEPHENSON DCS*

~ Angels Save a Dog ~

When you truly love an animal and do your absolute utmost to help them, the angels will be supporting and helping you. Your devotion enables miracles to happen.

I adopted a puppy from a shelter only to find that it had distemper and had to be put down. My heart broke. Then our three-year-old dog contracted the disease and three vets advised us to put him to sleep. My husband disagreed and the dog was regularly fed a concoction of liver and garlic, apple-cider vinegar and honey as well as antibiotics. I gave him reiki and many prayers were said.

One night I became aware of someone on the couch next to me. I caught a glimpse of something white, but when I turned my head I saw nothing. I said: "OK, I know you are here. Thanks."

By Sunday our boy dog was well again. The virus did not reach his brain. The diet, the reiki, the prayer and an angel watching over us all helped.

— *LITTLIE*

~ Crystal Skull and Telsa ~

Trust your animal's instincts. They are angelically guided and know what to do.

••••••

Edwin Courtenay lent Rosemary Stephenson his favourite crystal skull, Cora. Rosemary was not sure about the skull so she put it in her spare room. She wondered what her boxer dog, Telsa, would make of it.

Telsa stood at the door, cocking her head from side to side as she examined it. Then she walked up to it and eyeballed it for a minute before walking back to Rosemary and sitting looking at her. Rosemary felt that it was safe, so knelt down and eyeballed the crystal skull. As she did so she felt it downloading information into her consciousness.

— *ROSEMARY STEPHENSON AS TOLD TO DIANA COOPER*

~ A Pet's Message from the Spirit World ~

Your animals love you and want to keep an eye on you from the spirit world after they die, and protect you if necessary, just as your human loved ones do.

••••••

I attended a workshop with Carol Deakin. I cannot begin to explain how life-changing that was. I came home on wings!

When we got home I lay down to savour the experience. I reached for my little jewellery box – I don't know why. Inside was a lovely jasper necklace my sister had sent me, which I had forgotten all about.

Next morning, again I couldn't say why but I reached out to my windowsill for two large Dalmatian jasper stones that my mum had given me. I looked up jasper in my crystal books to see what it meant and a picture of our much loved dog who had died fell out. His name had been Jasper. The hairs on the back of my neck stood on end. Jasper was trying to tell me something.

The message was "Protect yourself – when you open yourself up to the light – protect against the dark." Wow! Asking the angels for protection every day is a natural part of my life now.

— *TINA GRAY*

~ Creating a Loving Home for a Puppy ~

I am always being asked what you can do spiritually to help animals who are being cruelly treated. This story illustrates how the angels can help you help them.

••••••

A Spanish couple with a young puppy moved in across the road from me. I could see into their courtyard, which had no shade from the hot midday sun, where the puppy was left all day. I talked to the puppy every day and stroked his nose when he pushed it under the fence. The couple didn't seem to walk him. I learned they had been reported to the police for ill-treating him.

I decided to ask my guardian angel to talk to the puppy's owners' guardian angels to tell them how to treat him and to understand that he wanted love, attention and walks. I did this every day and sent lots of healing. Within a few days I saw the owner give him food and water, make a fuss of him and take him for a walk. I would like to thank all the angels for their help.

— *SHERALYN TAYLOR*

~ Dog Obedience Signs ~

Here is a practical example of how Archangel Fhelyai can help.

••••••

Our dog, Lui, is peaceful and friendly. When I take him for walks he often runs away but I ask Archangel Fhelyai to help and he comes back. When I call in Fhelyai a white feather always falls from the sky.

— *RAMA REGINA MARGARETE BRANS*

ANGELS AND INSECTS

INSECTS are in a different evolutionary place from us so their frequency band is different from ours. They too are here to experience. Their group souls consist of about 1000. Some are third-dimensional, a few fourth and others fifth-dimensional.

~ Archangel of Insects ~

Our planet could not survive without insects. And the archangel in charge of them has to work very hard to help them.

••••••

Angels have brought so much joy to my life. During a meditation I was introduced to the archangel of insects, whose name is Archangel Preminilik.

He taught me to love and respect every insect I see as they all have a purpose and we have many lessons to learn from his beautiful creatures. He says they play a vital role in the survival of Mother Earth and need to be honoured by all humans.

— *LINDA DCS*

~ Beautiful Butterfly ~

When a bird, butterfly or animal does something three times it means it is bringing an important message.

* * * * * *

Years ago I was ill. My immune system broke down and it was hard, but it provided me with the fuel I needed to start a deep transformation and spiritual awakening. I spent time alone learning to cook healthy food to heal my body, writing in journals to heal my emotions and going on lots of nature walks. One day I spotted a beautiful butterfly with vivid colours. It obviously wanted me to notice it – it kept resting on the flowers and bushes in front of me. The same butterfly appeared later outside my bedroom.

When I awoke the next day it was still there, so I knelt down beside it and asked it if it was my guardian angel, and if so would it come towards me? The butterfly flew round me three times to make sure that I got the message. From that moment I have never doubted that I was guided and protected by the angels.

— *JILL WEBSTER DCS*

~ Conference of the Wasps ~

An illustration that we can communicate with wasps and they will respond, especially if we call in the angels.

* * * * * *

There was a wasps' nest outside our stable and whenever the windows were open they would fly in and scare the horses. I called in the angel in charge of insects and told the wasps that they had to stay out of the stable otherwise the spiders would get them. They didn't take me seriously at first and kept coming in.

I talked to the spiders and asked them to keep the stable free of the wasps. It didn't take long. A wasp was soon caught in the web with two other wasps flying around her. They then agreed to stay out and have not returned since; they still have and live in a nest on the outside wall. We now all live happily each in our own space. Humans and animals can live peacefully together.

— *ALEJA DANIELA FISCHER DCS*

~ Angels Move Bees Safely ~

Just as angels whisper to humans what is the best thing to do, they also guide animals, birds and insects – here, bees .

* * * * * *

I had a bees' nest in the compost bin and did not want them hurt but needed to feel safe. No one was willing to move them, so I asked the angels, explaining that I did not want them harmed.

I waited a day and then went to look. The bees had moved on and the nest dropped down onto the compost. Angels never let you down or cease to amaze.

— *MARION*

~ Cosmic Moment ~

This is an inspirational story about seeing the true beauty of insects.

• • • • • •

I was in at the Temple in Luxor for 11.11.11. I sat with many others in preparation and meditation. I did not know what to expect, but hoped something amazing would happen to me.

Just a few minutes before 11.11 a fly landed on my mouth and I thought, "Oh no!" Perhaps I was being told that I was not ready. The fly did not move and I realized that it too was part of the great shift in consciousness. As we moved into the cosmic moment it became golden and I was given the vision of all flies ascending and becoming golden.

It was a very special moment, which still stays with me as a reminder never to presume or judge.

— *ELIZABETH ANN DCS*

~ God's Creatures ~

Everything on this planet has a purpose and is part of the divine plan. We often forget this when we think about particular animals or insects that we view as less attractive. This story might help to open up our perceptions.

• • • • • •

I was in South Africa helping Diana on her tour. We were staying at a beautiful bed and breakfast overlooking the ocean near Cape Town.

I remember one afternoon looking out at the stunning scenery when a rat appeared on the grass in front of my room's window. The owner of the bed and breakfast was horrified and instantly said they would "destroy" it. I asked them not to as I was sure there was a purpose in me seeing the rat.

The next morning as I opened the curtains the rat was lying on the grass. It was clear to me that it had died. I went out to check, and as I did so a beautiful rainbow formed over its body. As I looked at it, I started to see its great beauty – it truly sparkled in the morning sunshine. I called in Archangel Fhelyai and asked that the little rat ascend. I sang it a song of love as I watched its soul rise out of its body. It was a phenomenal experience and opened up my compassion for all creatures on the planet.

— *ELIZABETH ANN DCS*

~ Journey to Shirdi ~

When we are truly awake to angelic guidance it can come in many forms, as this story shows.

• • • • • •

I was travelling by car to Shirdi in India. I prayed to the angels and the Hindu god Ganpatiji to protect us and our car. After we'd been driving for two hours we got a puncture. We couldn't find a garage so got out the jack to replace the wheel, but it had seized up and we couldn't use it.

I prayed to Archangel Michael and ascended master Shirdi Saibaba for help. A man appeared from nowhere, fixed the jack and replaced the tyre. He refused payment and instead asked us to offer a coconut to the temple of Saibaba at Shirdi.

Then I saw a beautiful butterfly – I knew it was the angels telling us that they had sent this man. When we found a garage the mechanic told us that a thin iron rod had caused the problem. Had we not stopped we could have had an accident.

I thanked the angels, Lord Ganesha and Saibaba for their blessings and for their support.

— *SAMEETA DCS*

CHAPTER 9

Angels Everywhere

There are angels everywhere. If you call on angels to help you or send them to help others, dozens of them may come to you. Angels carry anyone who has ever incarnated on Earth to visit or help people. They gather in high-energy points and they wait on street corners to hold the energy. We are blessed that so many angels are here now waiting to help us.

~ Buckets of Love Dissolve Anger ~

Ask the angels to pour love over someone who is sad, bad or angry and they can transform them.

. . . . . .

A lady who came to my workplace used to yell at my workmates for no reason and they started to become anxious whenever she appeared. I asked the angels to help me to pour love over this lady.

I was in reception when she returned. She came toward me saying angry words, and when she was near me I asked the angels to pour love over her. She stopped and stood still, and then left the building. She has not returned.

I now know that she has felt love at least once in her life.

— *ANNE LUNDQVIST*

~ Violet Flame ~

The following story is a reminder that an angry person can leave unpleasant energy in someone's home, which can make them feel ill. The violet flame angels of Archangel Zadkiel transmute lower energies so that higher ones can come in. If you ask for and visualize the gold-silver-violet flame, the lower energies will be transmuted and replaced with higher ones.

. . . . . .

A medium friend of mine had rung and left me a message. She was having problems with her landlord and was in a terrible state. She felt that her house had been filled with hatred and anger after his visit. She felt ill from the atmosphere. I asked the angels to clear the energy for her.

Within minutes she rang to say the energy had changed and felt much lighter and brighter. I also asked St Germain, keeper of the Violet Flame, to use the violet flame to help clear the negativity. I feel blessed to have the angels work with me and asked them to send love and light into the world.

— *SARAH*

~ Oneness ~

Every sacred place and every house or building has its own angel.

. . . . . .

Letty was very connected to the Himalayas and was sure she had lived past lives there. Once in a meditation group she found herself having a reverie that she was in the Himalayas, at the top of one of the mountains.

She started to meditate on the angel of the Himalayas; she was totally absorbed and became part of the energy of the angel. She experienced complete oneness, though she still had her own identity. She could even see her physical body below her.

When she eventually opened her eyes she knew she had had a very profound experience.

— *TOLD TO DIANA COOPER*

~ Faith ~

This is a story of faith making the impossible possible.

. . . . . .

My son got his ear pierced. I wasn't ecstatic; however, I helped him to bathe his ear regularly. After two weeks he said, "Mum, can you put this back in for me?" He had taken the earring out. It was supposed to be kept in for six weeks! It would be difficult to get it back in as his ear was very swollen. I had a look and realized there was no way it was going to happen.

"I'm sorry sweetheart; it's just not going to go back in," I said.

He said, "Can't you ask the angels?" I thought, "Oh no! Ask me to ask for things that are possible, not for things that are impossible!" I didn't want his faith in the angels to be shattered. But I said I'd try.

We both asked the angels and to my absolute amazement the earring went straight through first time.

— *ELIZABETH HARLEY DCS*

~ Be Careful What You Ask For ~

We have all heard the adage, "Be careful what you ask for – you just might get it!" Here is one example. When you ask be very clear about what you really want!

. . . . . .

I had bought a copy of *The Celestine Prophecy*. I started reading it on the tube from central London, kept reading it at the airport in departures and carried on reading it on the plane back to Glasgow. I was totally immersed in it! Before I knew it the captain had announced that we were ten minutes to landing. I had fifty pages to go and didn't want to stop reading.

I sent up a prayer to the angels asking to finish the book before landing. Almost immediately the captain came over the intercom again and apologized – we had missed the last landing slot and would be diverted to Edinburgh. Everyone grumbled and complained, and once it dawned on me what I'd asked for I had to laugh – at least it meant I could finish my book!

— *KARIN FINEGAN DCS*

~ The Angel Earring ~

The angels have wonderful ways of making things happen in perfect time to help you.

......

I visited my sister in Australia. She had recently moved there and was homesick. I wore my silver angel wings earrings on the journey and, at my sister's house that night, placed them on a stand for safe keeping. The following day I couldn't find one of them. It still hadn't turned up by the time I had to leave. My sister wanted to find it, but I said, "Considering it is an angel earring – it will appear when you need it."

On Christmas Day she took some clothes to her room, then sat on her bed and cried with homesickness. Then she noticed that on top of the bundle of clothes was the angel wing earring, and she recalled what I had said. She was truly delighted. The angels had cheered her heart.

— *EL GLEESON DCS*

~ Angels Support a Mother ~

We all have lessons to learn and very often it involves letting go and handing a situation over to the angels so that the highest good can come about.

......

My son fell in love, but I just knew this girl was not suitable. My son moved in with her and lost interest in his family, his friends and was losing confidence in himself and his work. In despair I begged the angels to dissolve this relationship.

I asked him to attend a counsellor and if he still felt the same about her afterwards I would respect his decision to be with her. After two sessions he came home to stay with me. It was short-lived, though, as she threatened to end her life if he didn't return to her. He said he wouldn't be able to live with himself if anything happened to her.

I asked my son's angels and guides to connect to his girlfriend's angels and guides and to help both of them realize that this relationship was no longer serving them. I requested that the outcome be for the highest good. I did this under the Law of Grace.

Three months later my son arrived home and told me he was home to stay. I blessed the angels. He later met his true soulmate and they married.

— *MARIEL*

~ Pretty and Pink ~

The angels nudge you through all possible manner of things.

. . . . . .

While out shopping I walked into one shop and looked at a table laden with goods on special offer. I noticed a pretty pink lip gloss and picked it up. I never bother about that kind of make-up, but something told me to turn it over and I did – and was astounded when I read the label: ANGEL DUST. WOW – thank you angels. As you can guess, I bought it, with a big smile on my face!

— *KARI NYGARD DCS*

~ Angelic Poetry Inspirations ~

This is a wonderful example of how Liz used her own experiences to guide and inspire others through her poetry. Once we understand that there is always a higher purpose in all our experiences we can create a positive future.

. . . . . .

I was diagnosed with cancer at the age of twenty-two, and went on to suffer from depression for years. Nothing ever seemed to go right and I had many challenges. My life changed when I embarked on a course in counselling and then trained as a reiki healer.

Through reiki I felt connected to the angels. I have developed my skills over the last ten years by reading about angels and healing and attending workshops.

One day I felt a tremendous sense of peace and calm wash over me and then I started writing beautiful pieces of intuitive, emotional and meaningful poems. Over a period of six months I wrote over 200 poems.

I knew that these poems would help others and I felt an urgent need to share what I had written. I met a woman who had her own publishing company and wanted to publish my poems. The angels helped because my book was published within six weeks.

— *LIZ EVERETT*

~ Circumstances ~

Angels can show themselves to you in many different ways – and when you want to connect with them all sorts of angel gifts appear.

. . . . . .

I wanted to connect more with angels, and bought books, cards and tapes to raise the energy of my home. Rather than seeing angels I started to sense cone-shaped wheels of energy flowing upwards from my heart centre.

Then an old friend of mine brought me some gifts . One of them was a charming chime: three crystal angels with golden wings, musical instruments in their hands and three engraved tubes to make an angelic noise. So even more angels came into my life!

— *KRYSTYNA NAPIERALA*

~ President Obama ~

The election of Barack Obama in 2008 created a wave of excitement throughout the world that pushed Earth onto its ascension pathway. He is the forty-fourth president of the United States and forty-four is the number that vibrates with the Golden Age of Atlantis. He was a priest in Atlantis and was trained there for his presidential role in this incarnation.

• • • • • •

When Barack Obama was inaugurated, I felt a sense of excitement among light-workers. I lit incense, made my kitchen a sacred space to watch the ceremony and sent out light.

As President Obama prepared to make his speech, I saw (with my third eye) a violet "Russian"-style hat on his head, protecting his third eye and crown centre. I felt emotional as he spoke. I felt a huge angelic presence around him and all the people in Washington, DC.

I know he has a challenging task to buoy up people's faith in him, so I make a point of frequently sending him and those around him angelic light.

— *SUSAN*

~ Perfect Christmas When I Trusted the Angels ~

If you want a joyful day, let go and trust the angels.

• • • • • •

I was hosting my family's Christmas lunch. In the past I would have been stressed and worried about fifteen people coming over, but I knew my angels would help.

I had ordered chairs and crockery from a catering supplier but when I went to collect my order the chairs were tatty and my crockery was out of stock.

It was two days before Christmas! I just took a deep breath and trusted my angels would help. I turned to leave and out of the blue the assistant said that he had some glass plates and fifteen gold and red chairs. I was delighted and took them home.

My original table cover didn't match; however, a gorgeous red silk sari I'd bought a few days earlier fitted perfectly. A friend appeared with a present for me – a stunning red glass table decoration. My sister-in-law brought Christmas crackers that perfectly matched the colour scheme. Everyone thought the table looked beautiful and I knew the angels had brought it all together.

— *MAIRI BECKETT DCS*

~ Wedding Day Angel ~

There is a reason for everything and the angels organize synchronicities and timing in our lives.

• • • • • •

Peter and I married in October 2001 and while we were in the church, which is in a very special area in Abbey Fields, we realized that one of our guests was delayed. We were aware that angels are always present during a wedding, and an angel is always appointed on the wedding day to help the couple throughout their marriage. Our ceremony was very special and we could feel the angelic presence. Our delayed guest told us that as she approached the church a beautiful double rainbow appeared in the sky at the exact time that our marriage was blessed.

If our guest had not been delayed, we would never have known about the beautiful double rainbow the angels had brought to our wedding ceremony.

— *JILLIAN STOTT DCS*

~ Treasure Trail ~

Follow the feathers and the angels will lead you to your dream.

• • • • • •

During my teacher-training with Diana Cooper, I was clueless on how to dress for angel ceremonies. I decided to go to the village one day to find something suitable. A few of us went shopping and the others found something quickly, but I could not find anything special and it was getting late. I saw a white feather and said, "Girls, the angels are here." Then I saw a bigger feather and said, "The archangels are here."

I followed the feathers and as I looked up there was the most beautiful shop with the exact dress I was looking for. I still wear it with pride, knowing that the angels led me straight to the shop.

— *CAROL DE VASCONCELOS DCS*

~ An Angel Holiday ~

Angels are with us all the time but sometimes they turn a special occasion like a holiday into something even more special.

• • • • • •

Angels are magnificent beings of light. They are part of my life and I connect with them all the time. I recently visited my sister in London. The angels assisted me with everything including my visa application – I was able to collect my visa just three days after submitting my documents, which is unheard of. While we were in London the angels always provided us with convenient parking, prompting my sister to say, "You must have asked the angels!"

— *LILA NORVAL DCS*

~ Signs ~

Coincidences are organized by your guides and angels to make you pay attention.

• • • • • •

I get lots and lots of signs! My sister, mother and I always see white feathers around. My mother found two white feathers in her bedroom underneath a chair and she doesn't have a bird – or windows! She didn't believe in angels until her parents passed and she started regularly seeing rainbows and white feathers in random places.

— *ANON*

~ Reversing the Car ~

This story was a reminder to me to ask the angels when I reverse the car.

•••••••

I could not reverse my car as the ground was uneven. After trying unsuccessfully a few times, I felt frustrated but then remembered the angels. I switched off the engine and calmly asked them to help me reverse the car. I then reversed effortlessly over the uneven ground.

— *ANON*

~ House and Cleansing Angels ~

This story is a brilliant reminder about the connectedness of all things.

•••••••

I received guidance that I needed to raise the frequency and work with the energy in my home. I called on my house-cleansing angels for assistance. While I was cleansing the rooms my house angels showed me that rooms can be viewed as different chakras.

I noticed that friends, family and I linger in certain chakra rooms more than others. With pure intent I told them to call in the aura cleansing angels to dust their auras with golden dusters and sweep up with their golden brooms afterwards. Later they called to let me know that things had changed positively.

I also feel a positive change in myself; I am healthier and happier working with the angels in charge of each chakra in my physical body and in my home.

— *MARION EDWARDS DCS*

~ Angelic Intervention ~

There is no such thing as an accident. The angels and guides arrange all "coincidences" and "accidental" happenings.

•••••••

On our visit to Legoland, someone accidentally took my sister's backpack while we were on one of the fun rides. I called on Archangels Chamuel and Michael to intervene and my sister's bag was returned to her with all her belongings including her purse and cell phone.

— *LILA NORVAL DCS*

~ An Angel Appears ~

When we are working with healing energies and in a pure vibration it is easier for angels to connect with us.

•••••••

I had just given my mum some reiki and we were sitting together on the floor talking about angels and what they meant to us. Suddenly an angel appeared in front of me next to my mum. There was no colour, just a black outline. I was not afraid, just surprised.

— *KATIE CURTIS*

~ Wonderful Energy ~

When you ask sincerely for energy you will receive it.

. . . . . .

One night as I said my prayers I asked the creator to send a column of white light to cover me from head to toe and protect me. I found myself surrounded by a pulsating energy. I lay absolutely still and the pulsating continued, down over my heart chakra and moving to my feet. My mind was blissful. I kept thanking the energy. It was a wonderful experience and I am very thankful.

— *ANON*

LOST AND FOUND

ANGELS OF LOVE help us find missing or misplaced items. If for some reason the item does not reappear I trust that the angels always have a reason.

~ Wedding Rings ~

Wedding rings are very precious and personal.

. . . . . .

While swimming one night the cold water made my fingers shrink and my wedding rings fell into the dark muddy water. I could not find them.

I asked my guardian angel for help and a miracle happened! The next morning my son came into our room and exclaimed, "Mother, I've found your rings in the lake!" The rings were side by side, glittering among the stones. I hope this story brings you faith in the angels, because they really are around us to help us.

— *AULIKKI JUURINEN*

~ Helpful Angels ~

Here is someone else unexpectedly reunited with her wedding ring after she asked the angels.

. . . . . .

After going shopping with a friend I realized that I'd lost my wedding ring. I must have left it in the toilets at the shopping centre when washing my hands. We drove back and searched everywhere, but to no avail. I was so upset. I put up some reward notices but didn't expect to see my beautiful ring again.

I asked the angels to find my ring. Later a lady called – she had found it!

— *RENE*

~ Lost Money ~

The angels have unexpected ways of keeping things safe for you.

. . . . . .

I had just finished working in my therapy room in the garden. I reached the house and put down my keys and cardigan. Then I noticed the 50-Euro note that had been in my hand was missing. I returned to my therapy room but there was no sign of it. There was no breeze so I knew if I had dropped it in the garden, it would still be there. I rechecked my therapy room several times.

I asked the angels to help and decided to walk round the garden again for a final check. I looked under my car and as I bent down I felt a scratch on my stomach. To my surprise the note was tucked into the waistband of my trousers. I had never felt a thing! I could not thank the angels enough for their help.

— *PAULINE*

~ Keeping Keys Safe ~

Synchronicities are organized by the angels.

• • • • • •

I was walking down my road when I noticed a man picking up a set of keys. He asked if they were mine and I said no. I suggested that he put them on the wall, in case the owner returned looking for them.

I asked the angels of lost property to help reunite the keys and their owner. Later that day I noticed a man searching for something and asked if he had lost his keys. He was surprised and said yes. I walked to the wall and handed him the keys. He gave me a big hug and called me an angel.

I smiled and said thank you to the angels. It made my day!

— *RUBY GOURI*

~ Heavenly Helpers ~

What an amazing experience to feel an angel take your hand and guide you to what you need to find.

• • • • • •

My daughter and her friend wanted me to attune them to reiki. In preparation I had to cleanse the room with sage; however, I couldn't find my sage stick. I asked the angels for help. I heard "It's behind." I looked behind but still couldn't find it. I asked the angels again.

Once more I was told "It's behind." "OK, behind what?" I said, then felt my hand being guided to a shelf and behind a box of flower essences was the sage stick! I thanked the angel helper.

— *CATHERINE MCMAHON DCS*

~ Safe and Sound ~

The angels save time when help is requested to return a debit card!

• • • • • •

I lost my debit card while coming out of the bank, but didn't notice until I was in a shop later. I asked the angels to find it for me, and by the time I got back to the bank someone had handed in my card. A bank teller who works in my village recognized my name and gave it to me. I was then able to give her a cheque I had forgotten to pay in – thus avoiding a long queue!

— *ALISON*

~ Finding a Receipt ~

I have a sense of awe when I see the way angels move objects and draw your attention to things to help you whenever you ask.

••••••

A friend of mine recently had a baby. I had been collecting items for her baby shower and, as I folded a pair of trousers into the parcel, I noticed a small tear. I needed the receipt for a full refund, so I said, "OK angels, I need this receipt, I know you can find it for me."

Later I noticed a leaflet sticking out from under the bed. I picked it up and underneath it was the receipt! Thank you angels.

— *CATHERINE MCMAHON DCS*

~ Lost Crystal ~

After you have asked the angels to help you find something, look again where you have already searched.

••••••

My husband lost his special crystal. We looked for it to no avail. I asked the angels to help and something caught my eye beside the plant pots – it was the crystal! We had looked at the very same spot a number of times and it hadn't been there, but now it was. Once again the angels had answered our pleas.

— *KARALENA MACKINLAY DCS*

~ Lost and Found ~

When you meditate and connect with the angels or archangels they may lead you to what you seek.

••••••

My husband restores classic Triumph sports cars and is passionate about his hobby. One day he came upstairs, very agitated. He could not find the spanner he needed to complete the work. Could I help?

We searched for two days, then I thought to ask Archangel Gabriel for help. I was given a flash vision of something falling down in the engine compartment. So I said to Gabriel, "Please show me where it is?"

The spanner was stuck on a ledge in the engine. Thank you Archangel Gabriel, thank you.

— *JENNY HART DCS*

~ Finding Lost Jewels ~

Faith and trust make the impossible become possible.

••••••

My friends and I were at a wedding with lots of energetic Scottish Highland dancing. As we prepared to leave one of my friends noticed that the large stone from her new ring was missing. It was a special gift from her husband and she was in tears. I told her I'd find it and asked the angels to guide me to it. I walked straight to where the band had been, and there was the stone. No one could believe I'd found it so quickly, and my friend and her husband were amazed and grateful.

— *KARIN FINEGAN DCS*

~ Lost Earring ~

The angels return lost items when the time is right.

• • • • • •

I lost one of my angel earrings. I was upset as it had a lot of sentimental value. I looked everywhere, but no luck. I gave up hope and kept the other one to hang on the Christmas tree. Months later I opened the front door – and found my earring lying on the doorstep. It was positioned as though it had been gently and carefully laid down. It was weathered but undamaged. I was astonished and very grateful. The message is "Never give up hope."

— *KARALENA MACKINLAY DCS*

~ Positive Affirmation ~

When we make positive affirmations the angels take that energy and help you.

• • • • • •

My sister and I were caring for our mum, who was in hospital. One day I returned home from the hospital by taxi and, the next morning, I couldn't find my purse. My sister hadn't seen it and the taxi company said it had not been left in the car. I constantly repeated the affirmation "My purse is found."

When I went to my sister's house my bright blue purse was lying on the grass verge. All my money and cards were intact. My sister lives on a busy street near a school, a shop and a bus route. My friend said that angels would have hidden my purse with their beautiful wings.

— *TRISH THORPE*

~ Follow Your Instinct ~

Angels impress on us to check in the most unlikely places.

• • • • • •

Before my son left to go to South Africa he couldn't find the packets of cigarettes that he had arrived with from Thailand. I said, "I'll ask my search angels," went into his room and opened the wardrobe. On the first shelf was an empty shoebox; I instinctively moved it and lo and behold the cigarettes were behind it!

— *ANGELA*

~ Search Angels ~

Sometimes the angels guide us to do a clearout and cleanse as they help us search for lost items!

• • • • • •

I was looking for my book to research a client's cold feet. The book was not where I thought it should be, so I asked my search angels. They led me to my healing room and a "clearing" ensued. When I had done the necessary clearing my foot-reading book appeared. Thank you once again my wonderful Angels.

— *ANGELA*

~ My Diamond Ring ~

The angels work in many ways.

••••••

My grandmother offered me my great-grandmother's diamond ring and I was very thankful. One day I placed it in my trouser pocket while cooking. When I went to put the ring in my jewel case later, my pocket was empty – no ring!

I asked Archangel Chamuel and the angels of love to help me. My inner voice told me to trust and that's what I did. Months later I decided to tidy under my bed. When I finished I saw something sparkling in the corner! It was my ring! I had no idea how it got there.

I started dancing and singing. I knew the angels were celebrating with me because I felt this "pure" happiness. I thanked Chamuel and the angels for their support.

— *JENNIFER LEA*

~ Gold Bracelet ~

Sometimes the angels arrange for precious things to be returned to us in special ways.

••••••

While shopping I realized that my gold bracelet (an eighteenth-birthday present from my parents) was missing. I retraced my steps to the car. No sign of my bracelet. I decided to check with the shop's customer services desk.

A lady came to the desk. I asked about my bracelet and she just handed it to me and walked away. She never spoke or asked for any identification. I had an overwhelming feeling that she was no "ordinary lady" but someone "special."

— *BERNICE*

~ Finding My Husband's Glasses ~

Prayer is so powerful and effective.

••••••

While on a sailing sabbatical, my husband dropped a pair of glasses into the water. While he dived and searched, I prayed to the angels. After two or three attempts my husband found the glasses. Proof that prayers work – I thanked the angels for their help.

— *BRITTA*

ANGELS ORGANIZE TIME

TIME MAY FEEL LINEAR but in fact it is not. When your consciousness is third-dimensional time goes slowly. When you raise your frequency to the fifth dimension, time flies. In the seventh dimension, which is the angelic energy, there is no time – everything happens simultaneously. Angels can utilize these frequencies to alter your concept of time, as you will see in the following stories.

~ Unexpected Stopover ~

Because angels always work for your highest good they may initially seem to be causing disruption – they might arrange for you to be late or miss a connection.

• • • • • •

I was flying from South Africa to the UK. The travel agent booked my flight with a stopover in Cape Town. When I went to book in for my London flight I was told the flight was overbooked and I could not fly until the following day, so I found myself with some extra time in Cape Town. My cousin invited me to lunch with him, his wife and his sister. I had not seen them for twenty-five years and we had a lovely time. I felt that there was a reason for this meeting, but could not quite work it out.

Three months later my cousin was diagnosed with a malignant brain tumour. As we had met up not long before, I felt better able to communicate with them during this difficult time. I am grateful to my angel for organizing that stopover.

— *ANON*

~ Lifted out of Trouble ~

I know the angels were doing this for my highest good.

• • • • • •

I was on my way to a meeting in London and had to pick someone up on the way. I asked Archangel Michael to protect my journey, as I always do, which was fortunate. I was listening to *The Time Traveller's Wife* as I as I drove down the M25, a route I knew very well.

I glanced at the clock and murmured to myself that it was exactly ten minutes to Junction 11 and I was in good time. Within what felt like a split second I looked round and I didn't know where I was. It dawned on me that I was further down the motorway in Kent! I knew I hadn't been driving unconsciously. I had been lifted out of time and this was triggered by *The Time Traveller's Wife*.

I managed to find the right direction and arrive to pick up my friend in time. Later my guide, Kumeka, said that the angels had lifted me and placed me further down the motorway because I would have been involved in an accident on the slip road. Because I was not there the accident did not happen. Once again I could only thank the angels and wonder at the amazing things that happen in the universe.

— *DIANA COOPER*

~ Perfect Timing ~

When you work with the angels, trust them to make things happen at the right time.

......

Mary has a great relationship with the angels. She is also a wonderful healer and tunes in at all important times to send healing or hold the light. Being her late eighties she needs a twice-daily carer, and on Remembrance Sunday she and her friend wanted to send out the light at 11 a.m. during the two-minute silence, so was very upset to find that her carer could only come once that day, at 10.45 a.m.

To her surprise and delight someone arrived unexpectedly at 10.15 a.m. She did what was necessary – and then discovered that she had come to the wrong person!

Not only did it mean that Mary could tune in and send the light at 11 a.m. but she also had the opportunity to tell the carer about the angels and how they worked behind the scenes to help us!

— *AS TOLD TO DIANA COOPER BY MARY*

~ Repair Angels ~

When you hold a vision and keep telling the angels, they will help to bring it about.

......

In November 2011 Scotland had severe storms. My mum was in Spain at the time but her property in Scotland was OK. There were more storms in December and Mum received an email from a neighbour to say her fence had blown down. Friends and neighbours were all having trouble getting their fences fixed – with the amount of damage caused, the repair companies were overloaded.

My mum asked the angels to help her to source a fence company and fix the fence quickly.

The fence company quoted her a price and installed her fence within a week, while some of her friends were still waiting on quotes. The angels definitely had a helping hand in it.

— *PAULINE GOW DCS*

~ Catching a Train ~

Ask the angels to help you catch a connection if time is tight!

......

A friend of mine came to visit, travelling down by train. The day she left we had plenty of time before her train and decided to do some shopping on the way. We set off for the station later, but I missed the turning. It was Saturday morning and there was a lot of traffic. My friend and I prayed to the angels that we would get to the station on time. We arrived three minutes before the departure time.

— *CORNELIA MOHR DCS*

~ A Very Short Wait ~

Let the angels help you choose the right queue – or even better, clear it.

••••••

We had to go to the town hall and normally you have to queue for ages. I asked the angels to speed up the process. There were two desks we needed to visit and when we got to the first desk there was no one waiting, but after we'd finished there was a queue of ten people! At the second desk we waited ten minutes and again when we left there were ten people waiting.

— *PENNY WING DCS*

~ Just in Time ~

There is often a spiritual reason why you get lost. Very often it is because the angels want your particular energy in a certain place.

••••••

The angels have very often helped me to get to a place in perfect time. Recently I was driving to Glastonbury to a teachers' reunion and I wanted to be there before they arrived. I left with forty-five minutes to spare (according to my sat nav) and asked the angels to help me get there in good time.

However, the sat nav directed me into countryside and I went round in circles; I could not get back onto the right road. By now I felt I was going to be late and wondered why this should be happening. I explained to the angels that I wanted to arrive before the teachers so that I could greet them.

Luckily a man with a dog came towards me, so I abandoned technology and asked him the way. He gave me perfect directions. As I drove towards the car park in Glastonbury I passed the coach with the teachers disembarking. So I arrived in time to greet them. The angels told me they'd wanted me to put golden energy into that bit of countryside, so in the end all was divinely perfect.

— *DIANA COOPER*

~ Catching Flight ~

Angels will distort time to help you, so ask them if you need to catch a plane or train.

••••••

I travelled regularly to London from Glasgow. One Friday night I was delayed on the tube and arrived at Heathrow tube station just twenty minutes before the last flight was due to leave. I only had hand baggage and knew if I reached the flight I would be OK. If I missed it I would have had to pay for a hotel and another flight, so I was desperate.

I sent up a silent prayer for help. I held the vision of me walking onto the plane. The angels must have made time stop; I reached the door of the aircraft ten minutes before it left. No one I've told can believe it only took me ten minutes to reach the plane. I sent up my thanks to the angels.

— *KARIN FINEGAN DCS*

~ Angels Speed Up Time ~

Angels can shift time, as this story illustrates.

· · · · · ·

Driving back from my daughter's house, I pulled out of a junction and as I did so a large 4x4 came speeding round the corner. I thought, "Oh my God this is it," but then suddenly I realized my car was quite a way in front of the other vehicle. It could only have been angel assistance – as I pulled out the other vehicle had been on a collision course for my car – and I have never forgotten it.

— *ANON*

ANGEL HUMOUR

ALL EVOLVED, high-frequency beings have a wonderful sense of humour. It keeps them light! It is always said that angels fly because they take themselves lightly. Here are some stories to illustrate their sense of fun and delight.

~ Angel Humour ~

This story really made me laugh. You do indeed have to be careful what you ask for!

· · · · · ·

I find this story very amusing as it shows me a) be careful what you ask for! and b) angels have a sense of humour.

One night I was at my grandparents' house. I put my glasses on my book on the bedside table and said to my angels, "Angels, if you really exist you'll make my glasses disappear."

Really stupid request since I can barely see without my glasses! I woke up the next morning and they were gone. I laughed about it for days (even though I couldn't see) and my mum wouldn't believe my angels had hidden my glasses! I was convinced they would turn up, and yes, a few days later they appeared (thank you angels!) under a table in the same room!

— *CAROLINE FRANKS*

~ Teenage Angel Story ~

A delightful story of the way angels help us.

· · · · · ·

My husband's granddaughter is just under fourteen and we do not allow her to watch movies for older people. She wanted to watch a movie that featured Angelina Jolie but it had an age restriction of sixteen!

She tried every trick in the book to get to see this movie. I asked my angels to help me stay strong. With every outburst I continued to give her choices of, *Home*, *Kung Fu Panda* or a Will Smith movie.

The cashier asked me what movie I was going to see. Turning to Justine I asked her what movie and she said, reluctantly, "*Kung Fu Panda*." She was absolutely furious with me and sulking, and walked to the back row while I sat in the middle of the cinema. I gave my worries to the angels, sat back and enjoyed the movie. As I met up with Justine and we prepared to leave, the credits started to roll and I saw that one of the voice actors had been none other than Angelina Jolie. I gave Justine a huge hug and said, "Thank you so much. You chose a brilliant movie which I thoroughly enjoyed and you got to hear Angelina Jolie's voice. How special is that!"

She said, "Ouma Faye, I am so sorry for my behaviour."

I wanted to share how angels help in every situation, no matter how small you may think it to be.

— *FAYE MOOLMAN*

~ Jumping Around ~

The angels look after us but we are expected to use our common sense!

• • • • • •

I told my sons that they have a guardian angel who always looks after them. One day my twelve-year-old, who'd been outside playing on the trampoline, came inside in a huff. He said that his guardian angel wasn't doing his job! He had fallen off and hurt himself. I sent out a question, "Angels what should I answer him?" Then the words came out, "You have to learn to look after your body!" Great insight from the angels.

— *KARI NYGARD DCS*

~ Religious Truths ~

The angels have a way of answering questions in a perfect and funny way.

• • • • • •

On my way to the shops a van overtook me and on the back door was the name BAPTIST. At the next roundabout there was a white truck opposite me with NAZARETH on the hood. Seconds later I turned in to the car park and the van beside me had a huge sticker of the Blessed Virgin Mary. I laughed as the previous day I had pondered over some religious truths and this is the response I got!

— *ANN QUINN*

~ The Angels Testing Me ~

Here is a psychic development exercise we can all practise – but in this case the angels are making it great fun.

• • • • • •

One day I was healing my eldest daughter, who is psychic. She said that Archangel Raphael and Archangel Michael were with us. I told her that I knew that. Then she said they want me to ask you which side they are at! So I told her.

My brother Pat who is in the spirit world came and I felt his presence strongly. Then my mother, grandfather, grandmother, my godmother, my dad and my stepdad, all of whom are in the spirit world, came forward, followed by Archangel Gabriel.

I was overwhelmed! Then they started swapping places. They were testing me to see if I could sense where they were – and they were having fun! Although I couldn't see them I knew exactly where they all were. It was truly an amazing day.

—*ANON*

~ Call or Yodel ~

I laughed my head off when I read this story.

• • • • • •

I've believed in angels since I was a little girl and feel a very close connection with Archangel Michael. One day I asked him to contact me. I said I'd like a call or even a yodel! I laughed the next day when I saw a big van outside my house with YODEL written on its side!

— *TRACEY*

~ Angels Love ~

There's nothing like a musical message from the angels to make you feel good.

• • • • • •

One morning I felt grumpy, tired and stressed about work. I said, "Angels, help me, help me, help me!" I did a short angel meditation to feel their presence. I started out for work, still not happy and not wanting any noise on the journey! I turned on the radio. A song came on, 'Who Loves You Pretty Baby'. My mood lifted and I smiled, said thank you and listened intently. In my mind I saw the angels dancing to the music. That day I was happy and not a bit stressed.

— *CAROLYN*

~ Angel Feathers ~

So you ask for feathers and what do you expect? We must be ready to laugh with the angels.

• • • • • •

My friend Deborah was upset as her angels never left her feathers although she continually wished to be given one. However, the angels soon showered her with feathers when her children cut open one of her pillowcases and feathers filled her home. Deborah was cross but her husband laughed and said, "You have been asking for feather for months so be careful what you wish for." The angels will always find a way to show you they are with you – it just might not be the way you hope for!

— *ELOISE BENNETT DCS*

~ Flying with Sophi ~

I love this story of Carol's angel's booming laughter and great sense of fun.

• • • • • •

I have done many meditations requesting that our guardian angels lift us up. I always apologize to Sophi, my guardian angel, for being heavy.

During a meditation we were required to levitate (with the assistance of our guardian angel) up to a temple. I had a clear vision of Sophi, radiant white, standing behind me, three times taller and stronger than me. I chuckled quietly as I allowed him to float me up the mountain. When we emerged from the temple I asked Sophi if we could do a little zooming around before we descended. I remember his delighted face, his deep laughter as we whizzed though the heavens before landing light as feathers. He remains close by. Thank Heaven for guardian angels.

— *CAROL COPPINGER DCS*

~ Angel Cards ~

We often actually know the answers ourselves and are surprised when the angels tell us the same thing!

· · · · · ·

I was at a time in my life where I need to make a few choices about relationships and I was a bit lost. I decided to pick some angel cards. The funny thing was I thought it would be typical if the cards I picked were forgiveness, (as I was annoyed with a certain someone) and choices. To my surprise I picked them both.

— *ANON*

~ Eagle Feather ~

When we talk to people about our guardian angels the most astonishing things happen.

· · · · · ·

My guardian angel is called Nicolas, and I constantly ask him for signs. One day, when I had to go to a lawyer's office to sign papers, I asked for an eagle feather. The office was decorated with native art and I noticed an eagle feather and asked the lawyer, "Is that an eagle feather?" He said yes and that I could have it. I started crying because I couldn't believe what had happened. I explained to him about Nicolas and we ended up talking for two hours about angels. An amazing day!

— *ANON*

~ Turkeys and Feathers ~

Ask the angels and the feathers come thick and fast.

· · · · · ·

I was driving my son and nieces to a tennis lesson. I'd had words with the girls before we set off – they had been asked to clean their bedroom and had found many excuses for not doing it. The atmosphere was unpleasant, but the only person it was going to affect was me so I asked the angels to help lift my mood. As I drove along the country road a livestock lorry appeared and there was suddenly a barrage of feathers, mainly white, heading in my direction. I knew the angels had orchestrated this. The angels certainly did what I asked. My mood altered immediately I just had to laugh!

— *PAULINE*

~ Dropping Pearls ~

The angels have a delightful way of using nature to provide proof.

My angel group was discussing angel signs and I told them how to set their own. One of the students asked if she could have pearls as her symbol. There was much laughter as I told her that the angels probably wouldn't be giving her actual jewellery! Instead she might see the name "Pearl" or an advert, a shop selling pearls etc.

The next day she texted to say "The angels have showered me with pearls today!" There had been a tremendous hailstorm and the hailstones looked like pearls covering the road as she drove!

— SUSIE

~ I Believe in Angels ~

Feathers come and feathers go.

I became curious about angels. I'd never had a personal experience, but had read things and I wanted proof. One night I "challenged" the angels to show me that they existed. The next morning an Abba song, 'I Have a Dream', specifically the lyric "I believe in angels," was playing in my head.

I wondered if it was just my subconscious. Then I saw a white feather – I was delighted that they answered my call.

I put the feather in a little trinket box. Later when I opened the trinket box the feather had disappeared as mysteriously as it had arrived!

Now angels often communicate with me through random song lyrics in my mind or on the radio. I feel blessed to receive their loving guidance.

— JANE

~ They Parked Us Side by Side ~

Angels love to arrange synchronicities for us to remind us that they are looking out for us.

I met Lila during a workshop and we got on well and arranged to meet for coffee at a shopping centre, with lots of different parking areas on different floors. As usual I asked the parking angels to arrange a safe parking space close to the entrance.

Lila was waiting for me at the coffee shop. Afterwards I asked her to come back to my car as I had a gift for her.

We could not believe our eyes when we realized that our angels had guided both of us to the same floor – and to parking spaces next to each other!

With eyes filled with tears of love we laughed at the angels' sense of humour and their synchronizing skills.

— HETTIE VAN DER SCHYFF DCS

~ Unique Signs ~

The angel sense of humour really shines out in this one.

••••••

In an angel workshop I was teaching we were talking about setting individual signs for our angels. I already have my personal sign, but I paired up with one of the students to do the exercise.

I heard my guardian angel laugh and say to me, "But you have your sign! What do you want now, a lollipop?" I saw the image of a large toffee lollipop with brightly coloured swirls. A few days later I was out shopping in town with a friend. We were attracted to a shop we had not seen before. Its name was Lollipop, they sold purses and handbags and on one of the bags I was surprised to see an angel's wing!

— *SUSAN RUDD DCS*

~ Nits – or Angels ~

I roared with laughter when I read this story.

••••••

Five years ago we moved to France. I kept feeling energy around the top of my head like pins and needles. It happened a lot so I said to my husband that the kids must have brought home head lice. I dosed the whole family with lotions even though the kids protested!

Afterwards the kids said, "It's just you Mum, none of us have a tingly scalp!" There weren't any lice. Later I saw a TV programme on angels and realized I had been sensing angel energy. I still get the same sensation, but I know now that it's not head lice!

— *ANN*

DREAMS

DREAMS are special states when the "censor" that protects your conscious mind is relaxed and you can retrieve information from your subconscious mind. At this time you are also available to messages from the angels and spiritual worlds. These can be very important moments.

~ Dream Angel Warning ~

Your guardian angel can introduce him or herself to you during your dreams and will also help you at this time.

••••••

I'm a big dreamer and record my experiences in my dream book. One night my dream began with someone touching me.

The person stood behind me and I never saw his face but he introduced himself as Daniel, my guardian angel. He pressed his hands against my back, my sides and my shoulders. He was giving me added strength during a challenging time.

Daniel told me that he had protected me and my family for many years but was now unable to protect my father. He showed me my father's heart. I woke up unsure of what to make of my experience.

A few weeks later my father-in-law was rushed into hospital having suffered a stroke! I had been convinced the angel was warning me of my dad. I never thought it could be my father-in-law, though I have always thought of him as if he was my own dad. I guess that's why my angel just said "dad." I knew that my encounter with my guardian angel was indeed real when the doctors diagnosed the stroke as having been caused by a blockage from his heart to his head.

— *ELLOUISE*

~ A Rainbow Angel ~

When you see an angel in your dreams it is as real and meaningful as when you see one when you are awake.

......

Some years ago I moved into a flat in a very spiritual area. I started to have dreams. During one dream my guardian angel came to me. He had huge wings of soft muted rainbow colours and two pairs of small fluttering wings on each side. This was so emotional for me that I cried whenever I told anyone.

— *CATHY BOLTWOOD*

~ Visit in My Dreams ~

Loved ones who have passed over sometimes connect with us in our dreams.

......

Since I was young, I have dreamed of angels visiting me while I slept. The dreams seemed real and told me things that made me believe it was really them coming to me from another world. There is no way that I can't believe in angels when I have seen them!

— *ANON*

~ Abundance Guidance through a Dream ~

Dishonesty creates karma and when you turn your back on that dark path the angels support you fully – as this story illustrates.

......

I had an angelic experience and received divine guidance through a dream. I had a financial need and was trying to figure out how to get extra funds. I realized that I could claim a few reimbursements, but only if I had the appropriate bills, which I did not have. A colleague suggested that I could use fake bills, but I was hesitant.

During an official dinner, I heard the directors talking about false bills and how management would take action to stop this practice. This confirmed my decision.

That night I invoked Archangels Gabriel and Michael to give me clarity and courage and Archangel Uriel to address my financial insecurities.

Archangel Michael and Gabriel were at my bedside table that night and I asked them to show me the right path. I had a dream that the CFO and the HR head were asking me to apply for a salary advance and an interest-free loan.

I wrote an email to the CFO and HR head requesting this advance. Within two minutes I got approval from both.

— *PIU BANERJEE*

~ A New Angel in a Dream ~

Here is a reminder that you are never left alone.

• • • • • •

During a time of despair and feeling alone I asked to connect with my guardian angel. I took an afternoon nap and had a wonderful lucid dream. A woman sat by my bed. She was filled with compassion and put her hand on my forehead. She had short dark hair and was dressed in the fashion of the 1930s. She was surrounded by a peaceful light. She reminded me that I had not been left alone during my difficult time. I guessed this was a new angel working with me. I woke up calm, peaceful and no longer alone. I feel blessed that I can so easily contact angels.

— *NORMA PARFITT*

~ Dream of a Unicorn ~

When you dream of a unicorn it has come to you to touch your soul and help you on your journey.

• • • • • •

I had a vivid dream in which I was walking down a forest path. In front of me was a white-gold, glowing unicorn. It turned and looked at me and I felt a wondrous feeling of peace and love.

— *SHARON RALPH*

~ The Name of My Angel ~

When you are asleep you are more open to angelic guidance.

• • • • • •

Two weeks after I saw the beautiful angel in my dream, while I was asleep its name came to me – Bellisimo. And now I call her Bella.

— *CATHY BOLTWOOD*

~ Your Angel Is with You ~

When you dream of a feather it is a message from the angels in the same way as seeing a physical feather.

• • • • • •

I had a minor car crash and was upset and shaken. That night I dreamed of a large white feather in a wastepaper bin. The feather was as large as the bin. I had heard that feathers indicate angels being around you but wasn't sure so I emailed *Spirit and Destiny* magazine. They confirmed what I had thought.

Later I was driving and my car radio seemed to change stations. I heard the lyrics "Your angel is with you" over and over. I'd never heard the song before and I'm certain it was a sign that angels were with me.

— *BEKI*

~ Counting Blessings ~

When you are wishing for one thing, the angels may be offering you something even better.

......

I read about a choir of angels singing over someone while they slept, and I really wished the angels would sing over me. I asked my guardian angel but nothing happened.

A few weeks later, I fell asleep in the afternoon. From two corners of the room emanated beautiful spirals of brilliant white light. They rose in massive arches and landed on my third eye, where they exploded gently as a butterfly's wings.

The light was joyful and playful – as if it wanted to show me how love can be. I was moved to tears and felt completely safe. A voice repeated, "Angels watch you sleep."

— *PIP*

~ Archangel Names in the Night ~

When mighty archangels want to draw themselves to your attention they will access you when you are "available".

......

I got up in the night while still half asleep and went into the kitchen. I knew I had been dreaming of an angel. Two names dropped into my head – Metatron and Sandalphon. I had never heard of them and did not know who they were but I knew it was important so I wrote the names down. Now I know who they are and it has all slotted into place.

— *CATHY BOLTWOOD*

~ Archangel Michael in a Dream ~

When you dream about Archangel Michael it means that he was with you.

......

I went to bed and had a dream about Archangel Michael. I did not believe in angels at this point, or know anything about this archangel. However as soon as he appeared I felt as if I was with an old friend. The next day I went to the gym and the owner said, "Archangel Michael wants to help you. You are sometimes very stubborn, he cannot help you if you don't ask him for it and allow his help! He loves you!" I was so shocked as there is no way he could have known of my dream.

— *SUSAN ELSAWI*

~ *Angelic Sleep* ~

This story is a reminder that when we send love, healing, protection or anything else positive to someone, the angels use our thoughts to help them.

······

I went to bed early to relax and think nice things. I drifted off to sleep, feeling calm, then after a while felt myself being gently lifted from my bed and then being placed back down. It was only a few seconds, but it felt nice, as if I was being protected.

I told my mum what happened and she said she had asked the angels to go into my room and protect me, send me love and show me they are there.

— *LOUISA BOWSKILL*

CHAPTER 10

Seeing and Hearing Angels

ANGEL VOICES

As we rise in frequency more people are developing their throat chakras and becoming clairaudient. More and more of us will start to hear the voices of angels and spirits.

~ Told to Let Go ~

When you hear the voice of spirit it always illuminates you in some way.

• • • • • •

I was going through a stressful time financially. I could not see the way out of the situation and when I went to bed that night, I felt panic and fear.

I heard the voice of a woman, saying "Just relax, don't be scared, let go." I wasn't sure who it was, but I felt comforted and decided to heed her advice. I fell into a deep sleep but in the early hours, I was awakened by the sensation of hands lying me back down on my bed. I felt calm and hopeful and I knew at that point that everything would be well. I am sure it was the voice of my guardian angel, responding in my time of need.

— *ANON*

~ The Time Is Now ~

The angels sometimes attract your attention by flashing lights on and off, whether your eyes are open or closed.

• • • • • •

Sometimes it feels as if there are bright lights flashing on and off in my bedroom but when I open my eyes, there are no lights on and it is pitch dark. Then I hear a soft, but firm, voice in my head say "Get up!"

— *FOLASADE LOKO*

~ Last Meeting ~

When the angels speak it is important to listen and do what is asked.

• • • • • •

Annie's daughter Mary was very ill and in hospital. Annie's family were away and she asked me to take her to the hospital to visit. I had my mum staying and my small grandson to look after and was feeling stressed and so said "No, sorry, I haven't got time." However, a loud voice in my head said, "Take Annie to see Mary," so I loaded everybody into the car and took Annie to the hospital. We didn't know then, but that was the last time Annie was to see her daughter – Mary passed on that night.

— *SUE WALKER DCS*

~ Principality Angel of Cheltenham ~

Operating at a faster frequency than the archangels are the principalities, who oversee big businesses, towns and large projects.

When I first started teaching angel workshops I was invited to Cheltenham to facilitate a class of thirty people. This was daunting as I was nervous about driving such a distance. I called on the strength and courage of Archangel Michael and went forth.

After creating a sacred space I sat outside to centre myself before my participants arrived.

Then something awesome happened. A huge angel who said he was the Cheltenham principality angel bent down and whispered, "Thank you for bringing your light and teachings to our city. We are very grateful." I was delighted and my worries melted away.

— *ELOISE BENNETT DCS*

~ End of a Marriage ~

When it is time for a relationship to end the angels will gently support and guide us to ensure that we make the right decision, even if it does not match what others want.

A few years ago I was in a difficult situation with my husband and our vicar. When he had married us he asked us to see him if we faced any marriage difficulties and now both my husband and the vicar were trying to convince me to give our marriage a last chance.

Inside I was screaming "NO" and felt myself leave my body. It was too painful. I wanted OUT... I heard a calm voice say, "Don't worry, all will be well." I relaxed and those words helped me cope until my marriage ended. I am forever grateful for the strength and love angels give us all every day.

— *LOUISE WEIR*

~ First Awareness ~

It is when we are at rock bottom and exhausted by life that the angels come to us and take out the panic, leaving us calm and ready to climb our way back to living.

I was going through a challenging time and felt mentally, physically and emotionally exhausted.

A friend persuaded me to try reiki. I arrived and started ranting to the woman about my life, but I was in the wrong house! She kindly sent me to the right address.

I got back to my car and realized I'd locked my keys in it. A reassuring voice said, "Be still and do not panic. All will be well little one." I felt so calm and so relaxed – I knew this was an angel. I phoned my husband for help.

A young man came and said he could help me get into the car. It was his mum's house I'd gone to originally. The son managed to open the car door.

Then my husband arrived and he couldn't believe the change in me.

Within a few months I was attuned to reiki and connected with Archangel Raphael and his healing angels. I have been guided by angels ever since.

— *MAIRI BECKETT DCS*

~ Dream Time Guidance ~

When angels give us specific guidance they generally give us the strength and determination to fight for what we feel needs to be done.

* * * * * *

I awoke three nights in succession with my angel telling me to take my mother to the doctor because something was wrong with her tummy.

I took her to the surgery. As we sat in the waiting room I asked the angels to guide me as to what to say. The doctor couldn't find anything, but I was so distressed that he said he would send her for a scan but it could take time.

I asked to go private and he called the hospital and said, "Luck must be on your side – an appointment is available tomorrow."

Within hours of the scan I was told to take my mother to a vascular surgeon immediately. She had a triple AAA aortic aneurysm and she was rushed straight to theatre for major heart surgery. The surgeon said my mother was lucky; she would have had only hours to live had the aneurysm not been discovered. Once again I thanked all the angels for their guidance.

— *MARIEL FORDE CLARKE DCS*

~ Angel Encouragement ~

However bad things seem, your angels are trying to get through to you to help you.

* * * * * *

One New Year's Day we went walking in the countryside at the foot of Mont Sainte-Victoire. I found a little outcrop of rocks and sat with my face to the sun with the breeze in my hair and meditated. It felt wonderful.

My angel spoke to me, telling me that I was never alone; she was there, guiding me and I was on the brink of something new. Earlier in the day I had found a beautiful leaf and decided to leave it on the mountainside for the angels to take to God. When we got back to the hotel I went into the bathroom and there on the floor in front of me was a little white feather.

— *SUSIE COOPER*

~ Time of Need ~

When the angels are with you they bring a wonderful sense of calm and peace and a knowing that all will be well.

......

Some time back I went through a stressful time financially. I could not see the way out and went to bed one night with a sense of panic and fear.

I heard a woman's voice saying "Just relax, don't be scared, let go." I felt comforted and decided to heed her advice. I fell into a deep sleep. During the night I felt hands underneath me supporting and comforting me and an overwhelming sense of calm and hope. I knew everything would be well. I am sure it was the voice of my guardian angel, helping me in my time of need.

— *JAYSHREE NAIDOO*

~ Voice of an Angel ~

When you can hear your angel's voice trying to help you, it really does make your life easier!

......

One afternoon I went to the supermarket and parked my car in a different spot from usual. When I'd finished shopping, I automatically went to where I usually park my car. I heard a very strong voice, saying to me: "We parked our car on the opposite side." I kept hearing the voice; it got louder and I turned to see who was yelling. There was no one there! Then it dawned on me: "It is the voice of an angel; my car is parked in a completely different location."

— *MARJETKA NOVAK DCS*

~ A Reminder of Love ~

The universe, Source, the angels, they never abandon or forsake us and here they demonstrate this.

......

I experienced a dark night of the soul. Although I knew it was this, I felt abandoned and doubted all connection from the divine and God. I said to Source, "You have abandoned me!" I heard a booming voice say, "I have never abandoned you, you have abandoned yourself." Still feeling raw and disconnected, I looked down my hall and saw a stream of pure white angels. They came to remind me of my divine connection when I needed it most. I stood in their purity and grace and allowed them to fill my heart with light.

What a powerful example of the truth that when life gets too big for your faith, then it's your faith that has to change. Since then my faith is grounded and rooted in remembrance of the love our angels have for us. All they want is for us to remember our divinity and truth.

— *REV MARIE LOUISE JONES*

~ Extra Hours ~

Never give up hope. If it is right, no matter how impossible it seems the job will be yours.

. . . . . .

I was working as a locum in a new surgery, which I enjoyed, so I asked if there were more hours available. I was told they would love to have me but they had just signed a contract with a long-term locum. I was disappointed but accepted it. A few days later I heard a clear message from my guardian angel that the locum could not do the work and the job was mine. The practice manager came to see me and asked me if I could do more hours as the locum could not work for them any more. I was delighted and am still happily working for the surgery.

— *DR BIRINDER KAUR*

~ Saved by Angels ~

If your soul has not agreed that it is your time to die, your guardian angel will make sure that you live.

. . . . . .

An attendee at my workshop told us a story from his youth. He lived in a basement that had no windows and one day, unbeknown to him, the gas heater started leaking. He thought he heard a voice in his sleep say: "Get up and get out." He ignored it at first, but the voice became louder and louder until he could not ignore it any more. Although affected by fumes, he dragged himself out and put his head out the door so the neighbours would rescue him. His guardian angel saved his life.

— *MARJETKA NOVAK DCS*

~ With Angels All Things Are Possible ~

So many of us have been in terrible situations and it is such a relief to know that the angels are helping in the background to sort everything out.

. . . . . .

I returned to Sweden with my one-year-old daughter after divorcing her father. I could not get a job without daycare. Because I had no job I could not rent an apartment. Because I had no apartment I could not get daycare … It was a nightmare!

Finally I managed to find a sublet and was accepted for further education. Sophie got a place in daycare and I was so happy! However I soon found out that I could not keep the flat. The government promised another one but none were available. Also the daycare and the gymnasium (where I studied) were in this area. If I had to move I would have to abandon my studies, and I didn't know how I would manage my daughter's daycare. I lay awake every night tossing and turning. Three weeks before my eviction I was sleepless as usual, when I heard a beautiful, loving, woman's voice saying, "Do not worry; everything will be OK."

I fell asleep immediately. Two days later I got a letter saying that I had a new flat next to the gymnasium and close to Sophie's daycare.

— *KAY GALLEN-KALLELA*

~ Loving Guidance ~

Here is a fascinating story where an angel audibly gives a specific timescale for the resolution of a situation.

• • • • • •

I was going through a painful marriage break-up and struggling to cope. One night I was sitting in my garden, crying and pleading for help. I was close to breakdown. I asked for the truth to be revealed to me so I might make choices and resolve the situation. I became calm and heard a voice saying, "Be at peace my child, in three days all will be resolved."

I knew I could trust this information and never questioned it. I slept for the first time in a long time. A close friend thought I was mad when I told her my experience. Exactly three days later, the truth came out and I was able to make my decision. Was it an angel, guide, master? It doesn't matter – I am eternally grateful and the experience sustained me. I knew I was never alone.

— *CAROL*

~ Love Endures All ~

If only we all knew just how much our guardian angels do to help us when we are disappointed or down.

• • • • • •

I was very disappointed not to get a part in a show that I wanted. As I had not had much success in the work arena it hit even harder. I was in tears, but I could feel waves of love heading in my direction followed by words of wisdom: "Count your blessings" and "Love endures all."

This has continued ever since and I know it is from the angels.

— *STEPHANIE*

~ The Ladder ~

If it is not your time to die your angel will make sure you get the message – as in this dramatic story.

• • • • • •

When I was a child of two years old I fell into a swimming pool. There was no one around and I sank to the bottom. A very comforting voice said clearly, "Open your eyes ... Now get to the ladder." I did and I am alive.

— *SHARON OLSEN GUAM*

~ Angelic Survival Instructions ~

Sometimes your angel has to work very hard to help you survive and heal! As in the previous example the angels are definitely looking after Sharon.

• • • • • •

I poured petrol onto a pile of wood without knowing that there were hot coals still in it. The five-gallon petrol container exploded! The same calm voice that had spoken to me in the swimming pool when I was a small child told me to take my shirt off, drop and roll. I survived and later realized my angels had been with me both times. I have very little scarring and people cannot tell that this incident happened. All this is because I prayed to my angels, not knowing their names but knowing they were there.

— *SHARON OLSEN GUAM*

~ A Hand On My Shoulder ~

An earthbound spirit is one who has not passed properly into the light. Their energy is often challenging and this can affect sensitive people, who need angelic protection.

· · · · · ·

I'd had a difficult year that left me feeling physically, emotionally and spiritually drained. I seemed to be extra-sensitive to negativity. I asked Archangel Michael for his protection.

One day I arranged to meet my best friend for lunch. While talking to her about my concerns she said she felt low, drained and quite poorly. As we chatted I saw an angel standing behind us. He was around 7 ft tall, all in white. He placed his right hand on my friend's left shoulder and his left hand on my right shoulder and said simply, "I'm here, you have my protection." I received a boost of strength and comfort and was overcome by the love of this angel towards me.

I believe in angels because I have seen one! Angels want to support you on your life's journey. Ask for their help and welcome them in.

— *THERESA MONSON*

~ Only Your Earthly Parents ~

Many people feel unloved and wonder why they chose their particular parents. More information on this is found in my book Transform your Life.

· · · · · ·

I was sad one night, asking why I never felt my parents cared for and loved me. Why had I chosen these parents? I felt a loving feeling come over me and heard, "We are your true parents. We love you dearly. They are only your earthly parents and everything is fine." I cried, for the feeling of love I felt was so strong.

Since then I have never felt sad about my parents.

— *KAY GALLEN-KALLELA*

~ An Angel Called My Name ~

Wow! What a wonderful confirmation from the angels.

· · · · · ·

After a stroke I have some paralysis and my husband looks after me. He takes some time out by visiting relatives in France, and when he is gone I am looked after by carers. The night before my husband left for his latest trip away, I said my usual prayers and asked my guardian angel to protect me and give me a sign to let me know they were there.

The next morning I heard my name called out by a voice I did not recognize. I thought it was one of my carers so I called that I was in the kitchen, but no one came. No one was there, but I had heard my name called so clearly. I knew that was the sign to confirm my protection. How wonderful!

— *VIVIEN BARBOTEAU*

~ Angel Elijah ~

Carol is a psychic who sees and communicates with angels on a daily basis.

••••••

Over the years I have had many angel occurences happen to me. One night I was getting ready for bed when a sound seemed to go through the top of my head and down my body. It was a high sound that spoke to my spirit. I fell into a deep sleep.

My angels had told me to keep records of everything, so later I went to write down my experience. As I started to write the sound came again, just like before. I put my journal down and went into the experience. I heard a deep male voice that seemed to come from a much higher place and carried a higher vibration than I had ever experienced. I received a powerful message: "I am the angel Elijah. You are to awaken and call forth all other Earth angels. You will be guided. We love you so. You are the mother of all."

The message was profound. I focused on my breath as the angels had taught me, as it brings your body, mind and spirit into alignment.

— *CAROL GUY*

SEEING ANGELS

THERE ARE many ways to connect with angels. People who see angels are considered clairvoyant and this chapter contains some lovely examples of this.

~ An Angel Appears to Two of Us ~

The wonderful thing about this awesome story is that Hannah-Belle and her husband both saw this angel, who she describes here in detail.

••••••

One summer morning I was sitting in bed with my husband having a drink and discussing the day ahead. The sun streamed in through the window behind Daniel. It hit the wall in front of us onto the chest of drawers. It got brighter and brighter and I could see a figure developing. I nudged Daniel and whispered, "Are you seeing what I'm seeing?"

He replied, "I am." We sat there speechless. The light being was 5 ft high. We could see its wings and feathers – even the halo. The light being got brighter and brighter for about three minutes, then faded away.

I'll never forget the feathers – they were perfect. I was so privileged to see this, especially with my husband there too.

— *HANNAH-BELLE ROBERTS*

~ Healing the Bereaved ~

In this story Lesley shares one of the most clear and beautiful descriptions of an angel that I have read.

······

My dear mum had been frail for a while but it was still a shock when she died. It was the most horrific grief I have known. I lay in bed and called out to my mum and God. I was saying sorry for not being able to stop her dying and asked God to look after her. I saw a bright light, which moved from the top of my head, down my body to my feet. I saw the most beautiful, 8-foot-tall angel. Its hair was silvery-white and the face was porcelain. Its eyes were closed in deep concentration. The gown was full of folds. The angel was holding a ball of light that shone on me.

I saw about six or eight hands touching the gown. I took this to be a message of healing. Were they sending a message about my mum being healed, or to help me with healing my grief, or both? I have seen spirits since I was a young child but I never imagined angels being real in today's world. I say a prayer for angels and archangels every night, just as I say prayers for my lovely mum.

— *LESLEY DARBYSHIRE*

~ Angelic Presence ~

What more wonderful confirmation and comfort at a time of loss than to see an angel?

······

I remember my mother telling us that when Granddad passed he was placed in the front room of our home. As we had guests my mother had given up her bed and slept in the front room alongside the coffin. She awoke in the night and saw a very bright light. As she looked towards the coffin there stood a large angel.

— *MARGARET GRUNDY DCS*

~ Bringing Hope ~

Angels make magic happen.

······

It was 1997 and I was in despair. I had four young children, a full-time job, a husband with a demanding job and my mother (who lived with us) had dementia.

I was exhausted and frustrated – I could not seem to get the right help for my mother despite all my efforts. One night I could not sleep; I lay in bed feeling I could no longer cope and remember saying, "Please help me." At the side of my bed a bright light appeared and a beautiful silver angel came forward, took my hand and said everything was going to be all right. I was then cocooned in a vibration of peace and love so powerful that I cannot fully describe it in words.

The very next day things started to happen – as if by magic the help I needed for my mum appeared. This powerful experience has stayed with me and inspired me to work with and teach others about angels.

— *ELIZABETH ANN DCS*

~ Car Crash Angels ~

If you refuse to listen to the messages of the angels your soul may agree to allow you to be given a harsher wake-up call.

• • • • • •

I had a bad car crash when a young man hit me from behind. My car was crushed and I was trapped. When help arrived, however, I walked free, unharmed. The police and ambulance crew were amazed and told me how lucky I was to be alive. That night I was visited by several angels. As I looked at them I was filled with a sensation of great calm and love.

One said, "What did we have to do to make you stop?" I was in a destructive relationship and a stressful job, both of which I needed to get out of.

The car crash and resulting back pain meant I had some time off work; during this time I ended the relationship and looked for a new job. The result – a new vocation and meeting my life partner. I am convinced the angels decided to visit that night to encourage me to take positive action.

— *CAITLIN ALLEN*

~ Seeing People's Angels ~

This is the story of someone who was very sensitive as a child and did not know how to cope with her clairvoyant vision.

• • • • • •

I've been able to see auras since I was small. I thought everyone could see them; it wasn't until I was ten that I realized not everyone could. About ten years ago light started to appear next to a person I was looking at, or in full-body form on its own, always bright white. I started to see facial features almost like a negative, which also happens when I blink, like a flash from a camera.

I've seen some amazing things. For example once I was watching four people walking out of the sea, only to realize eventually that there were only two people and the other figures, bright shapes behind them were their guardian angels. I know what I see are angels or guides. It is very comforting.

— *JENNIFER PALMER*

~ Reminder to Live ~

This is a profound message from the angels that we are here to live and embrace every moment.

• • • • • •

The last five years have been the toughest I've known. I have moved six times and suffered post-traumatic stress disorder. I found myself in a personal financial crisis ... surely nothing else could go wrong! One morning I got up and felt a lump on my chest. I was panicking – I have always had a fear of hospitals.

The doctor sent me for a mammogram. I was terrified. Waiting to see the consultant felt like a lifetime. Luckily it was just thickening of tissue and it was OK.

The following morning I had a vision. A female figure dressed in white with long flowing hair stood in front of me and said, "Yesterday you were dead and today you have your life back." Then she was gone. It was such a profound experience. My angel came to tell me I have to be here for a while yet.

— *JOAN CHARLES*

~ Road Safety Angel ~

How wonderful that Candace was able to see the angel who was protecting her daughter.

• • • • • •

When my younger daughter was studying, she went through a stage of going out until the early hours with her friends. Sometimes they drank too much. I used to lie in bed waiting to hear her car arrive.

One night as I waited for her to come home, I had a perfect image of her car coming down the road with a beautiful white angel lying on the roof facing forwards, as if she was hanging on to a sled. From that moment I knew my daughter was fine. To this day I imagine this white angel, whom I call Bianca, watching over my daughter and her car, keeping them both safe.

— *CANDACE*

~ Golden and White Angels ~

It is always good to receive feedback from clairvoyants about what they see during spiritual work.

• • • • • •

When we were all in the room during the filming for the Cosmic Moment and Diana was drumming the heartbeat of Lady Gaia, I saw golden and white angels in the room standing by everyone.

— *LINDA KELLY*

~ Angels Watching Over Me ~

Angels may appear in any form that makes a child feel more comfortable with them.

• • • • • •

My first experience happened when I was five years old and had a bad accident. I fell astride a manhole cover and had to be lifted off. When I got home from hospital I slept with my parents for a while as I was really ill. In the middle of the night I awoke to find three "nuns" at the side of the bed. I woke my parents asking them why the nuns had come, but they could see nothing and told me to go back to sleep. The "nuns" remained with me until I fell asleep. I realized later that the "nuns" were angels protecting me and sending me healing. I am 59 now and have never forgotten my first angel experience.

— *LESLEY MORGAN*

~ Angelic Imprint in the Sky ~

Katie showed me a glorious sketch that she drew of this angel.

• • • • • •

I was in the kitchen checking that everything was turned off. Suddenly I saw a hand in front of me telling me to stop. I looked out and saw a picture of an angel in the sky. He wore a knight's helmet and had beautiful wings.

— *KATIE CURTIS*

~ Angels Bring Hope ~

Angels are so full of love and compassion that they come to us when we are in distress.

• • • • • •

Seven years ago, I had an upsetting incident at work. When I got home I began to cry and refused to speak to anyone. I went to bed and threw myself under the bedcovers. I asked the angels for help and heard a very melodic choir singing.

Then I saw an 8-ft being in the corner bathed in gold. I had a sense that I was being watched over. I knew I had witnessed an angel.

The feeling has never left me and I know that we can call upon the angels in times of distress. I always urge others to seek out their angels, in times of need and times of joy, to share with them our earthly blessing.

— *TARA*

~ Angels in the Sky ~

As we are waking up or falling asleep the veils between the worlds are thin. These are the times when many people connect with the angels.

• • • • • •

One morning when I awoke it was still dark. I looked up to the ceiling and saw a night sky full of hundreds of stars like little LED lights. Across the sky were lots of angels of different sizes, moving quickly in all directions. There was one large central angel, which was still. They appeared as a silhouette of light like an aura. I closed my eyes and they were still there when I reopened them. I remember smiling at them and saying thank you and feeling very elated.

The next night I had another experience: I saw a large angel holding a dove.

— *PAT MCLURE*

~ Heat, Light and Healing ~

Angels and guides appear to us in many ways and it is always a privilege to see them.

• • • • • •

I was going through a difficult phase. As I went into my bedroom I felt extreme heat and light over my head. It was amazing to feel what I knew was healing on my head. That night I slept peacefully. When I woke up the next morning and opened my door I saw a huge man standing there and knew he was my guardian angel,

Pontius. Wherever I go I see the letter "P" in my mind's eye. I love him to bits! I feel him everywhere I go. Thank you to the angels! You are totally awesome!

— *SUMAYA ESSOP*

~ Challenging Situations ~

Once more the angels appear to take away fear and bring healing.

· · · · · ·

Seven years ago I was faced with my mortality. I had to undergo major surgery and was frightened. I had two young children so I had to make it through this. I prayed like I had never prayed before.

As they wheeled me into theatre I saw my (deceased) mom and the angels filling the operating theatre. Mom said they were all here to make sure that all went well. When I came round the nursing staff wanted to know why I was smiling. I told them that the angels were looking after me and had told me I would be OK. Angels do exist and they do help when asked.

— *ROSA FRAGA*

ANGELS SINGING AND ANGEL SONGS

AS THE FREQUENCY of the planet is becoming lighter more people are hearing angels singing, or even a choir of angels. They usually report that they feel healed or inspired.

If we have been 0m-ing or humming during a workshop we can very often hear the wonderful sonics of the angels as they take the sound of our music into higher frequencies. It continues long after we have stopped and in that time magic and miracles can happen.

~ Healing through a Song ~

If you want to connect with loved ones in spirit and the angels, listen out for the songs that you hear playing.

· · · · · ·

We run bereavement workshops. One young participant called Kali had lost her father ten months ago. During the workshop most of the group received a message but Kali received nothing. She felt that she had benefited from the workshop, but was frustrated. At the closing ceremony, the miracle happened.

I selected track 7 on the CD player. However the CD played track 9, 'I Believe'. When it finished I apologized for the mistake and Kali jumped up with tears of joy and shouted that her father had made contact. 'I Believe' was her father's favourite song and it was played at his funeral. Kali felt that the angels blessed her because through them she had received a message from her father. Kali radiated with love and light. She believes her father will continue to guide her through the angels.

— *MARIEL FORDE CLARKE DCS*

~ Healing Harmonics ~

Whenever beautiful harmonies are played or sung the angels sing their wonderful healing harmonics over the people present.

••••••

When Truda was seriously ill in hospital her son brought in her favourite music. She listened to one of the CDs, *100,000 Angels* by Bliss. As it played she could not stop crying because she could feel the angels around her and at that moment she knew she was going to make a good recovery.

— **AS TOLD TO DIANA COOPER BY TRUDA**

~ Angel Melody ~

When you open your mind and connect with the angelic realms, whether you believe in angels or not, you open to the seventh dimension and may hear their music.

••••••

After I completed my angel training I asked my good friend Stanka to help me prepare and practise for my first workshop by being my "student". Stanka was familiar with Diana Cooper's writing on angels. While she was a bit sceptical about the exercises, she went along with them and practised some of them at home. As she did so she heard a wonderful angelic melody. She will never forget it.

— **MARJETKA NOVAK DCS**

~ Heralding a Birth ~

Every single soul who is born here is welcome and loved.

••••••

My first angel experience was after the birth of my third child. He was asleep in his Moses basket when I heard him stirring. Being super-alert as one is with a newborn, I woke up instantly. The room was filled with uplifting music – trumpets, pan pipes and flutes. It was magnificent and I remember thinking, "This is every note I have ever heard played in perfect harmony." The feelings of the sound stayed with me for ages. As I moved to the foot of the bed the music faded. I picked my baby up knowing he'd heard it too – it was a special joyful welcome home!

— **ANN**

~ Hearing Angel Music ~

Teachers from the Diana Cooper School went into the Pipers stone circle near Dublin. There was a powerful and beautiful energy within the stones. This story is the experience of one of the teachers.

••••••

I teach piano and love music, so while we were in the stone circle it was wonderful to hear angels singing a melody. When I went back to the hotel I lay on my bed and heard the angelic music again. Suddenly it was an hour later – as if the angels had taken me somewhere.

The next day, while visiting the magical Newgrange, I heard the same music, but this time it was more earthly – as if sung by masters or ancestors. It felt as if cosmic wisdom was being given to me by the angelic kingdom and later grounded with music by those who had been human.

— *MARIE MITCHELL AS TOLD TO DIANA COOPER*

~ Trust ~

When the angels sing over you, you may feel pure love. You may also hear their choirs, especially during that state between waking and sleeping when the veils are thin.

· · · · · ·

One night in my bedroom the purest white light started flashing at regular intervals and there was a humming sound in the background – like a fan, but there was no breeze. There was a sense of intense love, as if I was being brushed from head to toe with love – I felt that everything was as it is meant to be. The message was TRUST. The following week I woke up to a choir of angelic music that faded away as I woke up.

— *ANNETTE O'DONNALL*

~ The Answer Is in the Song ~

Ask and the answer will be given to you in some way.

· · · · · ·

One evening I made a wish to the angels: "I would like to strengthen my intuition, I would love to hear, see and know your messages more clearly." The following morning I woke up with a melody in my head from the song that goes "Silence is golden, golden..." Instantly I knew what I had to do for strengthening my intuition.

— *CORNELIA MOHR DCS*

~ Listen to the Words ~

Think about the angels and thank them for all they do for you and they will communicate with you.

· · · · · ·

While waiting at the airport on my way home from a DCS angel workshop, I did some writing in my journal, remembering and integrating the adventures of my inner and outer journey. I felt the angels around me holding me in light and love. I felt grateful and full of light. I wrote:

"Beloved Angel, when I get home and back at work please go on supporting me with joy, lightness and serenity. Thank you!"

I closed my journal and became aware of music playing in the coffee shop. Amazed and delighted I took the words of the song as an answer from the angels: "Talk, talk, talk to me ..."

— *CORNELIA MOHR DCS*

~ A Choir of Angels ~

Occasionally people feel scared when they see or hear an angel. Often this is because we are unsure of what is happening and become anxious. Angels understand our concerns and will do their very best to gently reassure us.

· · · · · ·

As I went to sleep after a session meditating on my bed, I heard a choir of angels, singing in my ear. I felt so peaceful – but then my conscious mind got scared and I woke up, wondering what it was! This experience has helped me to feel more connected to the angelic realms.

— *ANON*

~ Angels Switch the Radio On ~

If the angels really want to make a point they will bring words or music through something that cannot play.

· · · · · ·

I came home and took the dog out for a walk. On returning I heard voices coming from the kitchen. I moved with caution towards the kitchen and realized that the radio was on. We rarely play the radio and keep it switched off at the plug. The song that had started playing was 'Spirit in the Sky' – what a sign from above!'

— *KARELENA MACKINLAY DCS*

~ The Message for Me ~

A thousand people may hear the same song and ignore it but if it is meant for you, you will know.

· · · · · ·

I was going through some spiritual expansion and felt I needed guidance. During a visit to my local shopping centre a song came on the radio with the lyrics "Send me an angel" – a song I remembered from my childhood. I knew instinctively that I was being helped and supported.

— *NADINE OLIVER*

~ Supported by Angels ~

When you believe the message in a song is for you and you take action, knowing you are supported by angels, your life can change totally.

· · · · · ·

I worked in a florist shop and had a high level of responsibility. However I was constantly put down and bullied by the owners. I was given menial tasks – to the point that I couldn't understand why they employed me.

One morning as I drove to work I felt like crying; the previous day had been terrible. The traffic was busy. I was half-listening to the car radio when a song came on about angels – I can't remember the name but the words are still clear in my mind: "I walked into an empty room/Suddenly my heart went boom ... an orchestra of angels, waiting there for me ... there must be an angel, playing with my heart." I burst into tears – not from unhappiness, from joy. I knew I had been given a message to say I was not alone and was supported. I left the florist and started a job caring for disabled people.

— *STEPHANIE BECKHAM*

~ *Unconditional Love* ~

Here is a story of true unconditional love.

• • • • • •

I started to read spiritual books and a new world opened up. My spiritual development accelerated but my husband didn't feel comfortable. He told me he had fallen in love with someone else who was his twin flame but he did not know what to do. He wanted *me* to tell him since I had read books on twin flames!

I told him I loved him and if he wanted to be with his twin flame that was fine; I wanted the best for him. That was one of the most fantastic moments in my life. What could have been a nightmare was so beautiful. I heard the angels sing; it was blissful – they wrapped their wings around us. That night I had the most beautiful angel dream.

— *WENCHE MILAS*

~ *Angel in Disguise* ~

We only hear what we need to hear!

• • • • • •

Arriving at work one morning, I went into my office and turned on the radio. A chirpy song was booming out and I could hardly believe my ears when I caught the words: "Open up your eyes ... angel in disguise ... open up your eyes ... angel of protection." Thank you angels, I said to myself.

— *KARI NYGARD DCS*

CHAPTER 11

Babies and Children

ANGELS AND BABIES

Angels love babies and the pure shining innocence they possess as they have so recently left the spirit world.

~ Babes Protected by Angels ~

The grandmother in this story is shown a vision of her unborn grandchild being protected by angels so that she could relax, knowing the child would be safe.

• • • • • •

A few days before my daughter Rosie told me she was pregnant with my first grandchild, I received a strong and clear image of two angel hands enclosing my grandchild in a loving, nurturing and protective manner. This vision stayed with me throughout the pregnancy. I knew that my grandchild was safe and protected by her guardian angel. Rosie recently gave birth to her baby, Jessica.

— *MARY THOMSON*

~ Birth of an Old Soul ~

I really like to hear of mothers who recognize their baby as soon as they look into their eyes.

• • • • • •

After giving birth to my son I realized there must be so much more to life. The midwife looked in his eyes and said, "Wow, you are an old soul!" I just knew she was right but could not explain why.

Then Diana Cooper released her book *Discover Atlantis*, which was a subject I had always been interested in, and that was it. Every word I read I already knew!

— *SANDRA PRATT*

~ Carrying a High Spiritual Soul ~

So many high-frequency souls are incarnating now to help the planet and bring in great light.

• • • • • •

My husband and I wanted to start a family. I believed it was possible to appeal to a high spiritual soul to choose me as their mother, so I prayed with all my heart. We were overjoyed when I conceived.

One night I was lying on my bed looking at the ceiling when I saw it change to a dark cloudy sky. The clouds parted and streams of multicoloured light poured down onto my body. It was the most beautiful vision. A huge white dove appeared, opening his wings slowly and gracefully. I realized I was carrying a highly spiritual soul. I thanked the angels.

— *HÉLÈNE GONELLA*

~ New Baby ~

The message from my guardian angel about my new grandchild filled me with joy.

• • • • • •

My granddaughter was expected while I was in Ireland at a DCS reunion. I secretly hoped she would wait to be born until I got home, but at the reunion I received a text to say that she had arrived safe and sound. Then I had to go into a meeting. As I sat down in the circle I noticed that my guardian angel was not beside me. As I observed this she came whooshing back to my side, so I asked her where she had been. Her reply amazed me: "I've been taking your love to the baby!"

I asked why Kailani had chosen to be born while I was away. The reply was, "She didn't mind because you have such a strong heart connection with her, she knows you are there for her."

I flew home and arranged to see her the following afternoon but in the morning I heard her calling me, so I dropped everything and drove over to give her a cuddle.

— *DIANA COOPER*

~ Angels Help a Baby Remember ~

A reminder that if you hold newborn babies as much as possible, your energies will help the angels to connect to them.

• • • • • •

For a week before my fifth grandchild was born I was aware of a huge column of light beside me. It felt incredibly beautiful and powerful and I was told that it was the energy of all the angels and God himself. Taliya was born by caesarean section and was a really cuddly baby. For the first week, whenever I held her the column of light moved so that it passed through us both and I could hear angels singing. The angels then said that I was to hold her as much as possible because they were helping her to remember where she came from.

— *DIANA COOPER*

~ Baby Love ~

What an amazing story about a baby communicating with his angel. How close babies still are to the spiritual dimensions!

• • • • • •

I always knew there were angels but one night they became real for me. My eldest son Alex, who was five months old at the time, slept in his own bedroom. I woke up at 4.am and heard a female voice from his room. My first thought was that someone was in the room and I had to "save" my son – but I couldn't move my body. I suddenly felt peace and knew that my son was all right.

The female voice spoke a language I recognized but didn't understand. The voice was angelic and I had a vision of a winged seraphim angel next to my son's bed. The voice stopped talking – and my son answered!

I will never forget that image, it was so beautiful. I believe that my son was having an important conversation with the angel. He still connects with angels and sees them easily. My sons have been amazing angel teachers in my life.

— *ANU WYSKIEL*

~ Baby Knows Her Name ~

Your name is chosen by your soul and when it is spoken the vibration of it draws your experiences to you.

• • • • • •

During my mother's pregnancy it was decided that if I was a girl I would be called Jane. Everyone knew this, including my father who was away at sea. I was called Jane for the first week of my life, until the registrar of births visited the nursing home. "What are you going to call your baby?" she asked. My mum opened her mouth to say Jane but instead out came "Ann."

By the time I was a teenager everyone was calling me Anna. I always think that poor naming angel must have had to work very hard indeed to make sure I got the right name – albeit at the last minute!

— *ANNA KNIGHT*

~ A Miracle Conception and Birth ~

Miracles happen all the time and they are often the spiritual consequence of getting the energy right with a lot of hard work!

• • • • • •

As I held the healthy baby boy for the first time recognition flowed through us from the angelic realms of creation. It was the first time I had met Annabelle, the baby's mother, in person, although for forty weeks we had spoken twice a week.

Annabelle had suffered a failed IVF miscarriage and aged 46 was told she would not be able to have a child. I agreed to help this wonderful woman become a mother.

I enlisted an archangel to heal Annabelle's emotions and physical body. We spoke twice a week. I called in the masters to allow regrowth of the reproductive organs. After five weeks Annabelle became pregnant. I took her twice a week to the angelic realms; Annabelle described the experiences as "amazing". With an angel beside her she gave birth to her beautiful son, Santino. I am known as his "angel daddy".

— *IAN PRIDMORE*

~ Looked After ~

This poignant story reminds us that every miscarriage or stillbirth is a beautiful spirit who continues to be connected to the family after they pass.

• • • • • •

Eight years ago I had a miscarriage. At the time my son was eighteen months old, so I kept myself busy in an effort not to dwell on my terrible feelings of loss. My sister-in-law was pregnant and I hated the jealous longing I felt when I saw her.

One night I went to bed and had a good cry. I awoke in the early hours as the hall light appeared to stream under my door and the bedroom door opened. A shadowy figure moved towards me and a voice told me not to be afraid.

The figure opened her arms to reveal a newborn baby girl. This was my baby – Sarah – I had named her when I lost her. I felt an enormous sense of relief. The figure told me it was time to take Sarah and go but that I would see her again and she would be safe.

The next thing I knew my husband climbed into bed after his night shift. I raced to check on my son; as I entered his room I felt deep peace and on the floor was a beautiful, snow-white feather. I ran to get my husband but when we returned the feather had vanished! I am blessed to have my son. Angels are looking after everyone and all children in spirit.

— ANON

~ Protection for My Little Son ~

The angels will protect your children and help them to feel happy when you are absent.

• • • • • •

When my son was seven months old I asked Archangel Michael daily to place his cloak of protection around him when he had to go to nursery. I believe this kept him happy and healthy.

Whenever my son was unhappy, I would ask angels to bathe him in light until he was calm. Now he is four I talk to him about angels. I have angel cards for children and love them for myself as well!

— BRITTA

~ Our Baby Thanks Us ~

Water is a wonderfully psychic and spiritual element.

• • • • • •

For a long time angels have kept our family and boat safe while sailing. Sailing on a calm day is the most beautiful thing. We took our son to our boat when he was two weeks old and for the first time since birth I felt myself relax. That night I dreamed I met my son's soul and he thanked me for the opportunity to incarnate with us. I thanked him for joining our family. This is the only time I remember having an inner-plane dream.

— BRITTA

~ The Gift of Hope ~

This is a truly moving story about three women creating such a powerful healing vibration that they all became pregnant despite long-term difficulties.

・・・・・・

Tereza, Katrina and Hilary did their reiki masters together. Within a year of completing, all three were expecting babies, having overcome long-term difficulties. Hilary said, "The masters triggered it for us all."

After two miscarriages, Tereza was scared. "When I started the masters course we did a meditation where I met an angel who gave me hope. That's what I continued to focus on."

Katrina's only way of conceiving was to use IVF. "The work gave me a deeper understanding of the situation; surrounded me in healing energy and helped clear the way for me to become a mother."

Olivia, Thomas and Alex were all born within six months of each other. They all have a purpose in being here now. They are a blessing to us and to the world!

— *ELIZABETH HARLEY DCS*

~ My Full-Term Baby ~

Here is another inspirational story of an angel miracle.

・・・・・・

Nine years ago I was very ill – I had uncontrollable seizures and two miscarriages. Doctors suggested that I should not have another baby and the neurologist warned me that if I continued to have seizures I could end up in a coma. My sister suggested reiki healing. I was sceptical but decided to try it. As I continued with reiki, I realized I was changing. I started to see angels.

A year later I fell pregnant. I continued to do self-healing and saw angels around me and felt them pouring light into me. It was awesome. Words cannot describe the love, light and peace I felt. My son was born in July, healthy and absolutely lovely. The healing, guidance and love of the angels blessed me with the gift of carrying my baby to full term. I know angels are always present and miracles continue to take place as we allow them to guide us.

— *LEOLA RAMMBLE*

ANGELS WITH CHILDREN

IT CAN REALLY HELP children when you talk to them about angels and remind them that they have their own guardian angel. They love to know that their angel loves them no matter what they do. Many children see angels or lights accompanying people and it is so comforting for them to know that this is normal.

~ From the Mouths of Children ~

When children talk about angels it has the ring of truth and those who are ready to listen will respond.

When my son was four and had started nursery he had a powerful dream. He saw angels and they put angel dust in his eyes.

I knew something significant had occurred as his energy was so high. He was full of light and could not stop talking about his dream and about angels. I was delighted and a little concerned about people's reactions at the nursery. It was 1993 and people were not as open-minded as they are now.

With some trepidation, I returned to pick my son up. I opened the gate and began to walk down the path. The place was buzzing! I stood in the doorway and listened. ALL the children and some of the staff were talking about angels.

— *ELIZABETH HARLEY DCS*

~ Let Him Be Happy ~

It is a parent's responsibility to put psychic protection round their children for it can help them enormously.

. . . . . .

When collecting my son Jamie from school I always ask him about his day and who was he playing with. For a few days he kept telling me he was playing on his own. I was sad for him and had a chat about mixing and playing with his friends.

The next morning when I walked Jamie to school I asked Archangel Michael to protect him and to help him mix with friends and be happy.

When Jamie came out of school he looked really happy. He gave me a big royal blue feather he'd found and said it was for me. From that moment on I didn't worry about Jamie any more. I thanked Archangel Michael that day and every day since.

— *CHRISTINA BYRNE*

~ Coming Out ~

Sometimes it's difficult to share your belief in angels when you are unsure of other people's reactions.

. . . . . .

I attended the very first Diana Cooper teacher-training programme in 2002. At that time there were very few angel books on the shelves and although I believed a hundred per cent in angels I found myself a little reluctant to share my ideas – particularly with people at work, who I thought might ridicule me.

I remember clearly assessing people before I told them I was an angel teacher. Well that all changed when I went to a health fair later that year. There was a little girl there who told me she was four. She asked me outright if I believed in angels and I said yes. Then she proceeded to tell me all about her own angels in such a matter-of-fact way.

I realized then that this four-year-old child was showing me something important. If she could speak freely then why couldn't I?

Ever since then when people ask what I do, I tell them proudly that I teach people about angels. I am sure the angels sent that little girl to the health fair to help me speak my "angelic truth". You will not be surprised to know that no one has ever ridiculed my interest in angels; in fact almost everyone I meet is fascinated by my work.

— *ELIZABETH ANN DCS*

~ Childlike ~

This is a story from a wise grandmother and shows just how much we can help our children or grandchildren by giving them encouragement.

••••••

My granddaughter was four and was learning about imagination. She said to me "Guess what, Grandma? This week I used my imagination and saw an angel."

I said I had never seen an angel, but that I would love to. I asked if she thought her angel would come to the room where I did reiki. She nodded and we went to the reiki room. She told me to lie down. Her eyes were wide open and she looked round the room describing what she saw.

That told me that she had not used her imagination. She had actually seen an angel.

— *SERENA*

~ Protection from Bullying ~

Parents and children can ask Archangel Michael to protect them from bullying and he will.

••••••

I was talking to my eldest daughter on the phone when suddenly there was a huge blue flash that sounded like an electric cable sparking. I knew it was Archangel Michael.

Later on a little girl came to me for spiritual healing and I discovered she was being bullied in school. I told her about Archangel Michael and said that if she was ever afraid she could call him and he would be there straight away. On her next visit she said, "I think I saw Archangel Michael." I asked what he looked like and she described him exactly as I'd seen him. I was so surprised and happy. It was confirmation that what I saw was Archangel Michael.

The girl's parents went to the school about the bullying. It was sorted out and they are all friends now – including the bullies. Thank you Archangel Michael.

— *ANON*

~ Naming a Car ~

Ask the children. They are so tuned in to the angelic realms that they come out with the perfect answers. Seraphina is one of the mighty seraphim and works with Archangel Metatron.

••••••

I recently changed my car and chose a beautiful pearl-white one. I always give my cars angelic names – the previous one was *Archangel Michael* – so I tuned in and asked what my new car's name was. I was told *Seraphina* – which for some reason I rejected.

Later that day my granddaughters Leah Beth and Nicole came to visit. I decided to ask them to name my car and said that I wanted an angelic name. Nicole (who was three at the time) immediately said, "You have to call your car Seraphina." I asked her where she had heard the name before – she did not know but was insistent that it was the right name. Needless to say my pearl-white car is called *Seraphina*! The purity and innocence of young children provide a clear channel for angelic wisdom and information.

— *ELIZABETH ANN DCS*

~ Saving My Son ~

My heart stood still as I read this story.

· · · · · ·

We were lying in bed one morning while our two-year-old son Justin was in our room playing with the four-drawer chest. He wanted to make a house to sit in and he was opening the drawers when suddenly he was pulled backwards about eight feet by some unseen force or being. There was a huge crash as the solid wooden chest of drawers fell over. If he hadn't been pulled backwards like that it would certainly have fallen on him. Clearly it was not his time and he was being taken care of from above. We are eternally grateful and I thank the angels for keeping our beautiful son safe.

— *SIOBHAN M.*

~ Angels Drive to Hospital ~

This is another magic story as the angels respond to calls for help.

· · · · · ·

I have always believed in angels and the following experience was truly miraculous and will always stay with me.

My seven- and four-year-olds were playing in our local park. My eldest, Eve, climbed the highest piece of play equipment, which had a three-metre drop. As I looked away for a moment, Eve fell. There was an ear-piercing scream and then she yelled that she had hurt her back.

The doctor sent us to Accident and Emergency. I asked the angels to help me reach the hospital quickly and to find a parking space at the entrance in case I needed a wheelchair. I felt the most amazing presence and I relaxed – it felt as if someone else was driving the car. When we arrived at the hospital, there was a parking space right at the entrance with a wheelchair nearby! I said thank you to the angels because I knew this was their doing. Even now, remembering the enormous love I felt that day makes me feel incredibly humble.

Eve was fine albeit a little bruised. All I can say to anyone reading this is "Just ask!"

— *MICHELLE BACCHUS*

~ Angels Play With a Child ~

Angels come to children in a way that is acceptable – and joyful – for a child.

٭٭٭٭٭٭

I was six, in my first year at school and my whole class had misbehaved except me. I was rewarded by being the only one to have afternoon playtime. I was shy and had no friends outside my class so I stared out of the window, wondering what I would do by myself.

I saw a glowing child my age open a door for me and he wanted to play with me! I had such fun. I had never seen him around the school before. He was so amazing. Then the whistle blew and he disappeared. I never saw him again. He was there for me when I was scared and to me the only explanation is that he was my guardian angel.

— *JEEVAN*

~ A Huge White Angel ~

It is natural for a child to be scared of the unknown, but now she is an adult Katie's face glows when she talks about her angel.

٭٭٭٭٭٭

When I was seven years old I saw a pure white figure standing at the end of my bed. It was huge, at least seven feet tall, and I was terrified. When I got the courage I ran across to Mum and Dad's bedroom. I have never forgotten that wondrous figure and it will be for ever. I think it was my guardian angel.

— *KATIE CURTIS*

~ Trust as a Child ~

This poignant story reminds us how important it is to tell children about the angels, so that they can call on their help.

٭٭٭٭٭٭

My parents worked, so after school my younger sister and I would go to the family across the road until my parents returned. The husband would take my sister and me into their garage one by one and molest us. I didn't understand and felt scared – he was hurting me and I didn't know how to stop him.

One day my sister and I were walking home from school. I remember praying for help because I didn't want to go back there again. Then suddenly a lady angel stood before me. She was beautiful and there was light around her. She had long golden hair and was all in white. She had the sweetest kindest voice.

She said, "Carol, take your little sister home now. You are old enough to take care of her. Take the key that your mother gave you and go home. Your little sister and you are now safe. You no longer need to go there any more. No one will harm you."

The angel smiled and I knew I was safe. I took my sister home and we never went back. I never told my mother or father about what had happened or about the angel. The reason I am sharing this story now is that it is important to let children know angels are there to help them; that they are safe and can trust their angels to guide them.

— *CAROL GUY*

~ A Christmas Story ~

Angels love children and this story illustrates how, because they are so full of simplicity, fun and laughter, they naturally draw in angel energy.

* * * * * *

I had my granddaughters and their parents over for dinner. We played some Christmas music and put tea towels on our heads to make us shepherds. We found toys to be sheep and turned the kitchen into a stable – it was magical. Then we hung a paper angel on the light and I told the children of Gabriel's light. The angels' glory really filled the room.

We gave Mary a golden cape and baby Jesus was laid down and we hailed him and gave thanks. This all took place on an old brown ram's rug. Later as I placed the rug back in the lounge I noticed a pure white, large feather. I looked at my husband and we knew who had placed it there and why. I was thrilled and it felt like I had received a big hug. Thanks be to the angels.

— *HANNAH BELLE ROBERTS*

CHAPTER 12

Angels Help with Finance

The angels bring you what you believe you deserve as long as you ask for it. Many of us limit what we have because of unhelpful beliefs about finance. However the angels will help us to manifest abundance if we do so with an open heart.

~ Flowers for My Nan ~

And here is a heart-warming story.

• • • • • •

When my nan died I wanted to buy flowers for her funeral. As I was divorced and bringing up two children alone, money was tight but I managed to order a small bouquet. On the day of the funeral, though, my flowers didn't arrive and I was very upset, so I asked the angels to help.

The next day I went into the florists and the assistant said there had been a mix-up with the order. She refunded my money and gave me a free bouquet, which I sent to my mum.

I realized my nan would have been very happy with this outcome. The angels were truly looking after me and my children.

— *JANIS ATWOOD DCS*

~ Angels Help Find a Way ~

Sometimes we have to wait for what we want – but the angels make sure we get it when the time is right.

• • • • • •

My intuition told me I needed a more spiritual way of life and specifically should be working with angels. I found the Diana Cooper School and I knew it was the right one for me. However I could not afford it so I asked my angels to help.

A year later my mum died. Her house was sold, her money divided and I had the money to do the angel course. Before she passed over Mum told me to spend the money on myself as for many years I went without things to help my daughters. Thanks to my lovely mother – and the angels – I am now a fully qualified teacher for the Diana Cooper School.

— *JANIS ATWOOD DCS*

~ Finding a Job ~

Many people are finding themselves without work and going through huge chal-
lenges. Praying with an open heart to the angels can yield instant results, as this
story demonstrates.

• • • • • •

One of my newsletter subscribers relayed this to me after they had been out of
work for a while and had started to have to use their savings.

"I prayed to the angels for someone to offer me a job and the very next day
I was offered a full-time position in a company close to my house. I know my
prayers are always answered but I was shocked at this – it was answered so quickly and I don't have any qualifications for that work. Furthermore I hadn't even
applied to work there, so to say I was astonished is putting it mildly."

— *CATHERINE MCMAHON DCS*

~ A Positive Solution ~

Tell the angels what you want and they will find a way to make it happen. This
works with big things – and small ones too.

• • • • • •

I ordered a Bach Flower Remedy wooden box set from Nelsons in London. Shortly
afterwards I discovered an internet site that sold the empty wooden boxes cheaper.
I was disappointed as it would have been cheaper to buy the wooden box. I didn't
need two sets, but ordered the wooden box thinking I could give my old set to a
friend. I was sure it would all sort itself with the help of the angels.

A few days later my wooden box arrived, but after three weeks I still hadn't
received my original set from London. I was just about to contact Nelsons when I
received an email from them saying that my package had been returned by Nor-
wegian customs and they gave me a refund. I know my angels helped and I sent
them a big thank you.

— *WENCHE MILAS*

~ Show Me the Money ~

There are times when we need to be clear and direct when we need something.
While what Florianna says may appear brusque, if it is said in gratitude then
angels will help, as her story demonstrates.

• • • • • •

Recently I had some financial challenges and I decided to have an estate sale. I
wanted to sell the property with all the contents; in particular two very old wood-
en angel sculptures.

One morning while feeling low I called upon my angel to "SHOW ME THE
MONEY!" Fifteen minutes later a young couple came and purchased the two angel sculptures. Talk about assistance from angels. Angels helping me sell angels, I
love it!

— *FLORIANNA*

~ Angels Manifest Money ~

Here the angels give a young mother exactly what she asked for – no more and no less!

. . . . . .

One Sunday on our way home for lunch, I was crossing the park with my three children. My eight-year-old daughter was misbehaving because I hadn't bought her something she wanted at the antiquarian market.

I explained to her that I didn't have the money and that I did not even have money for the food shopping.

Then I said, "OK, let's ask our angels to please find some money so that I can buy something for you and we can all have an ice cream." As we walked out of the park we found a 50-euro note. We jumped with joy and thanked the angels. We returned to the market to buy the children something and had an ice cream. There was enough money left to buy food the next day. All we'd needed was faith.

— *ANON*

~ Perfume from the Angels ~

Every little helps.

. . . . . .

I was getting ready for work and as I put on my favourite perfume I realized it was almost empty. I was annoyed as my husband had just returned from England and had I known I would have asked him to buy me some more –perfume is more expensive in Norway, where we live.

I said to myself, "I'm certain that somebody is going to go abroad soon and that they can buy the perfume for me." Later at work an electrician came into my office and said, "I'm going to England tomorrow, do you want me to get you some perfume?" I was delighted! Thank you angels!

— *WENCHE MILAS*

~ Angels Synchronize My House Move ~

When you are ready to do something that is in divine right order, the angels will ensure the money is there, so just ask!

. . . . . .

I received a message from the angels that it was time for me to move out of the city centre to the country, which would be more conducive to my healing and teaching work. Money was tight, though, and I didn't have the necessary funds. I asked the angels for help and within days I met a friend who I hadn't seen for a long time.

I explained my predicament and she wanted to lend me the money for my move. I accepted her offer. My flat sold quickly; the first person who viewed it made me an offer. The angels were very keen to assist me with my move and I was able to repay my friend.

— *JILL WEBSTER DCS*

~ Bread from Heaven ~

This lady needed bread so the angels responded to her thoughts and found a way to get it to her.

. . . . . .

When I got home from doing my food shopping at the supermarket, I realized I had forgotten to buy bread. Later I went to pick up my daughter from school. She handed her rucksack to me; it was heavy. I said, "What have you got in there? Why is it so heavy?"

I opened it up and couldn't believe my eyes: it was full of bread! This reminded me that the angels look after us.

— *ANON*

ABUNDANCE

THE UNIVERSE is delighted for you to have as much abundance and financial prosperity as you believe you deserve or truly want. It will even help you to transmute the underlying beliefs and patterns that prevent you receiving your good. There is no use saying you want a mansion and at the same time thinking you belong in your poorer area. Or that you want to be successful and saying that it is hard to get a business going. If you want a mansion, think big. If you want success envision it!

~ Faith Creates Positive Results ~

In the following story the lady tells the angels she only wants the money for the course if it was for the highest good.

. . . . . .

I wanted to do a particular course. I said to the universe, "If I am truly meant to do this course, please provide the finance for me." Unexpectedly, a couple of weeks later I was offered part-time work that completely paid for the course fees. This has happened to me twice now.

The message is that the universe is abundant and will provide if you ask for the right reasons.

— *KARELENA MACKINLAY DCS*

~ Funds for Egypt ~

The angels have wonderful ways of giving us answers and the finance to do what is right.

. . . . . .

When I was deciding whether to go on the Diana Cooper 2011 trip to Egypt I asked the angels for a sign. Later I got a phone call from my financial adviser who told me that an amount of money I was waiting for was actually £2,500 higher than expected! That was the answer to my question, no doubt.

— *PENNY WING DCS*

~ Unicorn Centre ~

Here is an example of asking and being open to what the angels bring you.

· · · · · ·

We had a nice house with a building in the garden called The Unicorn Centre where I ran courses and practised complementary therapies. My husband, Les, had a large garage where he could do his mechanical things. We also had a big mortgage and Les had a well-paid job but was only home at weekends.

I asked the angels for our mortgage to be paid; for Les to have a well-paid local job and also to help me to grow some vegetables in our small garden. I thought the angels would help us by having us win money on the lottery or something. I have since learned that they do not work this way!

It came as a great shock when Les was made redundant a week before Christmas 2007. He looked for another job, but there was nothing. It became clear that we needed to sell the house or we would get into debt. An estate agent said he knew someone who would be interested in our house and lo and behold the person bought it!

We looked for a three-bedroom house with a large garden for growing vegetables and space for a Unicorn Centre and garage. This was a tall order as we did not want a mortgage. We went to a tarot reader who said our new house would not be far away. It would be dirty and unkempt, but we should look under the dirt and see its potential.

We found a house fifteen minutes away. It was certainly unloved but it had potential. We could buy it without a mortgage and have money left for a Unicorn Centre! We are restoring it with love. It has a Unicorn Centre with two ley lines crossing, which heightens the energy. Les has a local job with time for his hobbies and we grow our own vegetables. We are grateful to the angels for bringing us abundance, even though it came in a way that we did not expect.

— *MARGARET MERRISON DCS*

~ Ask and You Shall Receive ~

Here is the story of someone who asked and what she received – in less than a week!

· · · · · ·

I wanted to follow my dreams but was worried about how to provide for my family. I asked Archangel Gabriel to help. The next morning I received a call from a man asking me to fix two computers. I hadn't had a computer to repair for weeks. I fixed them and he was ecstatic and has been recommending me to his friends. Then I got a call from a client who I had been chasing for payment for months – he wanted to pay his debt.

It's less than a week since I called on Archangel Gabriel for help and guidance. This has graphically demonstrated to me the truth of the saying "Ask and ye shall receive, knock and it shall be opened."

— *CLAIRE BUCKNALL*

~ Bringing Your Heart's Desire ~

If something is for our greatest joy then it is also for our highest good.

••••••

I love the sea and cetaceans. I've swum with humpbacks in the Silver Bank, but I had never touched a whale. A friend sent me a photo of someone touching a grey whale. I was mesmerized. I had to do this, but how? I would have to travel to Mexico but I had no spare resources at the time.

I asked the angels, "If this is for the highest good, then please make it possible." Two months later I received a letter from a law firm with a cheque for £4,500. Enough money for a month in Mexico, travelling to see both grey and blue whales.

I got to touch and kiss grey whales. One time the mother of a playful calf came right up between my arms. I received downloads from an ancient wisdom-keeper. I communicated with a blue whale in such a way a watching expert commented in amazement, "How on earth did you get a blue whale to bow-ride your boat?" And the best bit? The cheque allowing all this to happen had arrived on the morning I was running my "Angel Abundance" workshop.

— *ELIZABETH HARLEY DCS*

~ Unexpected Money ~

When you ask you never know where unexpected bounty may come from!

••••••

I went to the bank and found extra money in my bank account. I had no idea where it came from, but I had been praying to the angels for financial support.

I mentioned it to a friend and he explained that he had transferred the money into my account. He told me that one of my bank statements had fallen out of the pile of papers he had been carrying. He noticed how low my bank balance was and he wanted to put some money into my account.

He laughed and said that he almost put the initials "G Angel" (Guardian Angel) on the transfer slip. Each time I take a step towards rebuilding my life the angels in Heaven and Earth are right behind me offering their love and support!

— *JILL WEBSTER DCS*

~ Reward Card Buys Angel Cards ~

Whatever your needs, the angels will find a way to bring support to you..

••••••

When I became interested in angels I wanted to learn more about them so I read books. Our local spiritual centre showed me how to use angel cards and I wanted to get a pack but I didn't have the money. I asked the angels for help. Then the shop I worked in brought in New Age items to sell – including the angel cards I wanted. I realized I could buy the cards with my reward card; and I had enough points on my card to get my angel cards for free.

— *JANIS ATWOOD DCS*

~ Relax and Deserve Abundance ~

Life is not about working ourselves into the ground to earn money.

••••••

I had been struggling to manifest more wealth, but I worried that praying for money meant I was greedy or superficial. A friend gave me a book about angels and ascended masters. It mentioned Abundantia, a beautiful goddess who helps with finance and good fortune. I realized that I could ask for her help.

The next day I received a big order for my catering business. I was so happy I danced round the room in gratitude. I worked very hard to earn the money – and got a migraine. I did some soul searching. Why do I have this pain? I'm doing my best to earn money but I don't want to be ill.

I asked the angels for guidance. Abundantia appeared in my mind's eye. She was full of joy with golden coins raining down on her. "Be like me!" she said. Stop worrying, seemed to be the message and I started to laugh. As I got dressed I found a ten-euro note with a beautiful white feather wrapped round it! It was the confirmation I needed – they are helping me to achieve my goals. This experience has removed my money worries; when I feel anxious I just picture Abundantia.

— *JANIS ATTWOOD DCS*

~ Housing Abundance ~

Abundance comes in so many forms and with a mum like this you can enjoy the flow.

••••••

I have just heard that the fully furnished flat my son wanted in Brisbane, Australia has been given to him! There was another person interested in it but my son asked me to ask my communication/housing angels to secure it for him.

I asked the guardian angels of the estate agent and my son to chat and to favour him. It worked. I was not in the least surprised!

— *ANGELA*

~ A Gentle Lesson ~

Spiritual work is not about how much money we earn.

••••••

I decided to hold a two-day angel awareness event. It felt daunting but I knew the angels would help. I found the perfect venue – however, it cost £300 per day! I signed the contract, advertised the event and relaxed. Unfortunately I received no bookings and had to cancel both days. The hotel still charged me the full £600.

I knew that there was a lesson here but didn't know what it was. Later I received an insight: "It's not about you, it's not about money; it is what the day is about, healing the planet and everything on it." When I realized what I had been doing I felt quite ashamed. I realized that if I had only paid £20 a day for the room I would probably have just thought, "Oh well," and continued in the same mindset.

It was a wonderful way to help me recognize what is important. I went on to hold the angel awareness day at our local Spiritualist church and we had a wonderful day so "Thank You."

— *BARBARA HOWARD DCS*

CHAPTER 13

Earth Angels

Angels do not incarnate. However they sometimes over-light a human being or prompt him or her to help someone else. Here are some examples of people who have acted because an angel has whispered to them to do so. These are earth angels.Sometimes an angel will take a human form for a very short while and then vanish, so I include some of these fascinating stories too.

~ *Quiet Angels Heal* ~

Your guardian angel is always trying to lift your spirits and help you.

· · · · · ·

During the days when I worked as a chef and was also a part-time therapist I had an incident where I started to feel really ill. I had an hour of my shift left and two reiki treatments to do later. I felt weak and shaky but did not want to let my colleague or clients down.

I called the angels for healing and asked to be able to complete my work. Two seconds later I had a phone message from my sister Lorraine saying, "I believe friends are like quiet angels who lift us to our feet when our wings forget how to fly." I instantly felt energized and centred; the strange thing was my sister had never mentioned angels to me until that point in time!

— *ELOISE BENNETT DCS*

~ *Man in the Woods* ~

Angels sometimes impress their energies onto humans to cause them to act with angelic qualities, as with this couple.

· · · · · ·

I was walking in the forest when I met a man wearing pyjamas and dressing gown, bedroom slippers and a flat cap. Something was obviously very wrong so I stopped him and engaged him in conversation. He seemed vague about where he was going and where he lived. I felt he needed help.

Another person walking a dog appeared and the man said he was afraid of dogs and ran away. I asked the person with the dog if I could borrow his phone to call the police, but he refused and walked on.

I called on the angels to help the man. A couple appeared and I told them about him. They were concerned and said they would find him and talk to him. I said I'd walk in the opposite direction in the hope of seeing him. I did this, but to no avail.

The next day I saw the couple again. They had found the man and had taken him home. He had been wandering for some time and his wife was most relieved that he was brought home safely.

I never saw that couple again but I believe the angels brought them to help the man and returned them to reassure me that he was safe.

— *DIANA COOPER*

~ A Helping Hand ~

Yes, the angels influence family to help you too. If help is sent with love then accept it with grace.

• • • • • •

Sandra telephoned me and said she would love to undertake the angel teacher-training with me. During her foundation teaching course Sandra told me that she was finding money a little tight but was proud of how she was managing. She had no money for the angel course but would do it later. One day Sandra opened her post to find a cheque from her sister Susan and brother-in-law with the money to pay for her angel teaching course! Sandra was grateful and recognized that the angels had given her a helping hand.

It had snowed where Susan lived and when Susan looked out of the window she was amazed to see two perfect intertwined hearts in the snow. I suggested that the angels were saying a thank you to Susan and her husband for helping Sandra to achieve something that meant so much to her.

— *ROSALIND HORSWELL DCS*

~ A Story of Hope ~

Angelic comfort may come in words, actions or both.

• • • • • •

In the Scottish Highlands, I decided to take a walk in the countryside near Aviemore. I was having a lovely day enjoying silence and clean air, but unfortunately I took a wrong turning and two hours later realized I'd be late for the library and the bank.

I asked the angels which way to go and "To the left" was the reply. When I could not walk any further I realized that I was eight miles from Aviemore. I asked why I had been sent this way and was told, "Because he is there." At that moment a cyclist came by and we chatted. He said I would be fine; I had the right shoes and plenty of time and all will be well, and if I didn't make the bank there would be other days. I felt reassured and calm. As he cycled away I saw that on the back of his shirt was the word HOPE, which made me smile. Minutes later a taxi stopped, gave me a lift and would not take any money.

I made my trip to the bank, library and topped up my phone. While there I again bumped into my mystery Earth angel. I commented that I liked the name on his shirt. He replied, "That's me. That is what I am, Hope." I am blessed to have witnessed a message from the angels and will never doubt them again.

— *YVONNE WATSON*

~ *You Cannot Give Anything Away* ~

This is a story of spiritual law in action.

✶ ✶ ✶ ✶ ✶ ✶

While reading the previous story I remembered something that happened many years ago while I was training to be a hypnotherapist.

At that time I had very little money but there was a woman on the course who had even less. I woke up one morning with an overwhelming feeling I must send her some, so I wrote out a cheque for everything I had in my account. I hardly knew her but the feeling, which I now recognize as the prompting of my angel, was very strong.

She later told me that she had been absolutely desperate and could not pay her rent. A clairvoyant had told her the money was on its way and the next day she had received my cheque, which was the exact amount of her rent!

Some years later she phoned and sold me a ticket that won me ten times the amount I had sent her. Spiritual law says that whatever we give away unconditionally returns to us tenfold. That confirmed to me that I had originally acted truly on the prompting of my angel.

— *DIANA COOPER*

~ *Lost in Africa* ~

Angelic ones come in all shapes, sizes and colours and when you most need them.

✶ ✶ ✶ ✶ ✶ ✶

I had spent a lovely afternoon with a friend; however I left later than I would have liked and was not familiar with the roads in the area. I missed a crucial turn-off and realized that I was not on the correct road, but as it was going towards Durban I continued. I found myself in an African township. It was late and I was worried. I couldn't even contact anyone as this was a time before cell phones. I pulled in to a petrol station and asked how to get to Durban. The directions were vague and I just seemed to be driving further into the township.

I decided to return the way I had come. I was lost, afraid and it was dark with no street lights. In South Africa, a lone white lady in a black African township was a recipe for danger. I said to the angels, "Come on guys, I could do with some help here. I am lost. Please help me out of this."

I saw the petrol station again and pulled in. A huge black man came towards me and said, "You are lost, aren't you?" I said yes. He smiled and said I should follow the only street that had lights as it was the only road in and out of Kwadebeka. He said to keep going and eventually I would reach Durban. I followed his directions and arrived in Durban safe and sound. I was so grateful. I just know he was an angel – there was something very special and beautiful about him.

— *DAWN CONNELL*

~ An Unlikely Angel ~

Never judge anyone – they may be an angel in disguise!

••••••

I was shopping in Edinburgh and it was just before Christmas, so it was very busy. I had just left a shop when a girl walked towards me. I made an instant judgement because of her piercings, tattoos and bright pink and blue hair and because she glowered at me and banged into me. I glanced down and realized my bag was open and my purse was missing. In a panic I ran back into the shop. There, sitting on the counter, was my purse. If I had not returned so quickly it might have got taken. I'm absolutely sure that girl was an angel – and it also taught me that they come in all shapes and sizes.

— *LESLEY SORRIDIMI*

~ Angels Prompt Carer ~

When you follow the promptings of an angel you could save someone's life.

••••••

My mum lived alone. As she grew older we asked her to start wearing an emergency telephone button round her neck. One morning Kate, the lady who helped look after Mum, was driving through the village. It was not her day to visit Mum, but for some reason she decided to call on her.

Thank the angels that she did. Mum had just had a stroke and Kate was able to ring the emergency services immediately. This saved her life as nobody would otherwise have called at the house for another twenty-four hours and Mum had forgotten to put the emergency button round her neck. I will always be so thankful to Kate – a human angel – and all the angels, as Mum lived for another eight weeks, which gave us the chance to spend some very special time together.

— *SUE WALKER DCS*

~ Asking Angels to Help Others ~

When you ask for help for others the angels create perfect synchronicities so that help comes instantly.

••••••

I was out walking in very wintry weather and icy road conditions. A man drove past with his car and small trailer. As he navigated the bend the trailer turned over and landed in the ditch. I asked, "Angels please help him, for the best." And suddenly four other men came walking by. They gathered round the upturned trailer and huffed and puffed and managed to turn it upright. Thank you angels for helping them.

— *KARI NYGARD DCS*

~ *Traffic Safety* ~

This story reminds you to listen when you are warned and take care!

......

Many years ago Mary was warned by an astrologer not to drive on a particular day. Unfortunately she had to go out that day, but she was very nervous. She drove slowly and carefully. At one point she had to stop at traffic lights. When they went green she paused and started very slowly, looking carefully in all directions. Just then a young man on a bicycle jumped the lights and shot across in front of her car. Had she not been driving so cautiously, she would have been involved in a nasty accident. She thanked the angels for prompting the astrologer to give her the warning.

— *AS TOLD TO DIANA COOPER*

~ *Finding Soul Purpose* ~

A reminder that we are all magnificent if only we will open up and be our true selves.

......

For many years I did not know who I was. I believed I was not good enough. I saw myself as shy, unintelligent and unwise. My dreams were locked away inside me.

Then I met an earth angel called Michael. He introduced me to his enlightened, lovely wife and spiritual teacher. What a blessing for me! My life changed immediately: I had angel encounters and felt reborn. My dreams are blossoming: singing for 100 people, leading workshops about angels and going on trips.

The angels taught me that I am part of the big picture and I have a talent that would fill my heart with joy and enrich Mother Earth. I am free and serene with abundance on every level, like it should be for every one of us.

— *DANIELA SORAYA SHANTI MARCINNO DCS*

~ *Angel in Hospital* ~

And the blind shall see.

......

We have a five-year-old son and he has been blind in his left eye from birth. He had to have an operation to relieve the pressure on the lens and later he had a routine check-up, but it wasn't the usual nurse – we felt that it was an angel!

She was a small lady with gentle eyes. After she checked his pressure she put an external lens in front of his eye and asked him to read the alphabet. This had never happened before, and to our amazement he saw! Our son saw! He said every letter she put her finger on. I was shocked, because we had been told that he will never see with this eye. Our angel said, "You can see yourself ... he can see."

The doctor could not believe it and although our son still cannot fully see with that eye, we have not lost hope of a complete recovery. Miracles happen. We haven't seen the nurse again, but we are still blessed by hope, love and holy faith.

— *KATRIN*

~ Yellow Roses ~

Follow the prompting of the angels and they will use you to do their work.

• • • • • •

While delivering Christmas cards to my neighbours I was prompted to call at a supermarket to buy a plant, even though I didn't know at this stage who the plant was for. I was drawn to the miniature roses and could not decide which colour to buy. A very tall man stood behind my right shoulder and said, "Choose the yellow rose, as it is a message of new beginnings." I purchased the yellow patio rose.

Then I visited a neighbour who had recently lost her husband. I gave her the yellow rose. As we talked, she explained that her daughter, distraught at the loss of her father, had been for a reading with a clairvoyant. She was told to look out for yellow roses as a sign that her father was safe. I know that yellow rose was a message for the family.

— *GLENISE*

~ A Human Angel ~

You act like an angel when you truly listen to the still quiet voice of the angels.

• • • • • •

My husband Keith was very ill, suffering from dementia. I worked and a wonderful lady, Christina, looked after him in the mornings.

One morning Keith had fallen out of bed and was lying semi-comatose on the floor. He was extremely heavy and I could not lift him. Christina arrived, but even together we still could not lift him! I solicited the help of a labourer I managed to find nearby and Keith was soon tucked up in bed.

I arranged for the doctor to call on Keith and drove Christina to the bus stop. On my return Keith had fallen out of bed again. I made a bed for him on the floor but could not move him to it. I called out, "Dear God please help me." A man called Julian appeared at the door , so I told him my problem. He replied, "That's why I am here." Julian transferred Keith to the floor bed.

I asked Julian why he had come and he told me he had been working nearby when something told him to "Go up there!" Afterwards I referred to him as my guardian angel – my prayer was truly answered!

— *DIANA*

~ Hidden Blessings ~

If someone or something appears as an obstacle or challenge, bless it and it may transform into a blessing.

• • • • • •

When I was eighteen I travelled from England to Papua New Guinea. I got a job there, in Rabaul, working as a receptionist. After finishing work one day I decided to drive along the Kokope Road, a beautiful costal road overlooking the sea.

Driving out of town I came across a stop sign, but no one was around so I didn't stop. Out of the blue came a policeman on a motorbike. He said, "Madam you didn't stop at the sign, that's $40 please." I didn't have the money with me but had it at home. He said, "That's OK, I'll follow you home." I drove home, gave him the $40, and he left.

Later I noticed that the birds had stopped singing. Then there was a rumbling noise and the floor of the house started to move. Rabaul is an earthquake zone, so I knew that a safe place to stand was under the door frame; I did so. The earthquake was 8.5 on the Richter scale – very powerful.

The house survived and so did I. Later I discovered that those people who were driving along the Kokope Road when the earthquake hit were killed. I realized that the policeman who had made me return home earlier was an angel and that he had saved my life.

— *ROWENA BEAUMONT*

~ Mobile Phone Delivery ~

Thoughtfulness and kindness are angel qualities and there are so many wonderful people on Earth who carry these energies.

• • • • • •

My husband decided to buy a new mobile phone. As we live on Crete he ordered it via the internet and asked the angels to help deliver the phone safely to our local post office.

After three weeks it had still not arrived, so we asked the angels to find it. We received a call from a lady from another post office asking us if we were waiting for a parcel. The phone had been delivered to her post office twenty miles away.

The lady said she had a feeling that someone really needed this parcel, so she had decided to find us. She searched the phone book and found our number. She offered to leave the parcel at her friend's shop so we could pick it up safely. We wrapped up an angel gift, wrote a thankyou letter and left it with her friend. We thanked the angels for their help. Had it not been someone so caring we would never have received the parcel.

— *JANIS ATWOOD DCS*

~ An Angel in a Flood ~

Sometimes it's only afterwards that we recognize what has been an angelic intervention. This lovely example illustrates that angels support us in ways we do not expect.

• • • • • •

Very late one Sunday night my boyfriend and I were woken by our housemates, who had come home to find the boiler leaking. The kitchen floor was under a good couple of inches of water and the leak wasn't stopping.

We all searched for the stopcock but to no avail. I rang two emergency plumbers. One told me he couldn't come out at such short notice. The other didn't answer the phone.

As a last resort I rang the phone number on our water bill, but didn't hold out much hope as it was now around 4 a.m. To my amazement, a calm-sounding woman answered and directed me to a grille cover on the pavement outside, which turned out to house our stopcock. Once I'd opened it she talked me calmly through turning the water off.

The leak stopped and we all cleaned up the flooded kitchen and fell back into bed, exhausted. It only really struck me the next day how unlikely it was that someone from the water company should have been there at such an hour, let alone picked up the phone and known exactly how to help me. I have told people the story and found myself referring to the woman as "an angel"; I meant it light-heartedly but sometimes I do wonder ...

— *ANON*

~ Angel Saves Teenager ~

The angels had to influence a lot of people to get this teenager home safely.

As a teenage I had epilepsy, but it was well controlled. I used to travel on the train into Johannesburg to go to college. One day I had a minor convulsion and knew I had to get off the train. It was not my station, though; it was a station that was deemed dangerous. An angel sat me down again, saying firmly, "You don't get off at this station my girl – you get off at the next station."

When I got to my station and got off the train, my mom, who usually always waited for me in the parking lot, was waiting on the platform instead. Needless to say I got home safely thanks to my angel. I am forty-two now but I still remember that with such gratitude.

— *SHARON*

~ Canadian at Angel Glacier ~

Sometimes the angels can work through a person to give you a God moment.

I went on a twelve-day trip to Canada with a friend, Ita, to celebrate our fiftieth birthdays. On our third day we went to Angel Glacier, where the energy of Arch-angel Michael is strongest .

We decided to walk toward Mount Edith Cavell and a man invited us to walk to the summit with him. It was snowing hard and I kept slipping until I felt I couldn't continue; however the man gave me his spare hat and gloves and both he and Ita held on to me until we reached the top. It was such an achievement and a real thrill.

On the way down the snow became a blizzard. The man knew I was strug-gling and he went in front of me and helped me without saying a word. He held my hand until we reached a safe place. As he did this all fear seemed to leave me. I felt stronger and something shifted in the way I perceive myself in my rela-tionships with females in my life. It was liberating and empowering. It was like a

"God" moment. I tried to explain it to Ita later and she said she had felt the same thing. For me he was an angel who helped me when I was struggling.

— *MAURA*

~ An Act of Kindness ~

Here, the message is in the story.

. . . . . .

I arrived at London Heathrow in the early evening with no hotel reservation. Every place I called was either full or too expensive! Finally I found a room and was directed to take the 555 coach. I had a cracked rib, which made carrying bags rather difficult, but a kind gentleman helped me with my cases.

The bus driver told me we'd arrived and the kind gentleman helped me with my luggage again. It was dark outside and as the coach drove off I looked up but the hotel was nowhere in sight. In the distance, I saw the sign – it looked far away! I dragged one of the suitcases for a few metres, left it and returned for the second one ... This went on for a while. The larger suitcase tore and clothes started popping out. The hotel looked no closer! I searched for a taxi but they were all full. I looked up and asked my angels to help.

Out of nowhere a coach appeared. The driver asked if I needed help. I cried "Yes!", full of joy. He picked up my cases and took them all the way in to the reception desk! I expressed my gratitude and called him my angel. I asked if I could give him something. He refused, and said: "If everyone in the world performed one act of kindness every day, the world would be a different place." And with that my angel left. I will never forget his words.

— *KALLIOPE DCS*

VANISHING ANGELS

SINCE TIME BEGAN there have been stories of strangers who appear from nowhere to assist someone and then vanish before they could be thanked. Here are more examples.

~ An Angel in a Bobble Hat! ~

Earth angels sometimes send positive thoughts to get you home safely.

. . . . . .

I had driven to a crystal shop about an hour away from home. It had been snowing and then thawed, but more snow began to fall while I was at the shop, making the roads treacherous. I wasn't worried as I was going to be driving on main roads.

I left the shop with a large amethyst geode crystal on my passenger seat. I made steady progress past cars that had slipped off the road into ditches and abandoned vehicles until I reached a steep hill. I crawled up the hill in second gear, but regretted my decision when I smelled burning. All of a sudden my car was full of smoke.

I wound the windows down to find a kind elderly man standing by the passenger window. He was wearing a bobble hat and said he was out for a walk. Strange because it was 7 p.m. on a cold January night and miles from anywhere!

Although I had my handbrake on I started to slide backwards towards the cars at the bottom of the hill. I panicked and asked him what to do. "You must carry on going forwards, even though it is hard and you are frightened," he replied. I laughed and said I had been asking angels for help and with his positive comments and my prayers I might just make it. When I finally reached the top of the hill I looked in my mirror – but the man had gone.

The car smelled badly of smoke but when I took it to the garage there was no damage. I knew it was the angel in the bobble hat who had helped. My amethyst geode sits on a windowsill, reminding me that even when things seem impossible, frightening or dangerous, there is always help at hand from the angelic realm.

— *MAI WORTH*

~ Car Accident ~

Here is an amazing story of an angelic rescuer.

∙∙∙∙∙∙

When Yoram, my partner, first came to visit me I took him out in my car. I was nervous but wanted to impress him. I had to turn left at an intersection, so I moved forward but misjudged my timing. A car hit me and things were a blur for a while but then I thought, "I'm still alive." However Yoram was semi-conscious. In panic I pulled him out of the car onto the grass.

A man with a peaceful, gentle presence came over. He said, "Don't worry. Everyone is going to be fine. Only the cars are damaged."

I saw smoke coming from the other car and still felt panicked. The man repeated, "Don't worry. Everyone will be fine." The paramedics took us to hospital saying, "People don't usually go home from an accident like that."

Yoram had three broken ribs but was OK. I was worried about the woman in the other car and was told that she was fine. Apparently a man had come up to her while she was trapped in the car and pulled her out. Her car burst into flames immediately afterwards. I knew it was the same man who had helped me and that he was an angel.

— *PHYLLIS*

~ A Lady and Her Dog ~

The people on this shuttle certainly needed a little help with their sleepy driver.

∙∙∙∙∙∙

My husband bought me a plane ticket to Santa Fe, to attend an opening party for my favourite artist. I booked a shuttle to take me from the airport in Albuquerque.

As I boarded the bus, I noticed a beautiful woman dressed in white with a huge dog crate. She sat next to me, her dog's head in my lap. I asked her how long she had had her dog. She replied, "Not long." I asked what she did and she replied, "Cosmology."

The bus started its journey and after a while, I caught a glimpse of the bus driver in the rear-view mirror. His eyes were closed! The lady in white nudged me and said, "Did you see that?"

She spent the rest of the trip talking to him to keep him awake. When the bus arrived I turned round to thank her and she, the dog and the crate had vanished.

— *VICKI GRABICKI*

~ Rescued from a Terrifying Car Breakdown ~

If in danger call on God and the angels and someone will appear out of the blue to help you.

• • • • • •

In 1991 I bought my first car. After finding a car I liked I asked a friend to check the engine and the bodywork. My friend took me to collect the car and planned to follow me home. I was nervous but excited.

The route took me through a multi-lane carriageway with traffic lights. Out of the blue, the engine died on me! I had no option but to put the gear in neutral and pull in to the central barrier with my hazard lights flashing. I was trembling because I knew what a life-threatening situation I was in. There were no other vehicles around. I knew traffic would come up behind me when the lights changed. My friend had taken a different route home, so I was alone. I began to pray: "Oh God please help me."

Ahead was an exit with a blue car parked on the verge. A man and woman got out and rushed toward me. The woman said, "Don't worry, we had one of these cars and it happened to us." The man lifted the hood, worked away and within seconds said to restart the engine. The car started. I remember repeating, "Thank you, thank you." They ran back to their car and I drove away. The blue car vanished.

The couple had seemed to know exactly what to say and do. I have no doubt that they were angels. When you meet angels, you just absolutely know in your heart of hearts that you have. I thank God for them.

— *LINDA VERYARD*

~ Blowout on Seven Mile Bridge ~

Once more helpers appear and then disappear.

• • • • • •

We were on our way home from Miami Airport with my grandmother, Mary, eighty-six, and her daughter Anona.

It was 10. p.m. and we were on the Seven Mile Bridge to Key West when suddenly the station wagon came to a stop. We had a blowout on one of the tyres. We were very tired after our plane journey and were now stranded with no one in sight.

Out of the blue a car appeared and two young men got out. One of them said "Don't worry, we'll put you on the road again." They changed the tyre and said "We'll follow you to Key West." We couldn't thank them enough and went on our way.

Further down the highway I realized there was no longer anyone behind us. Where were our two friends? It was impossible for anyone to turn round or overtake us, so where had our knights in shining armour gone?

We believe those two young gentlemen were in fact, our guardian angels and had come to our rescue at a time of dire need.

— *BERNICE AND ANONA*

~ A Very Real Angel ~

When you have trust an angel will always assist you.

......

I took my dad, who is eighty-seven and suffers from angina and various complications, to see a healer. During the healing my dad felt ill. The healer called me into the room and I was shocked by what I saw. My dad was close to losing consciousness. I kept talking to him and my voice seemed to bring him back. We decided that Dad needed to be in hospital and called an ambulance. He is over 6 ft tall and a heavy man to handle, especially in a semi-conscious state. I called the angels to help.

A man appeared and said he was a paramedic. He said, "He is going to be fine, don't worry." I remember looking into the clearest blue eyes I have ever seen and feeling calm. He had the kindest face and smile I have ever witnessed. The ambulance arrived and took Dad to hospital. I looked for the man to thank him but he was nowhere. I asked at the hospital reception, but no one had seen a man matching that description. He simply disappeared! My dad has recovered and is fine. I believe that man was an angel.

— *YVONNE CLARKE DCS*

~ In Deep Water ~

The angels work with all the elements to help us.

......

The site we worked on was at the end of a lane, with one-way access. Following some heavy rain there was extreme flooding in the area and the entrance was flooded. Those of us who had managed to get to work were stuck there and worried about how to get home.

My colleague decided to drive his car through the flood water but his car broke down and he was marooned in the flood. He became aware of someone helping him out of the car to safety. This person then disappeared. My colleague wasn't able to say who had helped him, but I believe it was an angel.

— *ELIZABETH STUBBS DCS*

~ A Little Light on the Spiritual Laws ~

If you are ready to read a particular book the angels will make sure it comes to you.

• • • • • •

In 2001 my world changed when I lost my dear dad to cancer. Having been a holistic therapist for many years, I had beliefs that were of great comfort. While searching for inspiration I came across the book *A Little Light on the Spiritual Laws* by Diana Cooper.

While I was looking at the book a man appeared and started talking about it. "Her books are really good you know," he said. I smiled reluctantly as I wasn't feeling chatty. He kept talking until I put the book back and moved away. I waited until he turned his back, then went back and bought the book. I realized that the man was nowhere to be seen. I know now that he was an Earth angel, for that book opened a door for me into spiritual development and really changed my life.

— *DEBBIE PETTITT*

~ Guiding Hand ~

A profound story of how a guardian angel helps this person to recognize their alcohol issues.

• • • • • •

On Christmas week 1984 after nine weeks of drinking heavily I was the first customer into my local pub. It was early morning and I ordered a pint of beer, which the barman put in front of me. Then he asked me for £2.20. I was short by 15 pence. I pleaded with the barman but he would not give me the pint.

This barman knew me well and laughed as he took back the pint. I badly needed the drink. There were no other customers in the bar but from my right side a "hand" pushed some loose change into place alongside my money. It made up the price of the pint.

I looked at the barman, he put down the pint in front of me and I gently pushed it back over to him. I turned to thank the stranger but no one was there! Today I know that was my guardian angel, and I have never drunk alcohol again.

— *ANON*

~ A Human Angel Moves My Car ~

Here is another story of an angel disappearing after giving help.

• • • • • •

I used to live in Abu Dhabi. Parking is very different there and people park in places we would consider illegal. Early one Friday morning I went to collect my car. The middle of the road was full of parked cars and there was no way to reverse my car without hitting one of the parked cars – I was blocked in.

Friday mornings are very quiet (it is prayer day) and there was no one there to help. I asked the angels to help me instead. Out of nowhere an Arab man appeared and helped me manoeuvre my car out of the space. He was very patient

– it took many turns of the wheel! As soon as I was out of the parking space I looked around to say thank you but he had vanished.

I believe he was an angel in human form sent to help me.

— *JULIE GREENHALGH*

~ *Angel on the Subway* ~

Angels help, protect and support us in the most astonishing ways.

••••••

After graduating from college I moved to New York City, where I lived for three years while saving for graduate school. Money was tight so the subway was my transportation of choice.

One evening I was riding the subway with a friend. We were deep in conversation so neither of us noticed when a man stole my wallet. I was shocked when another man picked the thief's pocket and returned my wallet completely intact. I stammered my thanks then turned to speak to my friend.

When I turned back my rescuer had vanished even though the train had not stopped and there was nowhere for him to go. I believe the man who returned my wallet was an angel.

— *LAUREN BLOOM*

CHAPTER 14

Death and Dying

ANGELS HELP WITH PASSING OVER

No one dies alone. Angels are always with you when you are about to pass over. Your guardian angel is holding your hand and Archangel Azriel, the angel of birth and death, is also with you. They ensure that you feel no pain and a minimum of shock when you move into the light.

After you die the angels stay with you.

A spirit never travels alone even if they passed many years ago, so they are always accompanied by an angel. Not even a master is allowed to travel without an escorting angel.

If someone who has recently passed wants to visit their loved ones, an angel will go with them so that they can come back to give their loved ones and friends the message that they are safe.

~ Comfort ~

Here is a detailed account of a beloved father passing and seeing the angels before he did so.

••••••

After bravely fighting liver cancer my dad was admitted to a hospice. We were all with him in his last few days. Every moment we spent together became precious.

Every now and then, Dad would look towards the corner of the room, even though nobody was there. He would hold up three fingers but we did not understand what he was trying to tell us.

He could not speak but I knew he could see something that we could not. I thought he must have seen a relative who had passed over. "Can you see your dad?" I asked. He shook his head, no. "Can you see your brother or mother?" Again he shook his head, no. I was perplexed. "Can you see angels?" He nodded. I asked him how many angels he could see. Dad held up three fingers with his left hand. I was in awe. My dad had never believed in angels. I told him to go with them.

Every single day is important. Death makes you appreciate the people in your life more. It still comforts us to know that the angels took Dad safely to the other side.

— *RUBY*

~ *My Guardian Angel* ~

In this story the angels left a token at the moment of death so that Elouise would know the timing was exactly right.

• • • • • •

My family was devastated when my father-in-law suffered a stroke, and I was angry that the angels had let this happen. Every night I tried to communicate with my spirit guides and my guardian angel but nobody would respond. I felt cheated and hurt.

I received a phone call from the hospital to say his condition had deteriorated considerably. I rushed to my car and noticed a brilliant white feather lying at the door. I noted the time was 10 a.m. I made it to the ward by 10.30 a.m. but it was too late – he had passed away at 10 a.m!

By leaving the feather the angels were reassuring me that he had been taken safely. It reignited my faith.

— *ELOUISE*

~ *A Dear Friend's Passing* ~

Here are two stories in which the angels have helped the person to leave reassurance for their friends and loved ones.

• • • • • •

A dear friend had become very ill with cancer. I was at work one morning and went to the staff toilet – it was 3.am. The toilet does not have a window but on the floor was a white feather. I knew it was a sign that Jacqui had passed. As I sat with my family to have breakfast that morning, a song came on the radio with the words "Jackie what you doing now? You're in a better place." It was about the singer Jackie Wilson. My son caught my eye and said, "Mum, did you hear that?" We knew it was a message from Jacqui.

— *VIVIEN BARBOTEAU*

~ *My Nephew's Passing* ~

It always feels like a tragedy to us when a child dies. Their soul has agreed the length of their life and the experiences they are to have and it's comforting to receive confirmation that they have safely passed over into the arms of the angels, as this story demonstrates.

• • • • • •

My three-year-old nephew, Sage, passed away in a tragic pool accident. A week after his passing I felt him around me. I asked the angels to guide and support him and surround him in light and love. During a meditation I saw five beautiful angels come in, pick him up and then fly into the ether with him.

I asked the angels for a sign he was OK. Later that night, as I was about to go to sleep I saw something in the curtains. I thought, "This is strange." I saw an outline, then a pair of eyes appeared and I knew it was Sage! It was truly incredible and heart warming. When I told my sister and described the outfit he was wearing, she recognized it as the one Sage was buried in. She was elated that he was OK and in safe hands. I felt special and privileged to experience something so magical. Of course I thanked the angels.

— *NADINE OLIVER-PIAMSUPHASUP*

~ A Feather from a Friend ~

Sometimes tragedy opens you up to the spiritual realms.

•••••••

I had a lovely friend called Chitra. She was mad about angels and talked about them all the time. She said she always knew when angels were about because they left little white feathers as a sign. At the time I was sceptical.

Tragically Chitra was murdered. We were devastated and missed her terribly as she was a truly very special person. My daughter came to visit me; we had been talking about her and we were both feeling sad. My daughter found a huge white feather; we laughed and said it must have been one of Chitra's angels trying to cheer us up. It made us feel better just to know that angels were around and that Chitra was being looked after.

— *HEATHER*

~ Angels Come to Take Him Home ~

No child's life is wasted.

•••••••

My very first encounter with the world of angels was twenty years ago. I was working as a beauty therapist with a lady whose eldest son was undergoing chemotherapy for leukemia. It was an emotional time that touched the hearts of everyone. After he had passed, the lady told me of her son's passing over into the light. He was lying in her arms when he looked into her eyes and said: "Mum, I have to go now! They are waiting for me!" She answered, "Who are they?" and he replied, "The angels!"

At that moment I realized that we are more than just physical beings. This experience was MY angel awakening.

— *LORNA*

~ Passing of Eileen Caddy ~

Many archangels will collect you if you ascend when you die.

•••••••

I was with a group of teachers from the Diana Cooper School, preparing a new course, when the phone rang. It was to tell me that Eileen Caddy, the founder of Findhorn, the magical spiritual community in Scotland, had passed over. We immediately lit a candle to offer prayers for her but instantly all realized that we did not need to do this. We were aware of Eileen with hundreds of angels, all singing and radiating love. She had obviously ascended and the angels were singing her praises. It was a glorious moment.

With divine timing, the following day we were sitting at the same table, continuing with our work, when the phone rang again. This time it was bringing news of the passing of someone who we all knew. We lit a candle and tuned in to offer prayers for her. The contrast was immense; this lady needed all the help we could give her, so that the angels could carry her into the light.

— *DIANA COOPER*

~ *Saving a Beloved Soul* ~

Many people cannot find the light when they die and their spirit becomes stuck. They do not have an angel with them but an elemental called a wuryl guides them.

•••••••

I was incredibly upset when my grandfather passed away. I knew he had been terrified of dying and I felt his spirit was trapped and not in a good place. I had the strong feeling that I was supposed to do something, but I was clueless about what to do and felt burdened.

I started going to a class with a Jungian psychologist and told him about my grandfather. He recommended several approaches but the one word I remembered was "angels". I somehow knew that was what I needed to do, so I asked the angels for help.

I sensed the air around me fluttering. Then I heard a male voice say, "Do not be afraid. We've come to answer your questions." I thought, "WOW, lucky me!" but realized they were not speaking to me but to my grandfather. I felt him surrounded, protected, literally taken under great wings. I was in awe of the power and majesty of these beings. They had no hesitation in moving into dark energy to retrieve a struggling soul.

It was Michael and his angels who came that day. What a gift to see that no matter how lost we are from ourselves, we are never lost to God or His messengers. All we need do is ask, and the door is truly opened.

— *KRISTA PERGANDE*

~ *In a Day's Work* ~

There are many dark places where earthbound souls remain; they need someone to show them the light.

•••••••

My day job is construction, but I also do spirit release. For my day job I was sent to work on a project remodelling an existing building to turn it into a library. There was a presence of something that felt like a large dark cloud clinging to my back. I knew that the building used to be an institute for the criminally insane.

With my spiritual eyes I saw hundreds of earthbound entities moping around with a thick black cloud over them. My spiritual teacher said that someone had to make an opening to Heaven and open the light for them to go through.

The next Monday I arrived very early, before anyone else. I told the earthbound entities that if they wished they could go to the light that I had created in the centre stairwell; continue their soul's purpose and be free. I visualized a brilliant golden-white light for them to follow. I saw people arm in arm, holding hands, smiling and as they passed some would even pat me on the shoulder.

Later I was reflecting on what happened when I felt a large presence behind me. It was about 7 or 8 ft tall and was a warm loving presence, wrapping arms around me and thanking me.

My tears fell – this angel was hugging me with the love of God and the total thanks of these poor souls who were now free and happy. I now go where the angels send me.

— *JOE*

~ *Plane Crash* ~

This story illustrates how a child could see the angels gathering to collect and help those who were about to pass over in a plane crash.

• • • • • •

Simon told me that he had just interviewed someone whose father died in 1994 when the flight USAir 427 crashed and everyone on board died. As a medium he sensed what had happened but then wondered if he was imagining it. A friend pointed out that the number plate on his hire car was 427. Angels provide amazing synchronicities to give us proof.

Furthermore, the lady he interviewed told him that one of the relatives waiting for the plane was with her four-year-old son, who pointed to the plane before it crashed and said, "Mummy, why is that plane being followed by all those angels?"

— *TOLD TO DIANA COOPER BY SIMON LUDGATE*

~ *The Angel of Death* ~

Archangel Azriel is the angel of death who meets everyone when they die. He appears black because his light is all within him and does not radiate out.

• • • • • •

I took a reflexology course at college and for the case studies I had to do, I contacted people who I thought would benefit most from the sessions.

One lady had been through a harrowing experience and I sensed that she did not want to be here any more. Later she told me that she had known exactly how and when she was going to take her life.

As I put my hands on her I was aware that the angel of death was beside her. He wore black motorcycle leathers and was camp! I loved motorbikes and realized this was for my reassurance.

When the lady arrived for her next session she told me that she had ordered a new garden shed. Not something you do if you do not plan to stay around. When I laid my hands on her the angel had gone. He was no longer needed.

I took great comfort in knowing that there will be an angel there for each one of us at our passing and there is no judgement about the manner of passing.

— *ELIZABETH HARLEY DCS*

~ Surrounded in Light and Protection ~

This is a glorious story, reminding you of how much you can do to help those who are passing and how magnificent is their true spirit.

* * * * * *

My son was dying and he asked me, "Mother, what sins do I have?" I told him that he had none. He had been a good father, a good son, a good husband, a hard worker and an honourable man. I asked Archangels Michael, Raphael and my son's guardian angel to enfold him in a circle of protection.

On the day he died I saw Archangel Michael at his head, Archangel Raphael on his right and his guardian angel on his left and they stayed with him the whole time. Later in meditation I saw a white tiger with bright blue eyes lying across his body, looking at me.

The hospice chaplain asked if we would like a prayer and the family formed a circle. As the chaplain led the prayer the centre of the circle filled with bright white light and a figure was standing there. The light was so bright that I could not see his face, only his beard. I knew that this was my son's real spirit.

— SERENA

~ Confirmation Feather ~

Many people need reassurance that their loved ones have passed well into the light. Ask for a sign and you will be given one.

* * * * * *

After my mother passed away I drove to order flowers for her funeral. I was crying as I drove and asked for a sign that she was all right. At that very moment, the largest and most gorgeous white feather you have ever seen floated down and landed in the middle of the windscreen. Coincidence? I think not ...

— GLYNIS

~ Hail Holy Queen ~

The angels arrange synchronicities and for our divine wishes to be granted even after we die.

* * * * * *

One of my close friend's mothers passed away. She was called Mary and was a beautiful person with a strong faith in God. The night after her passing I heard a knock. Both my husband and I assumed that the noise was each other!

I had a sense that Mary was beside me surrounded by a band of angels. She was extremely happy and she said she wanted me to say the prayer 'Hail Holy Queen'.

I called on Archangel Michael for protection and said the prayer. Mary told me that it was her favourite prayer and that she wanted it said at her funeral. She was so happy and light.

I told my friend that Mary was happy and in the arms of the angels and she wanted the 'Hail Holy Queen' prayer at the funeral.

Coincidentally, when Mary's other daughter heard about her mother's death she went into a church to pray and the congregation was reciting the same prayer.

To me this is confirmation that when our loved ones pass over they are healed and protected by the angels.

— *MARTHA MCMANUS DCS*

~ *A Presence Takes Nana* ~

This woman saw the spirit of her grandfather come to collect her grandmother.

• • • • • •

I would like to tell you the experience that I had with my nana's death. Three nights beforehand, Nana felt that she was going to die. On the third night she was sweating a lot but was very cold. I gave her water and Rescue Remedy. After about an hour I felt a presence walk to my bedroom and pass by me. I turned and I could see it. Nana turned, hugged me and then passed away. The presence scooped up my nana's spirit in its arms. The presence was my grandpa, coming back to collect her.

— *SOFIA SILVA*

NEAR-DEATH EXPERIENCES

MORE AND MORE PEOPLE are reporting near-death experiences. They follow a pattern: the dying person leaves their body and floats through a tunnel into the light, where they are met by angels or loved ones who have passed over. Sometimes they receive messages. Often they are told they must return to Earth and if they do so they are changed. Occasionally they are given a choice but, of course, we only know of those who choose to return to their bodies.

~ *My Car Accident* ~

We make a commitment to our families before we incarnate.

• • • • • •

At the age of twenty-six I was involved in a serious car accident. A lady came through a stop sign at full speed and collided with my car. My three-month-old daughter was on the back seat in her carrycot and survived because a bystander climbed into the car and rescued her.

I floated out of my body and viewed the scene from above before being sucked down a corridor. I floated on a cloud surrounded with love and light and peace. My family flashed before my eyes and I was "told" that I had made a commitment to my daughter, that she needed me and that I had another purpose. Zap! I was back in my body – and in pain. After spending six months in hospital recovering, I gave no further thought to what happened that day.

Years later I revisited my experience. Had I connected with beings of light? What was my purpose living here on planet Earth?

The being took me on an amazing journey to meet my higher soul and open me up to life after death and a beautiful relationship with the angelic realms. This experience still sustains me today. Namaste, we are all One.

— *JENNY HART DCS*

~ Angels Bring Me Back ~

I know Truda well and was one of hundreds of people who were lighting candles and praying for her survival.

......

I was seriously ill, on the border of life and death. Everyone thought I was dying, including myself; I thought, "This is it!" With that thought I fell asleep and went down a dark tunnel. At the end was a bright light full of angels. At that moment I knew I was going to live. I made a full recovery.

— *TRUDA CLARKE*

~ Reborn ~

This is a fascinating and detailed description of one young man's experience of dying.

......

I was at my friend Stuart's house. One minute I was drinking a cup of tea, the next I slipped into a dream state. Everything went black and it was as if I was paralyzed. Stuart said later that it was as if someone walked up to me and switched me off.

I felt myself sliding down the wall and falling across the breakfast bar and stools. I hit the floor and carried on falling and everything went blue with shimmering white and silver flowing through it.

I had a vision of my town in which I was floating above watching people. There was a beautiful lady in front of me, glowing like a star. Her blonde hair was flowing in the wind and her gown shimmered in the light. She kissed my cheeks.

Everything went black and I heard a voice telling me to wake up. I heard Stuart's mum calling for an ambulance, and I thought of my mum and said to myself, "NO!" I felt myself being lifted up. I took a gasp of air and my eyes opened. It felt as if time had slipped and that I was born again.

The experience has never left me. I think I did die in some way and an angel helped me back to Earth.

— *WILLIAM JOSEPH HENWOOD*

~ Heaven Hospital ~

When you pass over, if you truly loved your work on Earth, you may be able to continue to practise it in the heavenly planes.

......

I had plantar fasciitis, a very painful condition of the feet. I had acupuncture from a medical doctor and after two treatments it disappeared.

Five years later it returned. However, my doctor had passed away. I lay on the bed and said, "OK Doctor Ian, I need you to help me again with the plantar fasciitis. Please do what you need to do." I felt he had been in "Heaven Hospital" long enough to help me from there! The next morning I was considerably better and a week later I again asked Dr Ian to do what he needed to do. Next morning – no pain. I have had none since. I am truly blessed.

— *CARMEL*

~ Spirit Surgeon ~

After death many surgeons continue to help heal on Earth.

● ● ● ● ● ●

I was admitted to hospital and after investigations and CT/MRI scans, was found to have contracted a rare virus. This was a life and death situation and I was on the brink. I was out of it for four weeks and in hospital for seven. I remember nothing of this time.

I had two operations on my brain within twenty-four hours. My condition deteriorated rapidly and I would need a third operation or I would die. After being on the critical list, amazingly I began to recover. I had to learn to walk and talk again and it was like being reborn. Four months later I woke up and there was a male figure standing at the side of my bed. I remember thinking how could he be standing at the side when it was pushed right up against the wall?

Why was he there? I was not frightened. He was wearing a theatre cap and gown. The next morning I remembered the dream vividly and what the "person" looked like.

A lady who dealt in these matters gave me her interpretation. She felt it was a "Spirit Surgeon" who worked alongside the consultants in the hospital theatre. He returned to check and possibly give me further healing!

I know in my heart of hearts that this happened. I felt privileged. I know in my soul that I was meant to see him.

— *BERNICE*

~ Angel Story ~

Sometimes at the point of dying, your soul can renegotiate the time of passing in order to stay and help the family.

● ● ● ● ● ●

My friend's father was seriously ill with emphysema. She told me that the doctor had said it was time to call the family together; he was very weak and it was time for him to go.

At the hospital I found her father in great discomfort. I took his hand and called upon Archangels Raphael and Michael and all the angels to send healing energy to him. He told me he did not want to leave his sick wife and family alone.

Later I saw a tube of light enfolding him with a huge angel holding the energy around him.

The next day my friend called and said her father was sitting up in bed and eating. Everybody was shocked as they had expected the worst.

The only person he remembered visiting him was me. He remembered being on the other side and talking to an angel. He was told to finish his business and to talk to everyone he had to make peace with. His family had eight extra months with him.

— *ANON*

~ Goodbye ~

The angels come in and give us a warm golden feeling in the heart when we are saying goodbye to someone for the last time.

* * * * * *

As a child we had a lovely family in our neighbourhood. They had four boys and we were three girls. The boys were older than us but their parents so loved to have us around – the daughters they never had. The husband and father of the family was a big man, like a cuddly bear and I remember how much fun we had with him.

One day when my mum came and fetched us, I wanted to say goodbye to him, so I hugged him very tight and kissed him on the cheek. It had never happened before; it just "came over me." That was the last time I ever saw him – he died the next week of a heart attack. I had felt so warm, so happy and such a strong need to hug him. I remember it vividly.

— *CAROLINE CAMERON*

~ Another Farewell ~

The warm feeling round the heart, however, does not inevitably mean the other person is going to die.

* * * * * *

I was in the car with my dad and all of a sudden I felt that warmth around my heart. I had the urge to hug him, to tell him everything was all right and that I loved him. Sure enough, two days later he died.

Of course I was worried the next time I felt the warm feeling around my heart – as I saw my little girl off for her school trip – but at the same time I knew she would be fine.

— *CAROLINE CAMERON*

~ Clearing a House ~

When a soul is stuck it does not pass into the light but stays in its familiar surroundings.

* * * * * *

After a wonderful angel workshop I had learned so much about the angels. I had an amazing experience when I returned home. The house where I have lived for twelve years has always felt very "heavy" and my family have had a lot of problems since moving there. I became aware of a stuck soul and Archangel Metatron came and offered to take this lost soul to the light. At first the lost soul was reluctant to leave, but once reassured that she would be returning to God's love she happily left with Metatron.

Then three more lost souls arrived and asked to be directed to the light. I called in the angels and they too were transported to the light. I thanked the angels.

The house now feels light and easy and life for my family has improved greatly.

— *ANUPAMA SINGH*

~ Eternal Bliss ~

Those who have a near-death experience often describe it as feeling like eternal bliss.

• • • • • •

My near-death experience happened in 2008. I was extremely low on iron and exhausted. Tablets did not help and I needed an iron transfusion. During my second transfusion I was lying in the doctor's office when realized I could not breathe any more.

As horrifying as I know this sounds, I remained relaxed and was at peace. The doctor injected adrenaline and tried to give me some puffs of the inhaler. I felt like an observer, watching. He pressed my lips together over the inhaler. Everything around was hectic but I was ready to go. Even though I could not breathe it didn't bother me. It felt blissful.

I had NO worries at all. I didn't even think of my kids. I was not as far gone as seeing my life flash in front of my eyes but I was at peace. There is nothing as peaceful as this moment.

Three years later I am still around and kicking, and have no fear of dying.

— *CAROLINE CAMERON*

CHAPTER 15

Archangel Michael

Archangel Michael is the best known of all the archangels and his mighty light spreads across the universes. He wears a deep blue cloak and carries his sword of truth, with which he will cut away or "uncord" attachments that are holding you back.

You can call on him to give you strength and courage and to help you in times of trouble. If you invoke his protection he will place his deep blue cloak of protection round you and your loved ones. It is good spiritual practice to ask for his deep blue cloak of protection every morning and evening. Also ask for his protection when you go on a car journey or do anything where you feel you need extra angelic help. It is more effective if you ask and then picture his deep blue cloak as vividly as you can.

In this chapter there are many remarkable stories of the ways in which people have had experiences with Archangel Michael.

~ Archangel Michael at a Funeral ~

Archangel Michael protects and also comforts and supports.

My dad, a well-loved and unorthodox parish priest, had died and I was dreading his funeral. I knew my heartache would be witnessed by many people; there were to be three separate services held over two days.

On the first evening close family and the vicar stood around my father's coffin. A piece of music from the opera *Dido and Aeneas* was playing and my daughter and I wailed in a way more appropriate to the Middle East than Middle England!

On the second day I opened my heart to Archangel Michael. His light came through and his dark blue cloak surrounded me. His arms wrapped around me and I was protected inside this link between Heaven and Earth. I took my place in a front pew. The whole time, Archangel Michael held his protective cloak round me and his sword before me. When you can't cope, it's a very special help that's needed!

I share this story with great gratitude to Archangel Michael. Whenever we feel overwhelmed there is always a wonderful strength of love available to us. Be love and love will be. It is there for us to know and be throughout our lives.

— SUE PENROSE-GOULD

~ Archangel Michael Helps a Child at School ~

Ask Archangel Michael to look after children while at school.

• • • • • •

My son was very frightened of his strict mathematics professor at school. Whenever the teacher asked my son a question he would be tense and unable to answer. I asked Archangel Michael to protect my son during his class. Over time my son became more relaxed and has now lost his fear of the teacher and the maths class. His marks have improved and he is now pleased to go to school. All thanks to Archangel Michael.

— *MARTINA MARIA SERAPHINA KAMMERHOFER*

~ Finding My House Key ~

Ask Archangel Michael to help if you lose something.

• • • • • •

My sister gave me a blue Archangel Michael keyholder. One day at the beach I did some cartwheels. When I returned home I didn't have my door key and realized that it must have fallen out of my pocket. I prayed to Archangel Michael that I find the key in the sand.

Despite the odds I did find my house key on the beach; the incoming waves had not quite reached it. Thank You, Archangel Michael!

— *YOURS ALMUT*

~ Archangel Michael Speaks ~

This is an awe-inspiring story.

• • • • • •

My uncle lived an "ascetic" kind of life. He worked in a factory and received minimum wage. He lived sparsely and ate next to nothing. He bought milk and bread and distributed the food daily at dawn, leaving it anonymously on doorsteps in his neighbourhood, which consisted mainly of poor underprivileged families

I first met my uncle when I was eleven and the first thing that struck me was this feeling of serenity around him – he seemed to "glow". He would spend the whole day in his bedroom praying. He was intensely spiritual.

One day when he was upstairs praying, I was very curious so I sneaked up the stairs. The door was half open and I peeked in. He was kneeling with his back to me and was "conversing" with the wall. I looked and couldn't see anything but I could feel a presence unlike anything I had ever experienced. I knew something marvelous was there. Uncle was conversing in a language unlike any other I'd ever heard. I quietly went back downstairs.

Later he called me over. He said he had been talking to Archangel Michael and Michael had told him I was at the door. He explained that he spoke to angels, including Michael, constantly. He knew I would understand because he spoke the language of the angels and not many people could hear it, but I had.

Archangel Michael had told him that I was "different" and this is why I was able to "hear" them talking. This was my first encounter with angels. Archangel Michael would make himself known to me again – which is my second story.

— *ELLIE EVENSONG*

~ Silver Shoes ~

Ellie's story continues many years later as she meets Archangel Michael again.

• • • • • •

I moved to Greece. There was a tiny eleventh-century Byzantine church dedicated to Archangel Michael in an isolated area half an hour from our home. The church is not visible from the road and is almost permanently closed.

I decided to visit the church. Approaching it, I felt a very strong divine energy. The door was locked so I peeked in the window. On the floor in front of the altar was a pair of silver shoes. They were unlike anything that I had ever seen; I could feel them drawing me like a magnet. The heel was near the altar and the toes pointed towards the door. The altar was separated from the rest of the church by a curtain. I felt I had seen something from outside our realm. I kept going back, and every time I returned the shoes were in a different position inside the church. I asked the priest about the church and he explained that no one went there and it was only opened in November on the feast day of the archangels. I asked him about the shoes. He said they had been there "always", and that they had been placed inside the altar, behind the curtain. No one had ever entered the church that he knew of. The shoes were a mystery.

I told my oldest son about them. He drove to the church but a swarm of bees hovered like a guard and wouldn't let him in. My son felt Michael's presence and wanted to go back to communicate with him. When he returned, the bees allowed him access.

I am convinced that Michael was taking refuge in this little church. Michael gave me the opportunity to feel his presence there. It was the same feeling that I had when I was eleven and he was in my house talking to my uncle. Did he move the shoes around to let me know of his presence? This beautiful experience changed my life and opened my eyes to the angelic realm.

— *ELLIE EVENSONG*

~ Michael Does the Driving ~

Archangel Michael is such a high-frequency being of light that he makes time go faster.

• • • • • •

When I have been driving long-distance late at night, feeling tired and just wanting to be home, I have felt as if Archangel Michael was driving the car and I was simply holding the steering wheel. I always seem to arrive home wondering, "Wow, am I home already?"

— *WENDY*

~ An Angel in Blue ~

When Archangel Michael appears he is nearly always seen in deep blue. He can sometimes appear as a person dressed in that colour.

• • • • • •

One foggy morning my younger daughter Tara was running to catch the school bus and was hit by a car. A neighbour came and informed us. I went to the bathroom and prayed quickly, "Someone please take care of her until I get there."

When I got there I saw someone beside her in a blue robe. The person turned to me and said, "Oh you are the moth—" At that point the words faded and I heard bells ringing.

My daughter had concussion and a swollen leg but was OK. I asked my husband later on about the accident scene and he swore there was no other person there except us and the police. Then I remembered my prayer and realized it had been answered by an angel.

— *SHARON GAUTHIER*

~ Asking for Angelic Presence ~

This is a reminder that when you ask for an angel to contact you, one will do so.

• • • • • •

I was told that if you want a spirit or angel to connect with you you should ask three times prior to going to sleep. I did this, asking for an angel to contact me.

Several nights later I awoke to my room being full of bright light and a young man standing at my bed. He was slim with dark hair. He leaned forward and touched my right cheek, gently drawing his finger the length of my cheek. All I could think was, "I can feel that!" I was left amazed.

Recently at a psychic development group, one of the group members had a message for me. She saw a young man. He stroked her right cheek and gave her the name Michael. I have taken this to mean that Archangel Michael was guiding me towards the spiritual path I am now on.

— *MARY THOMSON*

~ House Hunting ~

Angels truly do smooth our way and bring the perfect thing forward for us.

• • • • • •

I ask my angels whenever I need help and thank them afterwards. My mum and sister are more sceptical about angels, though. When my sister was heavily pregnant, she and her boyfriend desperately wanted to move from their cold damp flat to a seaside town in Cornwall. Their search for a rental property became frantic – every house they were interested in was immediately taken by someone else.

My sister rang our mum in tears – they had viewed four properties that day, to no avail. I suggested that my sister ask Archangel Michael for help. "What has she got to lose?" I said, "Just ask him."

My sister did ask Archangel Michael for help. The first house they saw that morning was perfect, just right for them – and they got it! They were overjoyed. The house was on St. Michael's Road - opposite St. Michael's Church! Of course she thanked Archangel Michael and she always asks for his help these days.

— *KATIE*

~ Angel of Light ~

When you open yourself to the light of an angel it can transform your life.

......

I was in the shower and noticed a shadow blocking the natural light from the window. When I looked up I saw a huge angel. I opened myself up to the energy and realized it was Archangel Michael. I felt overwhelming love and protection.

— *DIANE*

~ Message of Confirmation from Archangel Michael ~

And here is a wonderful description of Archangel Michael by someone who saw him when she called him.

......

I started to develop my spirituality and read books like *A Little Light on the Spiritual Laws* and *A Little Light on Angels*. I began to feel able to call on angels and God for their help in all situations. I was always particularly inclined to call out to Archangel Michael.

One day as I called Archangel Michael I "felt" someone turn round and face me. In my mind's eye I saw a tall, majestic being with a suntanned complexion, shoulder-length copper hair and deep piercing eyes, wearing an off-white long gown. His eyes looked deep into my soul.

As this happened at my work in my lunch break, I couldn't really spend time thinking about it. I didn't believe my experience was anything other than my own imagination. Later on the internet, I typed in Archangel Michael's name and saw the exact picture of the angel I had seen earlier. I was so moved and thankful to the angels and God for letting me see and feel them. I hope anyone who reads this is inspired to invite the angels into their lives and be blessed.

— *MELODY CHOPHLA*

~ Archange Michael Listens ~

When you pray consistently to a specific archangel they will be with you.

......

I was really chuffed because I read about praying to Archangel Michael in one of Diana's books and had been praying daily for him to protect me and give me strength. I had a reading with a medium and the first thing she told me was that she could see Archangel Michael with me! It was nice and incredible to hear confirmation, and reassurance that my prayers are heard.

— *ANON*

~ *TV Repair* ~

Angels will help machinery to repair itself. Have faith and be grateful when they do help.

· · · · · ·

One Sunday morning I switched on the TV to watch my favourite programme, *Spirit Sunday*, and was upset to see that the picture wasn't clear. I called my son to see if he could fix it but he couldn't come over.

As I walked down my stairs I said to myself, "I am sure there are electrician angels." I remembered that Archangel Michael helps to repair electrical appliances. I called on him and thought that it would be lovely if, when I got into the lounge and switched on the TV, it was working! I switched the TV back on – and it worked perfectly. It is wonderful to know that there are angels for everything.

— *CAROL DE VASCONCELOS DCS*

FAITH

ARCHANGEL MICHAEL'S TWIN FLAME is Faith. The twin flame of archangels represent the divine feminine qualities. So Archangel Faith represents the qualities of faith and confidence within all of us. Having faith is one of the most powerful energies we can show as the following story demonstrates.

~ *The Miracle of Showing Faith* ~

Here is a story of faith and trust and how Archangel Michael responded in a miraculous way to this energy.

· · · · · ·

I run a workshop called A Journey of Healing with the Angels. In the beginning some participants are sceptical. One participant found even the concept of angels too much to take on board at first; however as the weeks went on she started asking the angels for guidance.

One week she informed us that she was going on holiday with her family and was disappointed that she would miss a class. The following week she shared this story from her holiday:

They had just checked in at the airport when her husband asked if she'd locked the back door. She couldn't remember but said, "If these angels are as good as Mariel said let's put them to the test!" She asked Archangel Michael to surround her home and her business in protective light and keep it safe until they got home. She thanked Michael.

On returning home they were met with an awful smell of burnt rubber. The fuse box was burned onto the wall and all the cables burnt to a crisp. The electrician said it was a miracle the house and business had not gone up in flames.

She knew it was Archangel Michael who had kept her home safe and answered her prayer.

— *MARIEL FORDE CLARKE DCS*

~ Headlights Fix ~

Archangel Michael will also respond to faith by repairing physical things if you ask.

. . . . . .

I got into my car to go to a workshop, but noticed one of the headlights was not working. As I was driving to the workshop, it started to snow. I didn't want to turn back and miss my class, so I asked Archangel Michael to fix my headlight. Sure enough when I pulled in to check it, it was working and I never had problems with it again. I always ask Archangel Michael now if anything needs fixing.

— *CATHERINE MCMAHON DCS*

ARCHANGEL MICHAEL'S SWORD AND SHIELD

ARCHANGEL MICHAEL carries a sword of truth and light to cut away lower attachments and a shield to protect people from lower energies.

~ Clearing a Bedroom ~

If you feel anxious, or that there is a negative presence around, call in Archangel Michael to take it away.

. . . . . .

I live in a nice apartment in Munich. One evening I came in late and felt insecure and unwell in my beautiful apartment. I did not know why, because nothing bad had happened that day. I went to bed and tried to go to sleep, but I could not close my eyes and shut out the light even though I was very tired.

I said to Archangel Michael, "Archangel Michael, purify and clear this room and my apartment from all negative and low-vibrating energy!" Immediately a flash of bluish-white lightning appeared opposite my bed and the bad feeling disappeared. I now felt safe and able to go to sleep. That experience strengthened my belief that angels protect us.

— *DANI*

~ Releasing Ceremony ~

Releasing ceremonies are incredibly powerful and important.

. . . . . .

I was going to perform a releasing ceremony and wanted to set my altar up the night before and put all the items I needed on it. I was going to have to to wait for my son to go to bed as I was using a room we shared but, uncharacteristically for a school night, my son asked to sleep over at his friend's house. I knew the angels were conspiring to give me the time I needed to prepare. The ceremony went well and I received confirmation of the release in my dreams.

— *ANON*

~ The Power of Cutting Cords ~

The following four stories demonstrate spiritual law in action.

••••••

When I run angel courses I often lead people in a meditation with Archangel Michael to cut the cords to anything that does not serve their higher purpose. This is a private thing and I do not ask people what cords they are cutting, although I do let people share their experiences and I give help or advice if needed.

I received a call one day from a lady who had done a cord-cutting meditation with me. She was in tears because she had been made redundant. She had asked for the cords between her and her job to be cut because she did not like it. However, she did need the money! This made me realize just how powerful this exercise can be. I am happy to say that she asked the angels for another job – one she would enjoy – and one manifested quickly!

— *MARGARET MERRISON DCS*

~ Cutting the Cords to My House ~

You can cut cords to anything when it is time to let it go.

••••••

We had lived in our house for thirty-one years and now that our children had moved away, we needed to downsize. However, the house had been on the market for over a year and I was feeling unsettled about the future and wondering whether it would ever sell. Even though I was in constant touch with my angels I was at low ebb.

I sat on my patio and spoke to the angels and to my house – I said, "I love you so much and you have given me and my family so much happiness for all these years but I need to move house. I need to cut the cords that are holding me here so that I can move on and someone else will come and love you." I actually felt a great sense of release and knew for certain that I would be moving on soon.

Ten minutes later the phone rang and it was people who had wanted our home for a year. They said that they finally had a buyer for their house and they would be in touch. The sale went through so quickly our feet didn't touch the ground.

This is one of my lovely angel experiences – I think in my heart I actually didn't want to move because of what the house meant to me and this happened to teach me a lesson about moving on.

— *TINA GRAY*

~ Cutting Business Cords ~

It is often easier to remember to cut cords with people, but this story reminds us of the power of detaching from anything that we are holding on to.

••••••

One of my clients had difficulty selling her business and asked me to tune in to see what stopped the sale. I saw that she had thick cords attached to her business that prevented her from selling. Although she had not consciously attached these cords, her business had provided her with a stable income and the idea of her financial uncertainty was blocking the sale on an energy level.

With Archangel Michael's help we cut the cords and freed her from her attachment to the business. She felt sad but relieved that she was ready to move forward. Three days later her business sold.

— *CATHERINE MCMAHON DCS*

~ Uncording ~

When Archangel Michael cuts cords it releases fear, which allows you to feel stronger.

••••••

I was working with two ladies who were going through a difficult time, so we did an uncording exercise with Archangel Michael. One lady released a huge amount of fear and was completely calm by the time she left. The other lady described how she felt as the chains were cut and pulled from the various areas of her body. Both of the ladies experienced a profound shift and left feeling a lot stronger.

— *ANNABELLA ONTONG DCS*

~ Archangel Michael's Sword Heals Sacred Site ~

Here is a story about Archangel Michael's sword of truth being used to heal energy in a sacred place.

••••••

I feel very connected with Glastonbury Tor. I often go there or sit in Chalice Wells Garden just below it. On one occasion I joined a group of about a hundred lightworkers who gathered to put Michael's sword of truth through the top of the tor to heal the etheric crystal within the hill. Of course, this is a spiritual sword, not an actual three-dimensional one!

The ceremony was very powerful. That night I dreamed I was looking into a kaleidoscope and a million shimmering pieces came together to form the crystal in the hill. I felt that this was confirmation from Archangel Michael that our work had succeeded in its purpose.

— *TRUDA CLARKE (AS TOLD TO DIANA COOPER)*

ARCHANGEL MICHAEL PROTECTS

~ Archangel Michael Saves a House ~

What I love about this story is Melissa's faith.

••••••

I heard from a customer that there was a bad storm coming so I immediately asked Archangel Michael to protect our home. Half an hour later, I received a call from a neighbour to say that a huge tree had come down over my house. I grabbed my bag and headed for the door. As I left I said to one of our psychic readers that I could not understand it as I had asked Archangel Michael to protect the property. The reader replied that Michael had just told him that he had done so.

When I reached home I found that the oak tree that had fallen was so huge that it lay completely over the house. However, it was resting on its branches so that the trunk was lying clear of the roof. Not even one single tile was damaged. Archangel Michael certainly had protected it!

— *MELISSA ELLSWORTH*

~ *Michael is a Shining Light* ~

When you think about an angel or an archangel one comes to you automatically.

••••••

I was talking to my neighbour and she lent me some books about angels. I started reading one of them at bedtime and tried to ask for protection and some guidance for the future. I was thinking particularly about Archangel Michael for some reason.

At about 2 a.m., I woke up because of an unbelievably bright light that looked like an angel standing beside me. It wasn't long before it disappeared, but it was incredible; I was sure it was Archangel Michael and now I feel safe and protected.

— *ANU*

~ *New Zealand* ~

Here is a reminder about the power of giving the angels a clear message about what you need.

••••••

While travelling in New Zealand I found that I was continually travel-sick if I took buses, so I hitched my way round the country. It felt fine and safe and I met some amazing, warm and generous people. I had a strict routine of wearing particular clothes, calculating my journey time and always taking water, fruit and a sleeping bag.

One day though I decided to go to the next town, Takaka, and I broke all my own rules. I don't know why but I didn't research the journey or take provisions, not even water. It was further than I expected and I found myself stranded at sundown in a valley without a lift in sight. I grew tired and worried, so I called on Sananda, Archangel Michael and any other angels to help.

I placed my request clearly! I wanted a lift with a female. I wanted to sit in the back of the car. I wanted to be delivered to somewhere I could eat and drink – and all of this before dark!

A car stopped. There were two girls in the front so I had to sit in the back. We reached the most delightful pub/restaurant and had a brilliant evening listening to live music and dancing. There was a hostel nearby where I stayed for a few days.

I've never doubted the presence of angels and that I was protected in my life and travels. It was confirmation that if you ask you receive.

— *JUSTINE TAYLOR*

~ Michael Saves the Drivers ~

When you ask for protection Archangel Michael will look after you. Your faith and trust are mighty transcendent energies that enable him to help you.

• • • • • •

Every day I place archangel protection upon my house, cars and family. Late one evening my daughter was driving me down a main street near our home. From nowhere came a red sports car, going very fast. I was panicking and so was my daughter – we braced ourselves for the impact.

Suddenly our car was shoved into the next lane as if a huge angelic hand had pushed us out of the path of the red car. I saw the driver of the other car sitting on the pavement dazed and bewildered. He was fine but his car was upside down, spinning on its roof. I felt a tingle in my body and knew that Archangel Michael was next to me. I felt his hand touch my shoulder for a second and I knew that he smiled. I was glad that my daughter was with me, because no one would have believed me otherwise.

— *CATHERINE HARDIE*

~ Facing Fears ~

We pick up other people's fears and automatically react to them out of our own underlying fears.

• • • • • •

I was travelling by train to Oslo. Most people had got off the train and I realized that the only other passenger was a dark-haired man. I was uncertain about him and asked Archangel Michael for protection. The man started to speak to me, but I couldn't understand him. I trusted Archangel Michael to protect me, so I started to use my hands to try to communicate with the man.

He took out his mobile and called someone and then passed the phone to me. It was his brother, very worried that he would miss his plane as he had been lost for hours. I realized I had nothing to fear and that my fear was because I had been picking up on his fear of missing his plane. I got off at an earlier stop than usual and helped him to get to the airport. He kissed my hand and I felt the most overwhelming feeling of connection to him. I looked into his eyes and felt his gratitude. I realize now that we are all connected.

— *KARI NYGARD DCS*

~ Protecting Nature ~

Archangel Michael can also protect the natural world, especially places where the vibration is very sacred.

• • • • • •

My friend Heather and I were walking round the beautiful lake at Fernworthy, where the trees are huge. Heather had a sudden feeling that we were not supposed to be there. She saw a huge angel with his arms stretched out. On his head was a metallic helmet, like the one Archangel Michael sometimes wears. He was huge and powerful. He imparted that this was a very special, well looked after place and they did not want anyone to do any harm.

— *AS TOLD TO DIANA COOPER BY MARY*

~ *Calling on Archangel Michael* ~

This is another miracle performed by Archangel Michael!

• • • • • •

My youngest daughter Shelley was studying to become a nurse. She always asked her angels for help in her exams and practical placements. Like many students she arrived home every weekend for a bit of pampering and home-cooked meals.

Saying goodbye was always difficult and at the end of one weekend, I stood at the door and called for Archangel Michael's safety and protection for her. A storm broke, which made me anxious. I called more angels to keep her safe.

Later Shelley called, crying and in shock. She had been approaching some traffic lights and they'd turned green, so she proceeded, but a massive four-wheeler digger had come out of nowhere and her car was heading straight under its cab.

Suddenly a huge force took the wheel from her hands and steered it away from the digger. Other motorists saw what happened and couldn't believe that Shelley walked away from what looked like a near-fatal accident. Even the police couldn't believe she'd escaped.

Shelley knows it was the intervention of Archangel Michael that day. Now she keeps the passenger seat spiritually free for him!

— *MARIEL*

~ *Right People at the Right Time* ~

There are people with wonderful, warm and generous hearts everywhere and Archangel Michael makes sure they are in the right place to help you.

• • • • • •

I travelled to Stirling to meet my ex-boyfriend, but he didn't turn up and I only had £8 and no return ticket. I went to the police station and they told me to go back to the bus station but that if he didn't turn up they would put me up for the night – in a police cell!

I asked Archangel Michael to help and protect me. A lady with two children came and said, "It's terrible what has happened to you." I don't know how she knew my story; however, she was so sympathetic and walked with me back to the bus station.

My ex still hadn't turned up so I phoned my son, who told me to find a hotel and he would pay by credit card. But I couldn't find any that had vacancies! I met two girls in the street and I explained that I couldn't find anywhere to stay. One of the girls gave me the keys to her flat and took me there. She made me something to eat and sorted the bed settee for me. She was so kind.

The next morning I told her about the angels and how I had asked for help. She took me out for breakfast, got me back to the bus station and paid for my ticket home. I took her address and phone number so I could return her money. I bought the biggest thank you card and posted it to her with all the money she'd spent. I believe that Archangel Michael answered my prayers by sending her and that he is always here by my side.

— *JANET SKINNER*

~ Safe Parking ~

When you ask Archangel Michael to protect your car or home or a person, miracles can happen.

• • • • • •

I lived close to the airport so, when my cousin and her husband went overseas they left their car parked by my front door. They thought it would be safer than in the airport car park. When they arrived back I went to the car to pick them up and noticed that a stone tile had fallen off the porch roof, onto the bonnet of their car. Amazingly there wasn't a single scratch on either the car or windscreen, just a sprinkling of dust. I had asked Archangel Michael to protect the car while it was in my driveway. Thank you Archangel Michael.

— *PHIL HARTNETT DCS*

~ Earthquake in Bali ~

This story illustrates Archangel Michael's enormous power.

• • • • • •

I was in Bali for a retreat when, one night, I woke up to see my bed shaking and hear the wooden door shaking and banging very loudly, as if someone was trying to force it. I realized it was an earthquake and called on Archangel Michael for protection. Not only did he come instantly and enfold me in his large wings, but the Earth also stopped moving, as if quietened by his presence.

I called for protection for the whole island, and knowing that everyone was safe I went back to sleep, peaceful and blissful. Thank you Archangel Michael for showing me the love and power of the angelic ones and teaching me that I am always safe and protected.

— *ANISIYA SHEEHAN*

~ Blessing on the Highway ~

When you ask for protection the impossible becomes possible.

• • • • • •

On Father's Day I found myself driving a friend home early in the morning. As I made my way onto the highway, I had nothing else in mind other than to get home and celebrate with my family.

Halfway home, my rear tyre blew out. I tried calling my husband for help but he could not be reached. Feeling rather vulnerable and unable to reach anyone for help, I prayed to Michael and asked, "Please shield my car and protect me from the other cars."

A state trooper pulled over. The officer said, "Ma'am, we are responding to your call for help." I had not called the police! At the same time, my husband rang me. Knowing my husband was on his way, I thought the officer would leave; however he said, "It can be scary out here by yourself; I will keep my car lights on and shield you." In that moment I knew who had come to help me – it was Archangel Michael, who among other things is the patron saint of police officers. That day, I promised Michael that if there were ever a way for me to tell the story of my experience, I would write about it.

— ANON

~ The Protective Cloak of Archangel Michael ~

If you ever feel threatened pray for help. Never underestimate the power of this.

• • • • • •

I was on a train in London and an alcohol-intoxicated man was stomping between the carriages, muttering loudly. I quickly placed Archangel Michael's blue cloak of protection around me, asked for the Christ light to be sent to all of the people in my carriage and invoked the angels of peace to fill it with light. I also sent prayers to the man's guardian angel.

Then he came and sat across from me and a male passenger. He explained that he had been supposed to go to work that day but had got drunk instead. He slapped his hand down on the man's thigh in a gesture of frustration.

Silently I continued to pray for him. He raised his hand as if to place it on my knee, but when he was ten centimetres away he stopped and slowly withdrew his hand. We shared a smile. I was convinced that day of Archangel Michael's total protection. I hope that the man has since been listening to his higher self and his guardian angel.

— DIANA DUDEK DCS

~ Michael's Protection Really Works ~

There are many wonderful examples of how Archangel Michael's protection has saved homes and possessions. As Penny's example shows, remember to use it every day!

• • • • • •

Recently three of our close neighbours have had bikes and other items stolen from their gardens. On the night of the thefts we had heard our dogs barking but thought nothing of it. In the morning it was obvious that someone had been in our garden. My husband had forgotten to lock our shed so we rushed to see if anything had been taken. The door was shut but we could see that someone had tried to open it. My husband opened the door, hoping his beloved bike was still there. It was.

I am convinced Archangel Michael stopped the thieves from getting into the shed as I ask him to protect our house and garden every day!

— PENNY WING DCS

~ Blue Light of Protection ~

When one person calls in angels it helps everyone in the area.

• • • • • •

One night as I walked home alone along a dark road, I noticed two men in the distance standing beside a large expensive-looking car. It gave me such an odd feeling that I immediately asked Archangel Michael to put a blue light of protection around me and the whole area. I wasn't sure if the men intended to steal the car, but as soon as I had asked for protection I felt the atmosphere change and the men turned and ran away. I was able to walk on home feeling calm and protected by Archangel Michael.

— *KARI NYGARD DCS*

~ Archangel Michael Shields ~

Archangel Michael can render you invisible to those around you. This story is a perfect example of his work.

• • • • • •

I live in South Africa, and it is not always safe for a woman to drive alone. I have to drive through part of a township to get to my farm.

One night as I came round the corner into the township there were hundreds of people in front of the police station, protesting. They were blocking my way but I was tired and did not want to turn round and take another route. I asked Archangel Michael to put his cloak of protection round my car to make me invisible to the crowd and help me get home safely.

Something amazing happened: I started to drive slowly and the crowd stepped away to make room for my car. There was no banging on the roof, screaming or anything – it was like they did not see me. Now that is protection! I am so glad to have Archangel Michael always by my side.

— *MARISE VIVIERS*

~ Amazing Grace ~

And here is a truly remarkable story of grace.

• • • • • •

I drove to work and left my seventeen-year-old son Jehan at home. Unusually, and for a reason I didn't understand, I asked Archangel Michael and the ascended master Shirdi Sai Baba to look after him.

Later that day my husband called to say our apartment was on fire and Jehan was trapped inside.

Before I could reach home, Jehan called to say he was safe but our belongings were all destroyed. I was so relieved to hear his voice. When I got back, the fire chief said that Jehan seemed blessed – he had never known anyone emerge unscathed from a fire of such magnitude.

Under the top layer of soot, some of our belongings were intact. I noticed that next to the washing machine, which had exploded and caused the fire, was a wooden cabinet containing important documents. Above was a key-chain holder with a picture of Archangel Michael on it. The key-chain was on the wooden cabinet, which for some unknown reason the fire had bypassed. Besides protecting our son, Archangel Michael and Sai Baba also saved our important documents!

Since then I have grown to trust the archangels, angels, ascended masters and the forces of light even more and often feel their beautiful presence in and around me.

— *DR. COOMI S. VEVAINA DCS*

~ Saved at Sea ~

Archangel Michael can remove your fear and panic, so that you are calm enough to take appropriate action.

••••••

One morning a friend and I were heading to watch and meet the dolphins. While swimming I felt a burning pain in my left arm and leg. As I could not see anything to explain the pain I got frightened and started to worry about my safety in the water. I shouted to my friend that I would swim back to the beach. She was far behind me and I realized that something was wrong. As she came nearer she looked pale, her breathing was irregular and she said, "I feel so tired, I can hardly move. I can't swim back, I won't make it."

I called in the angels and especially asked Archangel Michael for his help. My fear and panic disappeared. I reassured my friend that we would both make it back to the beach and we slowly swam back. It felt as if we were both protected as we arrived safely on the beach. Thank you, beloved Archangel Michael!

— *CORNELIA MOHR DCS*

~ Landing Gently with Michael's Help ~

Archangel Michael can save people in amazing ways and here is another example of his power.

••••••

Our son, Chael, aged three, is named for Archangel Michael and I always pray to Archangel Michael for his protection.

One day my partner, Paul, and I took Chael to a park with a slide. The slide was extremely high – Paul is 6 foot 4 inches and the slide was at least twice his height. Chael was a little nervous at the top but Paul was with him and I was waiting at the bottom. On his way down he put his foot into the side of the slide to slow himself down but instead of just slowing, he came to a sudden stop. He tipped over the side and both of us were too far away to reach him.

We watched in amazement as the top of his head gently touched the ground and his body was laid gently onto the grass as if a large hand had supported him on his way down. He was as amazed as we were but was not hurt at all. We are convinced it was the work of Archangel Michael.

— *ANON*

~ *Calling out to Michael* ~

When you call to an archangel three times they come to you.

••••••

We had spent Christmas 2004 with our son and daughter-in-law and, on our homeward journey on the motorway, the road signs moved all vehicles to the outer two lanes, with a 40mph restriction.

As we moved to the outside lane to overtake, we felt a bump at our rear. I saw a car bounce off the central reservation barrier and hit us again. This time it caught us under the rear; the force threw our car up into the air and forward. As we rolled over, I called out, "Archangel Michael, Archangel Michael, Archangel Michael, save us, save us, save us!" We landed on the road, upside down but all in one piece.

— *ANN TYLER*

CHAPTER 16

Archangel Raphael

Archangel Raphael is the angel of healing and travel. He is a brilliant emerald green colour and you can sometimes see a flash of this when he is near you. If someone needs healing he responds when you call on him. If you are going on a journey or know someone who is travelling, ask him for assistance and one of his angels will be with you.

He is in charge of the development of the third eye, which is in the centre of the brow and is the chakra of clairvoyance.

This is connected to the planet Jupiter and its ascended aspect Jumbay. And this planet is all about expansion and cosmic abundance. So call on Archangel Raphael to help you with abundance in every area of your life.

Prayers and invocations are very powerful. When you pray with pure intention the angels always take them to God. Your love, compassion and intent will make all the difference. Here are some stories showing that prayer has resulted in wonderful healings and others where Raphael has made his presence known.

~ Miracle Healing with Raphael ~

This is a truly amazing story of Archangel Raphael bringing healing, night after night.

• • • • • •

During a pregnancy I suffered a separated pelvis and years later I still suffered great pain. My consultant advised a steroid injection and I went in to hospital to have the procedure. Three months later I was in even more pain and couldn't even make a cup of tea. The consultant said the procedure had aggravated my inflamed bones and the only option was surgery to plate the pelvis back together.

I have always been interested in angels and frequently ask the angels to help. The day I got home I read about Archangel Raphael and how to invoke him for healing. Later I did an angel card reading and Raphael appeared in that too.

I went to bed and followed the technique for invoking Raphael. Immediately the energy in the room changed. I asked for healing on my pelvis and felt a strange sensation around my pelvic joint – like millions of tiny spiders spinning a web across it. This went on for some time.

The next day the pain was not as intense. I continued to do this every night. Sometimes my pelvis got hot, other times there was a sharp pain and I had to tell Raphael to slow down. For two months I invoked Raphael and asked him to heal me. After two weeks I was able to drive short distances. After six weeks I stopped using my walking stick.

Several months later I am better than I have been for a long time. I totally believe that Archangel Raphael is healing me. I feel very privileged to be on the receiving end of my Raphael miracle!

— *ANNE-MARIE*

~ Raphael Confirms ~

A flash of emerald as Archangel Raphael uses the energy of your prayer is all that is needed to activate his healing.

• • • • • •

My friend Truda was seriously ill and hundreds of people were lighting candles and praying for her. I kept a candle permanently alight for her. One evening the report from the hospital was very bad; they did not think she would make it through the night. I played Gregorian chants and sat by the candle to send Truda healing. As I relaxed and started to send, I was startled by a bright emerald flash of light passing through my body. I knew it was Archangel Raphael taking the opportunity to send his healing light through me and later my guide, Kumeka, confirmed that Raphael himself had come through me rather than one of his angels. Truda made a total recovery.

— *DIANA COOPER*

~ Beautiful Healing ~

Simply an awesome story.

• • • • • •

My daughter was in hospital and faced a difficult decision. She was stressed and needed someone to talk to, but couldn't get hold of her husband or me. Eventually she made her own decision and went ahead with surgery. Next morning she talked with her angels and asked them for healing. She surrendered totally to their care. She felt herself rising up towards the light; there was a gate and two tables in front of it.

She was told she needed to go to the other table. She was directed through a door to a room with a marble table. She lay down and waited. Her guardian angel appeared and lay across her, covering her top half with her body and wings.

Angels filed in down each side of the room and rested their hands on her body. A larger angel came in and stood at her head. He wrapped something round himself, covering his wings, and placed his hands over her heart chakra in her aura. An angel came and pointed a beam of emerald green light at her body.

The angels left and she got up and saw two small children through the gate in the mist. She had miscarried twice. The little girl waved and the little boy looked coy. She sank back down to her bed and began to feel that she was in her body again. She wrote it all down and then called me. She truly believes in angels now.

— *SUSIE COOPER*

~ Amazing Raphael ~

A story of profound healing where, once again, faith in Archangel Raphael creates a miracle.

· · · · · ·

I have had cancer twice in the last three years. The first time was when I discovered a huge mole on my right leg. On removing the mole the doctors discovered that it was a malignant tumour. After the surgery I would envision Archangel Raphael wrapping a blanket of green energy round me and healing me. I received a clean bill of health.

Three years later I noticed some tiny bumps on my leg – I had melanoma again and needed immediate surgery. I asked Archangel Raphael to guide the doctors and to give me the best nursing care. I asked him to hold my hand through this process and remind me I would be OK. Of course, he did. I called him every night to soothe and heal me and to remove any other cancer. I asked him to wrap a green blanket round my leg and to give me peace of mind and the information I needed to heal myself.

On my third day in the hospital, I saw Archangels Raphael and Michael beside me. They were there to let me know that I would be fine. I felt at peace. My recovery was amazing and the doctors were stunned by it.

I continued to work with Raphael. Four months after surgery the oncologist said there was no explanation as to how I could have healed – it was not possible. I was two months ahead of schedule. I was a medical miracle. I know that having Archangel Raphael by my side is what helped me heal so fast.

— *HEATHER VAUGHAN*

~ Profound Angel Healing and Transformation ~

This incredible story of courage, love and faith inspired me so much.

· · · · · ·

In my early teens my kidneys started to fail and by the time I was sixteen they had stopped working altogether. What followed was seventeen years of dialysis, many years of hospitalization, innumerable operations and three failed transplants.

When you have a severe, life-limiting disease and have no choice but to live on a machine and with many unpleasant symptoms, it is difficult to see beyond the suffering – and impossible to believe that angels could help.

After the failure of the third transplant I ended up in a coma and had a near-death experience where I was shown that if I chose to live I would talk inspirationally to hundreds of clinicians at conferences. Then I saw myself next to two dialysis patients and as I spoke to them my presence gave them hope. Instantly I was back in my body. Something had changed in me.

Within a few years I accepted a role in chairing a kidney disease initiative designed to transform the quality of life of dialysis patients. I had a successful fourth transplant and began to give speeches to hundreds of doctors at medical conferences as well as helping those two patients I had seen.

My NDE has empowered me and helped to transform decades of unimaginable suffering into a gift of hope. However the angels had not finished with me! Chronic severe cystitis had left me tense, in pain and unable to sleep for days and nights on end. Nothing the medical profession offered could help. While travelling to a workshop the cystitis struck yet again. Something made me ask my wife to ask Archangel Raphael for help. He appeared all in green directly in front of her and sent a white, cleansing and healing light like a flash of lightning to the area and the cystitis was gone – never to return. I am cystitis-free still and count my blessings daily.

If you have a chronic illness, if you feel there is no hope, if you feel lost, in despair and alone please call on the angels to help. Just know that the moment you call angels will come – they want to help.

Ask them to show you the gift in your suffering and realize that illness might help you discover your true purpose.

— *JONATHON HOPE*

~ Raphael's Hideaway ~

The archangels show us in many ways that they have heard our prayers.

• • • • • •

Throughout 2010 I was ill with varying symptoms including chest and abdominal pain. After many visits to the doctor with no improvement I tried different therapies to heal myself, including affirmations and calling on the angels. Raphael featured strongly in my healing requests.

One weekend in my favourite place, the Lake District, I walked to Castlerigg stone circle. I asked the angels to show me a sign and was disappointed not to find any feathers. Walking back to Keswick we passed some lovely slate cottages and one of them was called – 'Raphael's Hideaway'. Enough said!

— *ANN DUNN*

~ Raphael's Healing Light ~

Call on Archangel Raphael to help and things may well go better than expected!

• • • • • •

In 2008 my father had a quadruple bypass and I called on Archangel Raphael to guide the doctors, heal my father and give me the strength to deal with it all. The doctor said the surgery went better than expected and my father would recover fully. Each day I sent my father powerful healing intention and surrounded him with a green light. He has totally recovered and is happier and healthier than I have seen him in a while.

— *HEATHER VAUGHAN*

~ Angelic Reiki ~

Amazingly the healer and her client sense the angels' presence at the same time.

••••••

A friend was having a tough time so I offered her some reiki. I asked the angels and guides to be with me while I worked on her, then gave her reiki. Near the end I asked Archangel Raphael to give me a green Orb of healing energy to put into her. I also asked Archangel Michael to put his cloak of protection around her.

As I looked at her I could see two angels with golden wings, one on either side of her. They wrapped their wings around her, lifted her from the couch and encircled her. She could feel them lifting her. We both started to cry. She asked me what I had done and I told her it was the angels.

It was the most incredible thing I have experienced in a long time.

— *JACKIE FLEMING*

~ Green Healing Light ~

Archangel Raphael appears as a green light in a dark room.

••••••

A year ago the mother in my "adopted" Egyptian family had a serious operation. I went to visit her and gave her healing. Mamma Senna is very receptive and agrees with me that healing comes from God. When I returned to my flat I started my nightly ritual of protecting my space with St Germain and asking Archangel Michael for his protection. I thanked the other angels for their input and finally asked Archangel Raphael for some healing for Mamma Senna.

A green light appeared. I could hardly believe it – I was seeing the presence of an angel. I gave thanks and went to sleep. Mamma made a very good recovery.

— *GLENISE DANIELS*

~ Thank You, Raphael ~

Reading a book about healing can open you up to receiving it.

••••••

I was travelling back from Crete with my husband, father and two sons after a wonderful week of sun and splendour. I felt a pain in my throat and realized I was coming down with a throat infection. I suffered from this a lot, especially when I was younger.

I was reading about Archangel Raphael and his emerald green healing energy. There were examples in the book of "miracle healings" and "refusing to be unwell". I closed my eyes and invoked Archangel Raphael to surround my throat area with his emerald light. I immediately felt a sense of relief.

The journey home was tiresome. The plane was delayed. It was ideal conditions for my immune system to get depressed and not work very well, but despite this my discomfort and pain had gone and I remained in perfect health. Thank you Raphael!

— *SUSAN*

~ Reiki with Archangels Raphael and Michael ~

Archangels Raphael and Michael both announce their presence and perform healing.

••••••

A client of mine told me that she was being treated for depression. I offered her reiki and she agreed. As I raised my hands above her head I heard a voice to my right say "Michael" and a voice to my left say "Raphael." I was nervous but looked in each direction and asked for help with the healing. Immediately I felt burning hot hands on my wrists and could feel them working with me as I gave my client healing.

When I had finished she asked me what I had done. She had felt an incredible heat entering through her head and she felt much lighter than when she'd come in. We both felt amazing – although at the same time I could not stop crying.

— *LESLEY SORRIDIMI*

~ Interpreting Dreams ~

Our dreams can give us much information about ourselves.

••••••

At the last full moon we received a lovely meditation from the Diana Cooper School. We invoked Archangel Raphael and I felt as if I was bathing in his green healing light. The next day I woke up with a pain and fear in my heart, although at the same time I could feel a strong light surrounding me.

I brought my consciousness to my heart and the pain was still there. I knew that there was healing happening on an energetic level. As I observed the sensations the pain vanished.

Two days later I woke up with an image of a messy drawer, stuffed with a lot of things. I realized that the messy drawer represented my mind: full of thoughts, images and ideas. I closed my eyes and focused on the causal chakra, then asked Archangel Christiel for help. Peace filled my being. I asked Archangel Michael if there was any message for me and something beautiful happened: joy and happiness streamed into my head. My body relaxed and softened. One peaceful moment was followed by another. After a while I felt the need to bring the energy down to Mother Earth to ground myself and gently awaken.

— *CORNELIA MOHR DCS*

~ Angels Were with Her ~

Prayers can be the link that ensures a person is in exactly the right place to receive the assistance they need.

••••••

I had an unexpected call to say that my cousin had been rushed into hospital for a brain biopsy. The family was in shock and didn't seem to understand how serious this was. I asked Archangel Raphael to be with my cousin and keep her safe, and all my friends to send light and healing and to guide the surgeon.

My cousin had a brain hemorrhage on the operating table, and afterwards the surgeon said to my aunt, "Angels must have been with her because if that had happened anywhere else she would not have survived."

— *MAIRI BECKETT DCS*

~ A Golden Aura ~

When you call in Archangel Raphael for healing and your heart opens with love, your aura becomes an angelic golden colour.

• • • • • •

When I gave a healing session to a young woman, I called in Archangel Raphael at the beginning to help me. During the healing I could feel a very special connection and love for her emanating from Archangel Raphael. We were surrounded by his light. Afterwards she told me in astonishment that she had seen a golden aura round me.

— *CORNELIA MOHR DCS*

~ Raphael's Healing Angels ~

A sign.

• • • • • •

I hadn't ever felt any connection with Raphael, although one of my friends and fellow teachers often talked about his healing angels.

I was out walking, worrying about all sorts of things and feeling down. I decided to ask Raphael to send me a sign that the angels were with me and life would improve. I saw a man and woman coming towards me, walking a small dog and with a couple of children running round. As they passed me I heard the woman say, "As far as I am concerned Raphael is worth it...". That was a very clear sign to me.

— *KARIN FINEGAN DCS*

~ Courage, Love and a Kidney ~

Here is an awesome story about the way the angels respond to a woman's faith, love, and determination to help a loved one.

• • • • • •

When I met my boyfriend we both knew we had found "the one." I noticed Bradley's eyes were not bright and he drank a lot of water.

I asked if there were kidney problems in the family and he said, "Yes, my mum has polycystic kidney disease." I knew this was hereditary.

Months later we discovered that Bradley had renal failure and his only hope of survival was a kidney transplant. I offered my kidney but I was not a match. However, some pioneering technology meant that my kidney could be made compatible. I asked the angels for help and miraculously, when Bradley was tested he had no antibodies against my blood. This is almost unheard of! So the operation went ahead. I woke up in a lot of pain and watched for Bradley's arrival. My kidney had not been stitched correctly and was leaking into his body. They took it out, removed a clot and then put it back.

Then the doctors told us that my kidney had died inside Bradley. They promised to do all they could to get another kidney. I was devastated and annoyed. I didn't go through all of this just to have the kidney die!

"Well I'm not having it," I said to myself. I wanted that kidney to work so the angels had better help me!

At the check-up the surgeon was astounded to report that the kidney was alive. It was a miracle! Two years on my kidney is going strong in Bradley's body. Thanks angels!!

— *NICOLA KELLEHER*

~ Archangel Raphael's Intervention ~

In a crisis call on Archangel Raphael first for he can help everyone concerned.

......

I was working at my computer with my back towards my two daughters who were doing somersaults on the sofa. Suddenly Paulina shouted that Artemisia had twisted her neck. I took her in my arms; her eyes started to roll and she fainted. She did not seem to be breathing.

I told Paulina to call for an ambulance while I invoked Archangel Raphael for help, but after a while realized that Paulina was not getting through to the ambulance. My neighbour had some medical training, so I shouted to Paulina to open the door so I could rush upstairs to her flat. Then Artemisia opened her eyes and started breathing again. I have never been so relieved and I am sure Archangel Raphael had miraculously intervened and helped me to stay calm!

I am very grateful to Archangel Raphael.

— *FRANZISKA SIRGUSA DCS*

~ Enjoying Life with Angels ~

When you work with angels their energy works through you and touches other people, as this story demonstrates.

......

I had been facing health issues and although I knew the corrective measures I did not apply them. I cried out loud, "Please heal me." Then I received through my dear teacher Shalini Kalra information about an angel workshop and I knew I must attend. The workshop was amazing and introduced me to the power of Archangel Raphael.

Later I prayed to him, "Please, heal me." In my sleep that night I saw a green hand touching my forehead. When I woke up I felt fresh.

I feel better now and have stopped taking my medication. I feel so much lighter and happier. It is so reassuring that the angels are always there and ready to extend their helping hand.

— *SHYAMALI DEY*

~ *My First Meeting with Archangel Raphael* ~

An inner journey that leads to healing powers.

......

I discovered a book about angel maps and decided to spread out all the maps in front of me. At that moment I felt as if I was in a deep ravine and there were angels holding me. I could see an entrance in the cliff face; the angels set me down carefully and I entered.

A large green angel appeared and gave me a beautiful green sequined dress. He asked me to lie down on a stone couch and the angels blessed me with their hands. Then the green angel said: "Now you have got the coat of healing and your job is to help other people." I was overwhelmed.

The angel who gave me his coat of healing was Archangel Raphael. My life went in a new direction and I became a healer.

— *MARTINA MARIA SERAPHINA KAMMERHOFER*

~ *Healing with Archangel Raphael* ~

Archangel Raphael will always help when healing is needed – but only when the person is ready.

......

I am a hypnotherapist and decided to call on Archangel Raphael when I worked. On the first occasion, I took my angel cards to work with me. One was protruding: it was Archangel Raphael, giving me reassuring confirmation he was ready to work with me.

Feedback from my clients afterwards was positive. Later, as I reflected on the efficacy of my sessions, I was told not to be too invested in the outcomes as that created ego-based doubt; my clients needed to take some responsibility for their own healing.

I invoke Archangel Raphael with all of my healing work now and each time I do this the energy becomes more powerful.

— *ANON*

~ *Blessing the Water* ~

When you swim in a pool, blessing the water raises the frequency to the fifth dimension.

......

When I go to the gym I try to fit in a swim. My practice is to bless the water when I enter the swimming pool and trust that everyone receives the light.

One day I was doing my last length when I realized I had forgotten to do so. I immediately called in a blessing and was amazed to see the end of the pool light up with a wondrous emerald green light. I knew that Archangel Raphael was telling me that the blessing had been received and would be used to heal people in the water.

— *DIANA COOPER*

~ *Connecting with Raphael* ~

Archangel Raphael makes you feel happy.

• • • • • •

I was reading a book about spiritual guides and decided to contact mine. I asked for his/her name and immediately got a reply: Raphael. At the same moment I saw a bright green light. This light has visited me ever since and it always comes when I am in a state of love and happiness.

I was reading about how to ask Archangel Michael for help and decided to ask him to help me. The answer came quickly – "No, not Michael – Raphael!" The green light appeared and I felt so happy. I looked up Archangel Raphael on the internet and found out that he shows himself as a green light and that you feel happy when he's close. I now know for sure that angels do exist!

— *MALIN*

~ *Archangel Raphael Stops the Bleeding* ~

When we invoke Archangel Raphael and ask that healing be for the highest good, miracles can happen, as is illustrated in Ann's story.

• • • • • •

I was taken to hospital after a car accident and I was told that I would be prepared for an operation to remove my spleen, which was bleeding. I said a prayer to Archangel Raphael to stop the bleeding and, if it be for my highest good, to cancel the operation.

I am glad to say, and I sincerely believe this, the operation was cancelled because of Raphael's intervention.

— *ANN TYLER*

~ *He Always Responds* ~

Trusting in Raphael's help.

• • • • • •

I always call on Archangel Raphael for healing. For example my son Nils had a stomach ache and said, "Mommy do something about it." I called in Raphael and a few minutes later Nils told me, "Everything is fine." His stomach was better.

— *RAMA REGINA MARGARETE BRANS*

ARCHANGEL RAPHAEL LOOKS
AFTER TRAVELLERS

ARCHANGEL RAPHAEL looks after all travellers and it is really helpful to call in his help and protection when you're going on a journey. More than once I have felt the comfort of his emerald wings round me when in a stressful situation while travelling.

~ A Car Protected by Raphael ~

It's a good idea to carry a picture of Archangel Raphael in your vehicle.

⁕⁕⁕⁕⁕⁕

When my partner Michael purchased his new car I bought him a little card of Archangel Raphael for protection whilst travelling. One day a few months later he got up at 5.30 a.m. for work – only to discover that his car had been broken into. They had stolen money, CDs and tools and tried without success to hotwire the car. Mike called the police, who said many cars had been stolen that evening and it was a gang who had pre-orders to steal certain cars. The officer said he had been very lucky and something must have scared them off. Mike found a large thumbprint on the Raphael protection card and the police used it for forensics.

— *ELOISE BENNETT DCS*

~ The Power of Meditation ~

This experience was a huge reminder to me of the effect of meditation; how it can refresh, restore and make what seemed impossible not just possible but fine.

⁕⁕⁕⁕⁕⁕

I woke at 3 a.m. with my sinuses blocked and my nose pouring. I had to sit up in bed to breathe. I had to catch a plane to Ireland and was doing a television programme at 10 p.m. I knew that I would be a wreck if I didn't get some rest.

I asked Archangel Raphael for help and decided to meditate. Now meditation is not my strong suit, but it has a similar effect to sleep and I knew that it was the only way I could be prepared and fit for the TV show. I decided to focus on calm on the in-breath and relax on the out-breath. I did not let anything else intrude and I felt the angels surrounding me.

I continued this for the rest of the night. I even followed this breathing in the taxi, through customs, on the plane and for the rest of the day.

A friend of mine was talking about aura photography on the same show and she took my photograph beforehand. My aura was light blue and mauve with golden spots. "Have you been meditating?" she asked, puzzled!

By the time I went on air I felt relaxed and clear, which was just as well as there was a challenging person in the audience. The angels had filled my aura with such peace that I was able to handle him calmly.

— *DIANA COOPER*

~ Space Behind Your Car ~

A helpful reminder that Archangel Raphael can persuade other drivers to give you space as you drive.

⁕⁕⁕⁕⁕⁕

My husband and I were driving back from Hamburg on our motorbike. In the town of Donau-wurt, we realized at the last moment that we were in the wrong lane. My husband swiftly changed to the other lane. It was a dangerous situation. The driver of the car behind was so angry, he followed us. I begged Archangel Raphael to watch over us and soon the car disappeared. I wished the driver a good trip home and thanked the angels for their help.

I now do this any time a car comes too close to the back of mine. I call on Archangel Raphael to take care of it and about two seconds later, every time, the driver of the other car slows down and the space increases.

— *URSULA*

~ Raphael Saves a Stuck Soul ~

In this case the "traveller" is a stuck soul hoping for help.

......

On a flight to Dublin for a Diana Cooper School reunion, I became aware of a presence of a pilot. I knew he was not alive in this world but was a lost spirit just waiting there, needing help. I sent a prayer to Archangel Raphael to come to the aid of this poor soul. I saw angel wings covering him and I knew that he was being looked after.

— *MARGO GRUNDY*

~ Travelling with Angels ~

A legend comes true.

......

I had the opportunity to travel to the Arctic region of Norway and wanted to place a charged crystal as far north as I could. Over several angel workshops we put positive energies into this beautiful crystal. It was going to carry and transmit the light of the angels to the Earth and all on her from the snowy Arctic.

The day I set out for the northernmost point was Midwinter's Day. There was no light, only a magical twilight and a full moon; just enough to let us see the surreal landscape. Our guide kept exclaiming how lucky we were. "It is very rare to get weather like this at this time of year. Usually it is very stormy with no visibility." This would have made it difficult for me to place the crystal. The guide continued in a serious tone, "You know, we have a saying here. When we get a day like this in midwinter, we say that we are travelling with angels."

— *ELIZABETH HARLEY DCS*

~ Help with a Holiday ~

Archangel Raphael helps with finance and synchronizes time!

......

I had been thinking about visiting friends abroad, but didn't have the money. Later that day I said to my angels, "If it is meant for me to go, you must help me."

When my husband came home he said, "I will treat you to a ticket. I have enough airmiles points for a trip for you." He rang the airline. Normally there is a long wait but they answered straight away. They had one ticket left for that day! Amazing! So yes, the angels arranged it for me. Thank you!

— *KARI NYGARD DCS*

~ *Mum's Travelling Angels* ~

You can send angels to help and protect your family.

· · · · · ·

My daughter Jacqui travels a lot for her job and was in New York for a conference. She had a long meeting and then went to the airport for her return trip to London. It was when the volcanic ash was causing havoc with flights.

She boarded her flight and only when she switched on her phone in London did she realize she had been on the last plane out and the rest of them were stuck at the airport. She phoned me to tell me that "Mum's travelling angels had brought her safely home." Thank you.

— *JENNY HART DCS*

~ *Up Escalator with Raphael* ~

This is a reminder to call on Archangel Raphael to smooth your journey.

· · · · · ·

I was very stressed as my flight to Ireland was cancelled due to volcanic ash. I had to rearrange my travel and was dashing by taxi, trains, boat and car to my destination. I asked Archangel Raphael to help me but for a while I don't think I was really trusting in him and nothing changed.

As I was crossing London for my train I called him again. Suddenly I was surrounded by an emerald green light. It spread over me and up the escalator I was on. I could feel Raphael's wings enfold me as he said, "Calm down. I am with you."

I relaxed and trusted I would get my connections and, of course, I did.

— *DIANA COOPER*

~ *Listening to Higher Guidance* ~

When you ask the angels for help and listen to their guidance it makes the journey through life much easier!

· · · · · ·

In 2003 I decided to become a teacher with the Diana Cooper School. This meant driving to Wales from Germany for the course. In preparation I asked my driving angel and my English-speaking angel to help me. Archangel Raphael made sure that my journey went smoothly.

When it was time to return home I visited the stone circles in Avebury, but my intuitive guidance was to go home immediately. I reached Germany late at night and was led to a hotel. I asked for a room and was told that I was lucky – they had been full, but one person had cancelled and they could give me the room.

Again I thanked my angels for their guidance. The next morning the radio said that there were traffic jams on the motorway that I was going to have to travel on. I asked Archangel Raphael to guide me, chose a different route with his help and Archangel Raphael brought me home safe and sound.

— *ALEJA DANIELA FISCHER DCS*

~ Angels Look After Luggage ~

Here is a reminder to ask the angels to look after your luggage when you are travelling so you can relax.

••••••

During 2009 I was lucky enough to visit Machu Pichu in Peru. We travelled through so many airports, on so many buses and through so many places that our luggage had to make several connections. Our return journey had been long, with delays and cramped spaces.

After waiting a long time for our luggage it became obvious that mine had not made it. My friend said, "Call on the angels and see your case arriving back here safely – hold that picture." After giving a description to the lost luggage people I continued to "hold the picture." Three days later my belongings were delivered to me. I always send an angel with my luggage now whenever I travel.

— *JENNY HART DCS*

~ On Time with Archangel Raphael ~

It really helps to have a clear rapport and connection with an archangel.

••••••

A few years ago my husband and I were invited on holiday by his company as a reward for his performance at work. We were busy right up to the last minute and left home later than planned. I asked Archangel Raphael to get us to our destination safely and on time and on the motorway our lane was free of traffic and we proceeded quickly. We made it on time, even though we didn't speed. Archangel Raphael always travels with me and helps me pick the right route to reach my destination on time.

— *ALEJA DANIELA FISCHER DCS*

~ Angelic Support ~

Always trust that you are protected.

••••••

I was travelling to Johannesburg and arrived very late at night. I had no one to meet me and was to make my own way to the hotel. As the plane landed I suddenly felt vulnerable and afraid. The pathway to the bus station was dark. I put my hand in my pocket and pulled out a picture of Archangel Michael. That instant everything changed and I felt safe and protected. A reminder to always trust.

— *ELIZABETH ANN DCS*

HEALING ANGELS

ANY BEING in the seventh dimension can heal, so angels can all channel divine healing into us. If you ask they will do their best to help you, depending on your karma. Certain qualities such as faith and grace transcend karma, though, so when you pray for healing with total conviction it will be done.

~ Angel Medicine ~

I often hear that the instant someone asks the angels to help, the discomfort stops.

• • • • • •

My daughter was ill with a chest problem and was up all night coughing, I asked her angel to help her to sleep and give her healing. No sooner had I said it than she stopped coughing and slept peacefully. I saw flashing lights and felt a massive wave of warm energy go right through my body. It stayed with me for about ten minutes. I believe it was angels.

— ANGELA NUR

~ Hospital Help ~

It is so wonderful to be reminded how many angels there are in hospitals, just waiting for us to call on them.

• • • • • •

I was in renal failure due to kidney stones. I was in hospital and had just had my third operation. That night I started shivering violently and was in a lot of pain. I decided I had had enough and that I was going to concentrate and make the shivering and the pain go away.

I felt myself give a small shiver and became aware of a brightness coming to the bottom of my bed. It touched me below the knees and I was instantly warm. It was wonderful!

After the nurse and doctors had visited my angel surrounded me again and it was absolute bliss. I do not know what the nurse or doctors saw but I know that even if I wasn't smiling on the outside, I had a big smile on the inside.

I felt safe, total love and happiness, protected and completely at ease. It was wonderful!

— CATRIONA

~ Angelic First Aid ~

Whatever form of healing you choose to do on yourself, the angels will back it up if you ask them to!

• • • • • •

I had travelled to London to meet a good friend for lunch. I was taken to a very lovely fish restaurant and chose scallops. After lunch we said our goodbyes. I had to catch a tube then catch the train to Leatherhead where my car was parked.

I started to feel nauseated and my palms were sweaty. I wondered if I had food poisoning from the scallops. I said to myself, "What are my choices? Vomit on the pavement, be ill and pass out at the tube station, find a hotel but they probably won't let me in?"

I had learned Emotional Freedom Techniques, so I thought I would put them to the test. I also called in my angels. I said, "If you are really there I need you to help me NOW!"

I stepped onto the tube feeling awful. The train stopped and the lights went out. What was actually three minutes seemed like hours! I know the angels were supporting me though. I was using my EFT and stating, "I am in charge of my body and my stomach is settling and I am beginning to feel better." I programmed myself with positive thoughts. The lights came on, the tube continued and I began to feel better. Thank you angels.

— *ROWENA BEAUMONT*

~ Answered Prayers ~

The angels respond to prayers that come from the heart.

• • • • • •

My angel experiences started in the very early hours of one morning, in a hospital room when my desperately ill son hovered between life and death. He was three years old and had fought illness all his life. The doctors told me that there was nothing else they could do, so I went outside and started to pray.

Someone had mentioned a prayer group and I called them and asked if they could mention my son in their prayers. On the way back into the ward something moved against my foot. I leaned down to pick up the most beautiful white feather I have ever seen. I knew at that moment that the angels had heard my prayers and that my son would pull through, and he did.

— *ANON*

~ Healing with Angel Feathers ~

This story demonstrates that there are many different ways to give healing and, as long as our intention is pure, the angels are there to help us.

• • • • • •

When I started healing I felt I wasn't being effective. I asked for a big sign to be given if I was meant to do this work. I was upset, angry and doubtful. I was scared I would be poor and I was worried people would perceive me as flaky.

I stepped outside and on my doorstep was the biggest white feather I had ever seen. It was eight inches long and beautifully fluffy. It was so light I could hold it in my palm and not feel its presence. It had a beautiful flower-like perfume. I kept it safe and continued my training.

I often use the image of my special feather to go "inside" people's bodies and clear out blockages.

— *REBECKA BLENNTOFT*

~ Healing Statue ~

When any object is imbued with angel energy it holds it and can heal.

• • • • • •

My mum is getting old and has trouble walking distances. While she was on holiday in Blackpool her hip was causing her pain. Her friend gave her a gift of an angel statue and she was carrying it in a bag on her wrist. She felt a heat against her hip coming from the bag. As the day progressed she started to be able to climb stairs and the pain in her hip lifted. She truly believes the heat from the angel statue was healing her hip.

— *LESLEY SORRIDIMI*

~ *Bright Light Angels* ~

Everyone sees angels differently. Many see them as Orbs, circles or lights.

• • • • • •

For over a decade, at night in the darkness angels have been appearing to me a couple of times a week. I see them as bright light circles or clouds making their way towards my body, giving help and healing. I understand that other people may have difficulty believing this story but I know for certain that it's the truth.

— *PAUL WILKINS*

~ *Angels of Healing* ~

There are many angels who help and heal us.

• • • • • •

I am a reiki practitioner and, after reading various angel books, I started to call upon angels during my consultations. I was amazed at the team that would come forth. Some days I would see a beautiful golden emerald glow from Archangel Raphael, or the purplish-blue sparkles of Archangel Michael. My favourites were the Golden Glories, small angels just like the cherubim. They specialize in healing arthritis and joint ailments; I would see them with little feather dusters transmuting the toxins in the joints and filling them with golden light.

— *ELOISE BENNETT DCS*

~ *Angel Pictures Help Heal* ~

Fill your room with angels and listen to their whispers and you may just get what you want!

• • • • • •

Many years ago I worked as a therapist. Although I trained as a reiki healer most people wanted massage or reflexology. I knew reiki, angel and unicorn healing energy passed through my hands even if I did not ask for it. People would comment on the warmth of my hands, or how unusually relaxed they felt after having a therapy with me.

I worked in a leisure centre, which was not ideal, it had white tiles on the walls and the heating never worked correctly, so it was always either freezing or too hot. I had asked management several times to sort this out but now I decided to ask the angels. I was disappointed when nothing happened.

Two weeks later the angels gave me the idea to put pictures of them on the walls. This would enhance people's awareness of them, as well as cheering up the stark white walls. I got some beautiful pictures of Archangels: Michael, Gabriel,

Raphael, Chamuel, Uriel, Zadkiel and Jophiel. What a difference! The heating started to work. More people asked for treatments.

I saw many more angels around the room in the form of bright sparkles of pure-coloured light. Clients started talking about angels and one lovely old man confided that he believed in them, but made me promise not to say anything because he had never told anybody.

— *MARGARET MERRISON DCS*

~ *Grieving Space* ~

The grief of bereavement holds you back as well as your loved one in spirit.

• • • • • •

My hubby and I have been running workshops to help people understand the grieving process. We use angels as the bridge between the two worlds. These workshops are always blessed by the angels and many miracles have happened.

One participant was an intensive-care nurse. She was twelve years old when her mother died and her father was so angry at the death of his wife that he decided the only way to survive was to block out all memories of her. She was not allowed to grieve or talk about her mother. As an adult she was exposed to death and dying every day on duty. Every death was like a repeat of her mother's death.

During the workshop people go on a visualization to Heaven and meet their loved ones. She had the most amazing conversation with her mother, who told her that it had been her time to go and she watched over her and was proud of her. Her mother asked her to open her heart and allow love in.

She cried tears of joy and happiness. She said this was the most precious day of her life.

— *MARIEL FORDE CLARKE DCS*

~ *Solving Brotherly Squabbles* ~

There are many kinds of healing. Call in the angels when your children are quar-relling and see what happens.

• • • • • •

Last summer a good friend of mine came for a visit. When she arrived she was angry with her oldest son because he would not look after his brother. They had argued and fought all day. I suggested we call in the violet flame of transmuta-tion. Additionally we asked the angels to help her to feel peace and love and sup-port her intention to bring the highest outcome.

Her husband called and she told him about the situation at home. He was as-tonished, because he had phoned the boys and they'd told him that they were sitting together and the older one was reading to the younger one and it seemed peaceful. My friend and I felt that a miracle had happened and we thanked the angels!

— *CORNELIA MOHR DCS*

~ Bathed in White Light ~

When we cry out to the universe the angels respond.

• • • • • •

Four months after a relationship meltdown, I was crying out to the universe for my life to have meaning and depth. For one whole night I was bathed in bright white light. I was fully healed and for two years after that I had constant angelic help.

I was taught an amazing language that I am still learning today. My life has meaning and depth way beyond the material plane. I am now writing the story of my amazing voyage.

— *STEPHEN MEAKIN*

~ Healing with Golden Green Light ~

Visualizing the colour of the angels and holding the intention of healing allows the angels to make magic happen.

• • • • • •

On a sailing sabbatical, my husband fell into the water when trying to jump ashore. He hurt his thumb and it immediately became stiff and swollen. I invoked the golden angel light, asked Archangel Raphael if he could please assist healing and visualized golden green healing light. We found a cab to a hospital and by the end of a fifteen-minute ride, the swelling was down and my husband was able to move his thumb fully again. He was extremely grateful.

— *BRITTA*

~ Past Life Regression Healing ~

This is a beautiful example of a past life regression where the angels and unicorns entered to give their help.

• • • • • •

Three of us prepared together for the healing. We meditated and I could sense a host of angelic beings arriving and surrounding the room, bringing in light, love and protection.

A column of white light descended into the centre and as it reached the floor three separate scrolls of light separated and linked to each of us individually. The light became a rainbow and as it flowed, etheric white feathers formed a circle around us.

Fairy beings tapped gently on our heads with magic wands, creating silvery stars. Then the scene changed to a pool of water with dolphins leaping with joy and happiness. Unicorns entered, bringing in their beautiful energies. The message was joy, happiness, lightness, fun, laughter and love. A crystal formed in the centre of the room and created a mist around us. The angels came and tapped us with their wands creating beautiful stars. This was an amazing experience and it gave great comfort to the person receiving the healing.

— *LINDSAY BALL DCS*

~ Pain Relief ~

Many people do lightwork during the night, rescuing lost souls, healing and help-ing in many ways. When you call in the angels to heal you they will.

· · · · · ·

One morning I woke up feeling as if I must have been working the whole night. I had a headache and was tired and disheartened. In my meditation I called the angels in and could feel their presence. I was grateful for their love and support and tears ran down my cheeks.

I asked for healing and could feel them working at my head. It felt as if my head was pulled up and I had some pain in my crown chakra. My head made a small movement like a loosening. Then I felt a lightness and all the worries and the fears of the morning were gone.

— *CORNELIA MOHR DCS*

~ My Carnelian Necklace ~

The angels do not always necessarily come to you themselves

· · · · · ·

I had an unexplained rash on my chest and had had no success getting rid of it. One evening I felt so uncomfortable that I sat up in bed and decided to read. I opened up a book on gemstones.

The chapter I opened the book to was about carnelian. I learned that it can assist with any physical situation that is stubborn or not reacting favourably to other therapies.

The next morning I relayed the story about the carnelian to my friend as we were driving home from a meeting. She got excited and could not wait for me to pull in to her driveway. As the car stopped she gave me a bag. Inside was a gor-geous carnelian necklace.

She explained that she had been going through her jewellery box and thought I might like it! I put it on and by the second day my rash was totally gone.

— *CONNIE SIEWERT*

~ Angels Take Away the Pain ~

Ask the angels to help with pain relief. If your soul agrees, they will.

· · · · · ·

My friend had breast cancer followed by stomach cancer. She had to have very painful injections to drain fluid away. Another friend told her to ask the angels to remove the pain. She asked them and throughout the rest of her treatment she had no pain and passed over peacefully.

— *CHRISTINE MARSHALL*

CHAPTER 17

Helping Relationships

When you ask, the angels can change your perspective, bring new information and help you to resolve challenging situations. Sitting down quietly and asking them to assist you can transform your relationships.

~ Helping Resolve Arguments ~

Conflict creates a low vibration. When the parties or even one of them raise their consciousness, it must cease.

· · · · · ·

I have very good experiences with calling in the angels when my husband and I are arguing and cannot resolve our differences. Both of us are reiki teachers so we sit down to give reiki to the situation and I call in the angels for help. It feels different afterwards, like a rising of our energies.

The issues that were behind our discussion come clearly into our subconsciouses, or we feel lightness, peace, tolerance or love. It is a miracle and I advise it to the couples and clients I work with.

— *CORNELIA MOHR DCS*

~ Help Me See My Son Again ~

Even when a situation seems hopeless, ask the angels and trust.

· · · · · ·

I asked the angels to help me see my son Kingsley. I had not seen him for years due to conflict with his father. I was not even sure what he looked like! That afternoon I went into the town centre and heard a boy talking about his friend Lewis. This was the name of my son's best friend. I turned and it was Kingsley talking. That was the start of a change and my son now lives with me.

— *CHRISTINE MARSHALL*

~ Clarity At Last ~

If you need clarity about a situation, ask Archangel Gabriel to help you.

· · · · · ·

A long-running and complex romantic situation that was confusing me finally led me to throw my arms up and ask the angels to please, bring me clarity. I told them that I could no longer see clearly and the grief was too great. I stopped

trying to deal with matters by myself and surrendered the situation to the angels. Later I received a message from someone that revealed truths I had not known. It helped me take appropriate action and set myself free from the situation.
— *GRAIL SIDHE*

~ Angels Heal Conflict ~

Angels bring peace into a room and enable conflicts to be resolved in the highest possible way.

●●●●●●

A few years ago I was at a meeting at Findhorn with a group of people who were all interested in angels. During the meeting it became clear that there was unrest and tension in the group – we found it difficult to agree and were unable to make decisions.

When we stopped for lunch I decided to stay in the room and I asked Archangel Uriel to help us resolve our differences in a way that honoured everyone's view-point. As I was sitting quietly I saw a lovely shimmering angel. She was weaving her way round the room, creating a beautiful flowing figure of eight around the chairs. As she did this the energy in the room became light and vibrant.

When we recommenced our meeting it was very different. We seemed to be able to cooperate and listen much more easily and as a result we reached decisions that empowered everyone. I felt privileged to have witnessed this. Now I always ask my angels to join me during meetings and discussions.
— *ELIZABETH ANN DCS*

MOTHER MARY

MOTHER MARY is a great universal angel whose light and work spans many universes. She is known as the Queen of Angels because of the love and compassion she radiates. She overlit Isis in Atlantis and Egypt, Ma-ra in Lemuria and Mary, mother of Jesus. In the era of Golden Atlantis she radiated a beautiful high-frequency aquamarine light. Nowadays she is surrounded by a deeper blue light that we often see depicted in pictures of her, but her aquamarine light is being seen again too. We also observe from Orbs that she sometimes works on a deep pink ray of divine feminine energy. Further information on Orbs can be found in Ascension through Orbs and Enlightenment through Orbs.

~ Mother Mary Heals the Heart ~

This story tells of my very first experience with Mother Mary, which I found awesome. From that moment I have held her deep in my heart. I call on her in times of crisis and she always helps.

●●●●●●

Within two years of my first angel visit I started a practice as a hypnotherapist. While working with a client called Mary I became aware of her angel; it was with her. It telepathically imparted to me that I had to open her heart chakra to heal her problem.

As I helped her to visualize her heart opening a most extraordinary thing happened. A magnificent bright pink light shone from the client's heart like a rose-pink searchlight. It filled the room and I looked out of the window, thinking there must be a physical explanation. There was nothing outside though and the light continued for a few minutes. I knew it was Mother Mary who was enabling this healing to take place.

When I told the client what happened she was not surprised – it transpired that she often talked to the angels. Her problem disappeared.

— *DIANA COOPER*

~ Angels of Mother Mary Visit ~

In the era of Golden Atlantis when the consciousness of the people was very high, Mother Mary radiated a high-frequency translucent aquamarine light.

• • • • • •

Serena told me that she is very connected to Mother Mary. One night she went to the bathroom and looked out of the window. She was entranced to see several balls of beautiful aquamarine light about six to eight inches in diameter bouncing all over the outside pool. She fell asleep watching them.

She was intrigued and delighted when I told her they were angels of Mother Mary connecting with her at a high level.

— *DIANA COOPER*

~ Archangel Chamuel and Mother Mary ~

Archangel Chamuel is the angel of love and for a time I was connecting with him as a spiritual practice. Each day I breathed his bright pink light into my heart and as I breathed it out again I visualized it sending love to people, trees, elementals and situations.

• • • • • •

One evening after a month of working with Archangel Chamuel I stepped outside and clicked away with my camera into the dark night. I saw a bright pink in the light of the flash, which turned out to be a heart-shaped Orb of Mary, Chamuel and an angel of love.

My guide Kumeka said that this Orb enfolds you with the deepest loving comfort and knowing that you are OK.

The following day I walked in my local woods, imagining that I was in the centre of this amazing Orb and that the pink light radiated around me. I know I had the energy of Mother Mary, Archangel Chamuel and the angels of love with me for a squirrel stood a few inches in front of me and danced for five minutes. Then a deer lay by the path watching me with his big eyes. I sent the love to him and he was quite content to let me stand right beside me.

— *DIANA COOPER*

~ Mother Mary Heals Babies and Children ~

I will never forget the time Mother Mary visited me as I was giving healing to my daughter, and what she told me about babies and how she helps them. This story is not only about a baby or child but about the inner child in all of us; this inner child often needs healing and most certainly will if you were ill as a youngster.

· · · · · ·

When one of my daughters was a baby she had meningitis and we were told that she would be severely disabled, deaf, blind and a vegetable. She was in hospital for a month, miraculously made a full recovery and is now a mother herself.

One day I was giving her healing and as I laid my hands on her, Mother Mary appeared beside me. She poured her beautiful blue light into my daughter's aura. She told me that when babies are near their mother they are enfolded and protected in Mary's blue light. However if they are separated for any reason, they miss out on the nurturing, protective energy. So she had come to replace the blue energy that was missing from my daughter's aura because of her time in hospital as a baby. I feel that it really helped her.

Mother Mary also said that if you have to leave a baby or young child you can call on her to place her blue light in the youngster's aura.

— *DIANA COOPER*

~ Mother Mary Helps My Son ~

Mother Mary carries mother energies. She protects and enfolds mothers and children, even when the child is an adult!

· · · · · ·

Some years ago my son was in humanitarian aid and worked in all the trouble spots of the world, including three visits to Afghanistan. I never worried about him as I felt he was very protected. However, when he phoned to say he had to go to Afghanistan again a terrible feeling came over me and alarm bells rang. I phoned a couple of psychic friends and they both said he would be ambushed and captured by the Taliban with terrible consequences. I asked if he could cancel the visit as I had a bad feeling about it. He immediately said, "Mum, you've never said anything like this before. I'll see what I can do."

He phoned back to say the contract was signed and he had to go in two days' time but please would I give him as much information as possible so that he could be vigilant. I told him what I could but still felt very uneasy.

I went to a local hilltop near Wellington, Somerset. It was completely deserted so I said out loud, "Mother Mary I ask you as a mother, please help my son." Later I discovered I was standing on the exact point where the Mary and Michael ley lines cross.

The following morning my son phoned to say that the trip had been cancelled and I knew Mother Mary had interceded.

— *DIANA COOPER*

~ Church Prayers of a Child ~

Children are innocent and pure and Mother Mary's angels always respond when they call her.

••••••

I can remember one Sunday afternoon when I was five years old; I was in church with my mum for an hour of silent prayer. There were a few other people in the church, all praying silently. It was beautifully peaceful and quiet.

I prayed to Mother Mary and felt the most beautiful love filling me. It poured in and the feeling was incredible. I was completely loved and accepted. I wanted it to stay for ever but it faded before we left the church. I kept thinking about it afterwards and wanted to feel it again. The memory will stay with me forever.

— *ANITA*

~ Mother Mary, Archangel Raphael and My Mother's Passing ~

Every archangel has a masculine and feminine aspect and Mother Mary and Archangel Raphael are twin flames.

••••••

Mother Mary is an important saint in my family. From my first guided meditation I felt a wonderful connection to her and to Archangel Raphael.

I lived in Canada and my home in Germany seemed far away, but whenever I did this meditation I felt a spiritual connection to my family.

My mother was ninety-three years old. I got a call saying she was in hospital and not expected to survive. I did the Archangel Raphael meditation and asked Mother Mary for help. I asked for the grace to see my mother before she passed, and felt peaceful and calm. Her condition improved; she recovered and celebrated her ninety-fourth birthday with family and friends.

Two months later I received a call to say my mother was near the end and we returned to Germany. Again I did the Archangel Raphael meditation. To my delight my mother was alive when I arrived and we spent a wonderful afternoon together. We sensed that this afternoon was a peaceful farewell.

I asked Mother Mary, Jesus and the Archangels Michael, Raphael, Gabriel and Azrael to stay with her so she was not alone. She passed away shortly after I returned to Canada. I know that she is in the light and there is peace all over.

Thank you Mom for your love. Thank you Mother Mary, Jesus, the Archangels Michael, Raphael, Gabriel and Azrael for all the support and guidance.

— *MARGARETE KOESTER*

~ The Love of a Child ~

Mother Mary loves children and they have a very special bond with her.

••••••

My first memory is from when I was three years old. I remember walking on the beach in front of my parents' house with my dog. I was singing to Mother Mary asking Her to give me a sign of Her presence and I found a little gold medal, flower-shaped with an image of Mother Mary and angels around Her. I was amazed and tied it round my wrist with a white string.

Later I lost it, and my sister remembers trying to help me find it without success. I still know though that Mother Mary appeared to me through that medal just to let me know She was with me.

— *CINZIA TAFFURI*

~ The Fateful Journey to Medjugorje ~

If you feel drawn to visit a sacred place then there is usually a powerful message or insight for you there, as Marjetka's story illustrates.

••••••

In the early 1990s, I discovered reiki and started teaching. During that time, Medjugorje and its miracles were much talked about and I went to visit as I wanted to find out if the stories about the Virgin Mary's appearances were true.

I asked her to send a sign to convince me, so I looked at the cross and said: "Mary give me a sign." The cross's middle arm started to change shape and rotate. A flame of hope burned inside me. Then I stood in front of Mary's statue and asked for help with some of my troubles.

Once home, all my prayers were answered. This encouraged me to continue to connect with Mary and other divine beings. I started praying and asking angels, archangels and the Virgin Mary for help in my healing work. People were thrilled with the healing , which was further proof to me that I was doing things right. Since then, angels have been my steady companions.

One day I read a book by Diana Cooper and felt the presence of angels while reading it. Afterwards, I decided to enrol in her school. It goes without saying that angels have improved my life in all aspects. I hope you invite them into your life and allow them to help you.

— *MARJETKA NOVAK DCS*

~ Helping My Marriage ~

It is wonderful to know that Mother Mary helps people with their relationships and that you can always call on her to help.

••••••

I cried out to Mother Mary in real desperation after a bitter fight onboard a boat. She filled me with love and light; to this day that remains the most wonderful moment of my life. The dynamics onboard changed completely afterwards, and I am still grateful for this experience.

Since then Mother Mary has helped me a number of times simply by enfolding me with love. She is non-judgemental and gives me the confidence I need to find appropriate ways of dealing with situations. Somehow, enfolded in her love, I can look for a new and better solution, whereas before I would just feel overwhelmed.

— *BRITTA*

~ Giving Birth ~

Archangel Azriel, angel of birth and death, is present at every birth and Mother Mary will appear if she is needed.

• • • • • •

When I was in the hospital giving birth to my son, there was no progress for a long time. The doctor said to me that she wanted to force the baby to come out by pushing and pressing on my belly.

I felt Mother Mary standing next to me saying "NO" very clearly. So I declared "No" to the doctor and my husband supported my decision.

They had to perform a caesarean; however, everything went fine. A year later I fell on my tailbone, which had to be X-rayed. The doctor said I could never bear a child in a normal way because of an old tailbone fracture from my childhood.

Immediately the pain both emotional and physical was gone and I was very, very grateful to Mother Mary for her protection.

— *MARIAM*

~ Love of Mother Mary ~

Unconditional love means being able to send blessings to both victims and perpetrators and knowing that all of us are part of God.

• • • • • •

I woke up feeling sad, but didn't know why. Later that day I heard about a mass murder that had taken place that morning. I kept thinking about the children and adults who had been involved in this event and felt tired and emotional. I decided to meditate.

I called in the angels and Mother Mary and after twenty minutes I grew peaceful and calm. I felt love in my heart and with the help of the angels could send love and light to everyone involved. Thank you beloved angels and beloved Divine Mother!

— *CORNELIA MOHR DCS*

~ Mother Mary's Help ~

Mother Mary has such an energy of compassionate healing that you only have to mention her name and healing flows to the person you are thinking of.

• • • • • •

A friend of mine telephoned me; her young grandson was very ill and needed life-saving surgery. She asked me to pray for him.

I immediately asked Mother Mary to surround him and guide him through his operation. As I focused on this, in front of me appeared a beautiful blue light and a feather dropped down.

I knew my friend's grandson was going to be OK. His surgery was successful and Mother Mary is still surrounding him in her light as he recovers.

— *ELIZABETH ANN DCS*

~ Mother Mary's Statue Materializes ~

It can happen in a flash. A statue becomes human or angelic and you alone can see it.

* * * * * *

Ever since I was a child I have had a huge devotion to the angels and Mother Mary and always recited my guardian angel prayer. At the age of fifteen I had a profound spiritual experience at a grotto in an old monastery.

While I was praying, the stone statue of Our Lady materialized in human form before my eyes. She moved her beautiful head and smiled. Though this grotto is no longer there I can still remember the feeling of being inside it. The water trickled down the damp stone walls, forming a pool in the rocks beneath her feet. The candles glowed, creating a pulsating energy that I cannot explain.

I began to trust my intuition. My devotion to Mother Mary has brought me through many challenges and helped me to remain centred. Now, forty years on, I feel able to recount my experiences.

— *MARIEL FORDE CLARKE DCS*

~ Mother Mary and Archangel Raphael ~

Mother Mary is everywhere and you could see her or hear her voice at any moment.

* * * * * *

I went to Hawaii for a spiritual retreat. While preparing for a ceremony I saw a beautiful aquamarine and emerald green light. I knew I was connecting with the energy of Mother Mary. I felt her love and heard her say that she was with me. I took a photo and captured the energy of Mother Mary and Archangel Raphael. Afterwards we held the ceremony at that spot and the energy was wonderful. Thank you Mother Mary.

— *MARTINA MARIA SERAPHINA KAMMERHOFER*

~ Wishing ~

Calling in the energy of Mother Mary can create miracles.

* * * * * *

I ran an angel night class. One evening we were working with Mother Mary and each person had to ask her and her angels for a wish. One young woman asked Mother Mary to help her conceive a child; she had been trying for years with no luck. There was such a sense of love around her as she asked and some students saw a beautiful blue light. Six weeks later she was expecting! Miracles do happen.

— *ANON*

CHAPTER 18

Archangels and Masters

Archangel Butyalil ~

There are many archangels over-lighting this planet as we move into the fifth dimension. Understanding and working with them will help our ascension immeasurably.

. . . . . .

I had a spiritual reading in which I was told that my guide was Archangel Butyalil, who is in charge of the flow of the universe. For days I talked to him but felt it was a one-way conversation. At last in desperation I asked for clarity about who I should talk to, and then I picked an Orb card. It was Butyalil. That was all the confirmation I needed.

— *SHARON RALPH*

~ Angelic Beings from Other Dimensions ~

This wonderful story offers expanded perspectives on the angels.

. . . . . .

On 11.11.11 I was at Avebury. I walked down the causeway with friends and family. We were accompanied by crows, which in the olden days would have been an omen of death, but for me it was a message of transformation.

When the cosmic moment arrived I saw a light come up from Hollow Earth full of higher beings at a spot nearby. I sensed they were familiar with Archangel Metatron's energy and were from another dimension. They merged their energy with me and from that moment on I have been in touch with UFOs and Commander Ashtar.

A stairwell also descended from Heaven and angels were descending up and down it. This portal is located near the central feature stone. I was honoured, humbled and grateful to witness this.

— *JEEVAN*

~ Angels Light the Way ~

While Archangel Michael protects, Archangel Zadkiel is in charge of the violet angels who transmute all lower frequencies.

. . . . . .

I was travelling to Mozambique with two women I had never met before. I was driving and was exhausted – I hadn't slept for four nights and we started our journey at 3 a.m. I asked that one of the other women stay awake to talk to me and stop me falling asleep, but they both fell asleep and I felt very alone. Before starting the journey I had asked the angels to protect us and as I was driving I prayed to them again, and in particular to Archangel Michael, to keep us all safe and to stop me from falling asleep. I know that the angels were with us that night as whilst I was driving on the highway, the white line on the edge of the hard shoulder glowed violet all the time. Incredible!

— *LESLEY MORGAN*

~ *Archangel Uriel Burning Our "Stuff"* ~

Archangel Uriel works with the solar plexus and he helps us dissolve and transmute our lower energies.

• • • • • •

On the day we were at Diana's home filming the webinar to prepare us for the cosmic moment, we went out onto the patio to burn all our negativity and I sensed a huge angel, who I felt was Uriel. He helped us all to release our "stuff."

— *CATHY BOLTWOOD*

~ *Archangels Michael and Metatron* ~

When you have a regular spiritual practice it helps you to open up to the energy of the archangels. Archangel Metatron's vibration is a vibrant orange that many people can see or sense around them.

• • • • • •

I was aware of some negative energy around me, so I asked Michael for protection. Every night before I went to sleep I asked him to surround me, my family and my house with his blue energy.

After a few weeks of doing this I began to see a blue energy fill my bedroom. One night I saw a bright blue Orb in the corner above the door. To this day I continue this practice and find the visual energy very strong.

Now there is an orange colour mixed with the blue. I know this is Metatron working with me.

— *MARY THOMSON*

~ *The Story of a Shark's Tooth* ~

Archangel Gabriel is a pure white angel who brings clarity, joy and much light into your life. In this case he brought abundance too.

• • • • • •

I decided to go for a walk on our local beach in South Africa. I've found dozens of fossilized sharks' teeth over the last ten years. Mostly, they are chipped or broken and their colour ranges from grey through gunmetal blue to black.

The tide was high and I walked on the wet sand. I was contemplating my future, wondering how I was going to be able to follow my passion and fulfil my life purpose while supporting my family.

I decided to connect with Archangel Gabriel for guidance. As I did so my eyes were drawn to the right and there lay a perfect shark's tooth. It was such a pale colour that it was barely visible against the white sand. Since Archangel Gabriel's energy is white, I knew it was a message from him. I was filled with gratitude and excitement. I picked it up and said "Thank you."

The tooth was a confirmation that I was on the right track and that Gabriel was clarifying my direction. Within a few days I received unexpected abundance and I realized that I asked for help and it had come!

— *CLAIRE BUCKNAL*

~ Solar Archangel's Touch ~

An archangel of the sun is a beautiful and powerful golden being.

• • • • • •

I was at a Lightworkers gathering near Glastonbury. Our teacher Patricia Cota-Robles said, "You are now going to be touched on your shoulders by a solar archangel." I felt my shoulders touched by huge but light hands; joy and bliss washed through me and every cell in my body lit up. I became light. I cried with joy. It was the most beautiful experience and I remember this in my heart and give gratitude for it every day of my life.

— *ROWENA BEAUMONT*

~ Angelic Reiki ~

The archangels love to give us proof of their presence just as the angels do.

• • • • • •

I teach angelic reiki. The angels are always there and I feel their magnificent presence, as do a lot of the people who attend the courses. One day after a course I took photos of the group. We were standing in front of the wall where I've hung my picture of Lord Melchizadek.

When I looked at the first photo I noticed that a ball of light was coming in from the edge. In the second photo the ball of light was right in the centre of Melchizadek in the picture. Wow! One participant that day had said she'd felt Lord Melchizadek's powerful wisdom and the photos were proof. What amazing confirmation of his presence.

— *ROWENA BEAUMONT*

~ Archangel Gabriel Walks through My Hall ~

Archangels appear as they want to; they will not necessarily conform to your expectations but they are always on a mission to help you.

• • • • • •

I was walking down the stairs at home when I saw a man walking through the hall, looking deep in thought. I nearly jumped out of my skin. Suddenly he vanished. My dog Venus was completely unperturbed. I have noticed that she barks at spirits but not at angels. I could not understand who he was for he did not show himself as radiant light like an angel but he did have an angelic quality.

Then my guide Kumeka told me that it was Archangel Gabriel coming to examine my home to see how he could help me on my path! Wow! The love and caring of the archangels never ceases to surprise me.

— *DIANA COOPER*

~ Angel Help ~

When you ask Archangel Sandalphon to place the fifth-dimensional bubble round yourself or someone else, it raises the frequency. If someone is not ready for this vibration it raises their energy too quickly, so do not place it round houses or people without the person's permission.

• • • • • •

My sons had been acting up so I asked the angels to put a bubble of fifth-dimensional light round the house. My youngest, William became depressed, refused to go to school and would not even be with his friends; and that's a bad sign. He wasn't hungry and had insomnia.

I was despairing and asked the angels to take us back to the third dimension, and instead put Archangel Michael's blue around the house. Instant result! William at last got up, had lots to eat for breakfast and went off to his part-time job. So I guess we still have work to do in our house in preparation for the fifth dimension!

— *KARIA*

~ Archangel Metatron Works on My Chakras ~

Here is another reminder that when you ask, the angels and archangels will come forward to help you and work on you.

• • • • • •

In February 2012 I found out the names of some of my angels and met a wonderful person who channels angels. I started talking to my angels as I wanted to find my own true path. I asked my angels to clear my chakras and help me hear their messages.

One night while lying in bed I heard bells. I turned off the television but could still hear them. It was a very soothing sound and I felt calm. The next day I found out from my angel channel that it had been Archangel Metatron and some white angels working on my chakras. I was overwhelmed with joy and love. I know that if you ask, the angels will help. It is so wonderful to know they are there.

— *STACY KNOX*

~ The Metatron Cloak ~

Archangel Metatron is in charge of the ascension of our planet and the entire universe. If you have been a high priest or priestess in any civilization in any lifetime you can wear the Metatron Cloak in your auric field. If you have not been a high priest or priestess before and your soul deems you are ready, you can access it.

It enables you to attune to the wisdom within the Pleiades, Orion, Neptune and Sirius and to connect right into the Great Pyramid of Hollow Earth.

••••••

I passed the golden-orange Metatron Cloak to a number of people at a Saturday workshop. On Sunday one of the attendees returned absolutely glowing with delight. She said that it really worked. She had been with some people and literally seen their darkness come towards her. As it reached her Metatron Cloak, it simply stopped and could not get any nearer. Their negativity could not impact on her or take her energy.

— *DIANA COOPER*

~ St Therese ~

The great masters also oversee us and help us. Like the angels, they can give us messages and signs, as this story illustrates.

••••••

When I began teaching reiki I suspected I was helped by guides and masters but wanted proof! I was told one of my guides was St Therese. I knew she was associated with roses; during her life she had said, "After my death I will let fall a shower of roses. I will spend my Heaven doing good on Earth."

On the morning of my next workshop I asked her, if she was guiding me, to give me a sign. I was attentive all day, but nothing occurred. I was a little disappointed, but let it go – perhaps it was about learning to trust or increase my sensitivity. That evening I went for a meal with my friend. I decided to finish with ice cream. It was beautiful – sculpted in the shape of a rose! I said to the waitress, "Please thank the chef – the ice cream was carved beautifully." She said, "It wasn't carved, madam, I served it with a scoop." I got my message.

— *ELIZABETH HARLEY DCS*

~ Calming the Weather with the Elementals ~

Human thoughts influence the elementals. We can work with them and the higher beings in charge of them to change the weather positively.

••••••

When the news announced a hurricane in our area I immediately put up protection around our property and the whole village. I also took the practical step of putting away everything that was moveable. I contacted the nature elementals to calm the winds and asked Archangel Zadkiel to cleanse the area with the gold-silver-violet flame so that the wind did not have to do it. We never saw the storm; it was just a bit more windy than usual and everything was fine.

Tiles fell off our neighbour's roof and in the next village trees had fallen over. So the storm obviously passed very close by us. I thanked the elementals and the higher beings for their help. If we stay calm, take responsibility and visualize how it should be then we can influence the weather.

— *ALEJA DANIELA FISCHER DCS*

~ Archangel Metatron ~

This story illustrates that by focusing on our feelings and asking the angels to help, together they and we can dissolve pain and emotions of all kinds.

••••••

One morning I woke up with fear and the impression of "inner shadows". I meditated and I invoked Archangel Metatron; I felt his presence strongly. Although the fear kept growing bigger, I kept focusing and visualized golden light flowing into my brain. I asked Archangel Metatron for guidance and he told me that the fear was my fear of power.

As I kept sitting silently, watching my fear, it diminished. I became aware that the issue around this pain was connected to my divine mission. I asked Metatron for support in developing and fulfilling my divine mission – and the pain went!

— *ANON*

~ Divine Love ~

Archangel Chamuel is the wondrous pink archangel of the heart who directs the angels of love.

••••••

I was on holiday with my husband and after a lovely evening, we went to bed late. I fell asleep but woke up when I heard voices. However, these were no normal voices; I knew they were angels. I had an amazing feeling of love. The divine love flowed through my body and I felt as if I was floating above the bed.

I felt Archangel Chamuel come close and say, "I give you the strength of divine love for your new life work." I had already undergone the angel teacher-training with the Diana Cooper School and from that time on I knew without a doubt that I was connected to angels.

— *MARTINA MARIA SERAPHINA KAMMERHOFER DCS*

~ Archangel Love ~

Archangel Zadkiel is violet and helps to transmute lower energies to open us up to higher light.

••••••

One morning I was woken by the most wonderful energy. I felt profound and overwhelming love and thought: "This must be an archangel." I asked who it was; and in my mind's eye I saw the text Z A D K I E L and I felt the name on my lips.

I had never heard this name before. I looked it up on the internet and discovered that there was an Archangel Zadkiel.

When Zadkiel came to visit me I was going through a tough soul-searching period, but after his visit I felt so joyful and blessed. Thank you Zadkiel!

— *WENCHE MILAS*

~ Daughter's Car ~

The archangels love to give us proof that they really have done what we have asked.

••••••

My daughter Nicola is psychic and is frequently in communication with her angels. Her passion is cars and her favourite car at this time was a purple Hyundai coupé sports car. She was going to Australia for five weeks and her only concern was this car. She asked the angels what she could do to keep it safe.

The night before she left we went outside and stood by her Hyundai. We invoked the violet flame of Archangel Zadkiel and St. Germain to totally seal and protect it. We asked that it was invisible to everyone.

Nicola went off on her trip happy! After she returned she took a photograph of her car. When she showed me the photo there was a beautiful ribbon of purple/violet light surrounding the car. She was astounded and said it was the angels' way of letting her know that they were supporting and protecting her and her possessions even when she was thousands of miles away.

— *MARIEL FORDE CLARK DCS*

~ Healing Hearts with the Violet Flame ~

The violet flame is a very powerful healing tool that transmutes the old or stuck energy into a higher (positive) vibration.

••••••

Two years ago my sister had a heart attack. She had never been ill, not even with a cold. After having an operation she had a stent placed in an artery. As she recovered I sat one morning and worked on her with the violet flame.

Two days later she rang me and said that she had had a funny experience that afternoon. She heard a voice and she'd closed her eyes and said, "WHAT?" Then she saw two angels carrying a heart. She asked what was happening. They said, "We are taking your heart to make it better." My sister knew nothing of my angels and spiritual work. She was astounded and now comes to all my workshops.

— *MARGOT GRUNDY DCS*

CHAPTER 19

Unicorns

Unicorns are seventh- to ninth-dimensional ascended horses, fully of the angelic realms. They are known as the purest of the pure and their light is shimmering white. They look for the light over your head and if it shines with the message that you are ready to help others, they will work with you. They help bring about the dearest wishes of your soul.

Read more about them in my book *The Wonder of Unicorns.*

~ *A Unicorn with a Message* ~

When a unicorn appears to you it is a life-changing moment.

• • • • • •

Many years ago I built a "medicine wheel" on a fairy mound deep in the woods. One day I was sitting meditating with my eyes open, when a "window" opened up in front of me. There stood something I had always thought was a myth: a unicorn! I didn't know what to do, say or think. A great feeling of love emanated from the being and it telepathically said "Be True To Yourself!" Then the window vanished. I was stunned – in awe, because I had never believed in such creatures nor had I read about anything like that happening.

— *DAN CHANEY*

~ *Connecting with Gabriel and Unicorns* ~

The unicorns and angels have wonderful ways of giving people messages!

• • • • • •

When I heard about an angel workshop at the Mind Body Spirit Festival I knew I had to go. I had been searching for a moonstone ring without success, but I found the perfect one at the festival. I know that the moon and silver are connected with Archangel Gabriel, who is very close to me – an encouraging start to the day!

During the workshop we had to picture ourselves in a field and I saw a beautiful white unicorn coming to me. I rejected the vision, though, thinking it was just my ego. I wanted to buy *The Wonder of Unicorns*. However, the books had all been sold. I felt disappointed and took it as a sign that I wasn't worthy enough to get to know the unicorns.

As I went back to my seat I noticed one unsold copy of the book left on the stage. Diana had written a message in it: "Gabriel and Your Unicorn Are With

You, Diana." Joy, gratitude and surprise filled my heart as I bought it and read it: I felt enfolded in pure love and loving voices encouraged me to trust myself and my visions.

Whenever I have fear or doubt, I look at this wonderful gift and glorious light shines in my heart. It reminds me I am loved. Thank you angels, thank you unicorns and all you beautiful beings of light.

— *MARTA ISABELLA*

~ Birthday Present ~

Unicorns, by their very presence, give hope.

• • • • • •

I have always loved unicorns. One dreadful time my partner's heart stopped and he went into a coma. I was with him at the hospital when my sister visited. She knew nothing of angels or unicorns or of my love for them.

It was my birthday, so she went to get a cake and present for me. She came back with the most beautiful unicorn figure ; when I saw it I knew that my partner would be all right. And he was.

— *NANCY, AS TOLD TO DIANA COOPER*

~ A Unicorn Card and a Dream ~

Unicorn cards are very high-frequency and give assistance with unerring accuracy.

• • • • • •

I started visiting Diana's website and choosing daily unicorn cards. One morning I awoke from a strange dream with a bad headache. I had dreamed that it was dark and I was walking to a clear stream in a wood; but the stream turned into a fast-flowing river, rushing over rocks, that had burst its banks.

I went to the website and clicked for a unicorn card. HELP was the one that came up. This card shows a man sitting on the bank of a river; he cannot cross because the bridge is broken – and he is holding his head! A unicorn is standing nearby. I took this as very relevant considering my dream and headache. It gave me such reassurance and validation.

— *KAREN SPRING-STOCKER*

~ Goals and Unicorns ~

If you want someone to do better, ask the angels and unicorns to help them.

• • • • • •

The captain of our national soccer team in Switzerland had some difficulty in scoring goals. He is the best player we have ever had but for over a year he could not score. For weeks the press and fans had given him a hard time. I decided to send him a unicorn and lots of angels for the next important game. Needless to say, he scored two goals that night!

— *SABINA*

~ A Unicorn Rainbow ~

This is a lovely story of love and the comfort brought by unicorn signs.

· · · · · ·

While visiting my elderly mother, I trapped my little finger in the car door. Instead of feeling pain, though, I experienced a deep emotional reaction. Suddenly I knew finally it was now time for my mum to come and live with us. She was very independent but she was nearly ninety years old now.

As my husband and I are both retired, we agreed it made sense for her to live with us. However, we live in the north-west of England, she lived in the South and it would be a big wrench for her to move so far from her family and friends. I thought I had accepted the implications of my mum living with us so my emotional reaction came as a painful shock.

The next day I still felt emotionally delicate. My husband and I went to an exhibition at Tate Modern. While he was taking some photographs outside the building I spotted a cloud formation like a unicorn statue. I took some photographs of it. Then I spotted a little rainbow in the clouds and, looking for the source of the light, I saw the unicorn directing his horn to create the rainbow. He was pointing to it with a front hoof.

I had a strong connection with unicorns and knew it was my unicorn sending me a rainbow to let me know things would be all right. I was comforted and I have my special unicorn rainbow photographs to remind me if I need further reassurance.

My mum now lives with us and has settled into her new lifestyle. My little fingernail is now growing back quite nicely too!

— *KATHY DCS*

~ Our Own Little Unicorn ~

As horses evolve they become white in colour. This one truly is preparing to become a unicorn.

· · · · · ·

I love working with angel cards and books. However unicorns were a bit suspect for me and I didn't feel very drawn to them until the day I was in a bookshop to buy another angel book and saw some unicorn cards. I couldn't look away! I HAD to have them and the book they came with.

My husband, daughter and her friend went to a horse sale. They arrived home with Milly, a young black Shetland pony. I wrote a book about Milly the unicorn princess and put beautiful pictures of her in it. Why did I invent this story? I didn't know at the time.

Spring came and all the horses changed their coats, but not Milly. Overnight, all the fur moulted and more white hairs could be seen underneath . When Milly is fully grown she will be snow-white, even though her parents are brown and black – impossible but it's true! Now we have our own little unicorn!

— *ESTHER WILLEMS-KRÄMER*

~ Surprise Unicorn ~

If the time is right a unicorn will impress itself into your mind.

. . . . . .

Over the past year I've received messages that I need to pay attention to my spiritual path and psychic abilities. On two occasions I have been told to start working with angels.

I have made the decision to get off the corporate ladder to retrain as a counsellor. I've also decided to pay attention to the messages I've been getting, develop my psychic abilities and learn to channel angelic energies.

I was doing a guided meditation where we had to visualize an animal. The first thing that came to mind was a unicorn! I was amazed. I have much to learn but I know how special they are. If anyone had said "Think of an animal" normally, unicorns would not have been at the forefront of my mind!

— *HILARY ALEXANDER*

~ All Shook Up! ~

The unicorns have a sense of humour.

. . . . . .

Liz Roe French is a medium and healer who works with an e-LIBRA machine. When you plug into it, it tells you what is going on in your physical and subtle bodies and aligns them. She came to a lecture I gave where I helped everyone connect with their unicorns.

Next day she plugged into the machine and it came up with this description of her condition – anterior horn disease! When she told me this we laughed! Clearly her unicorn with its horn – which is of course at the front or anterior of its head – had shaken her energy fields around.

— *MARGARET MERRISON DCS*

~ Unicorn Meditation ~

This story is a reminder to trust the images that come to you.

. . . . . .

I saw a unicorn in my meditation. It was so bright and beautiful – very vivid, yet still I could hardly believe it and thought I had imagined it. Later I was having a reiki treatment. To my astonishment and delight the healer said I had a unicorn with me. Then I believed it!

— *ANON*

~ Unicorns and Black Panthers ~

Black panthers are fifth-dimensional creatures, symbolizing great strength.

. . . . . .

My good friend Cathy was treating me to some reiki. When she started I felt as if my legs were being held down and something was lying on me. In my mind's eye I could see a black panther and I felt great protection from him.

Then I felt that my arms were being tied down by black leashes. The pain was incredible. I asked my angels to take the leashes away, which they did, but they kept being replaced. Each time my angels dissolved them with white light. I asked my higher self why this was happening and a friend who was trying to control me came to mind. Just when the pain became too much a beautiful unicorn came galloping towards me and the pain disappeared. He filled me with total love and rested his head against mine. He used his horn to sever the leashes again. Then off he galloped. After the treatment I chose some angel cards and the unicorn card came up!

— *ROSIE*

~ Rainbow Unicorn ~

Unicorns bring creative inspiration.

······

I was meditating and was shown a bay horse. The horse turned towards the moon and transformed into a unicorn whose horn was made of crystal. It was drawing energy from the moon, creating many rainbows.

I was invited to climb on its back and we floated into the colours. I received healing from the colours. I felt inspired by what I had seen.

— *JULIE GILBERT*

~ Violet Flame Brings My Unicorn ~

The unicorns sometimes come to us in sleep and dreams.

······

Diana Cooper and I had decided to have a few days' holiday in the Scottish Highlands. It rained and rained but the energy was beautiful. We were staying in a hotel in Roybridge. I fell asleep quickly but woke at 3 a.m. I was wide awake and decided to use the time to send the violet flame to people, places and the planet. My third eye started to buzz and I saw a beautiful pure white unicorn, smiling and dancing around me, full of love and energy. It moved towards my face and put its spiral horn into my third eye. It was a beautiful experience; it relaxed me and sent me to sleep. In the morning I felt energized and alive. I knew the unicorn had come in to help me with a major project that I had to fulfil. How blessed we are to have the help of these powerful but gentle creatures to guide us in our missions.

— *ROSEMARY STEPHENSON DCS*

~ Following Unicorn Signs ~

Positive vibes attract the unicorns and they give you signs.

······

I love the support I receive from angels and unicorns. Diana's books and unicorn cards are a valuable source of guidance.

I recently had a huge life change with the loss of my career. The unicorns had sent me a sign about how to rebuild my life; the cards indicated that fresh opportunities lay ahead. They had also warned me when to leave a damaging situation in my workplace. I followed their signs and it led me to undertake retraining and move away from a very unsettling situation. The right opportunity and course presented itself when I was unsure of which way to turn.

Now if I am worried about the future I call in the angels and unicorns. I would urge everyone to work with them as they provide inspiration and help when you least expect it. Be open to signs and trust your instincts. Sending out love and positive vibes helps to attract them.

— *JOANNA*

~ *My Unicorn Guide* ~

Debbie's clients have said their healing sessions have become stronger as the unicorn energy comes through her.

· · · · · ·

Walking in the forest, I recognized a lady walking a puppy and realized it was Diana. Our dogs played together as we chatted about healing, travel and spiritual things. Diana told me I had a unicorn guiding me. I didn't know much about them but went and read her unicorn book. It told me to look for signs – white horses and feathers. I am always surrounded by feathers so I thought the white horse would be something new!

My brother had planned for us a mammoth cycle trip fifty-five miles up a mountain. I was going to need all the help I could get. I called the unicorns to be with me and help me up the steep hills. When the day of the trip came, everyone was amazed at how well I was doing, especially me!

We headed down a winding road with mountains on either side. As we rounded a corner I saw on a steep ledge a magnificent white horse looking down on us. I shouted to my husband, "Look! The sign!" "Oh yes!" he cried and I nearly fell off my bike in amazement as he could see it too!

Life is full of signs and I believe angelic forces are guiding us all the time. When you trust and ask, they will be there. I am aware of my unicorn guide and excited about the future as I continue to learn and develop spiritually to help and empower others.

— *DEBBIE PETTITT*

~ *Electromagnetic Energy* ~

It is important to understand the impact of electromagnetic energy and Margaret's example can help raise our consciousness so that we can all create a healthier planet.

· · · · · ·

I have been working with electromagnetic energies and auras and I feel that people need to know the effect of electromagnetic energies, particularly those generated by mobile phones, on their auras and that of the Earth. For mobiles to work they need a base station, which constantly pumps electromagnetic energy into the Earth's aura. The Earth is struggling to raise its vibrations through all this electromagnetic smog.

People's auras, too, are depleted by the use of mobile phones but can be restored – actually to more than their original strength – by calling on the angels for protection. Auras become even stronger if you call in unicorns for protection while using your mobile. Ask the angels and unicorns for help to protect the Earth's aura and ours!

— *MARGARET MERRISON DCS*

~ *Unicorns Comfort* ~

The unicorns really wanted Debbie to know they were there for her!

• • • • • •

I was feeling very heartsore about a personal matter while visiting Florence with my husband Neil and our son. I saw some paintings of horses and said to Neil, "Look, the horses again." Five minutes later I walked past a hotel and guess what it was called – the Unicorn Hotel! I took a picture. Then we visited a palace. My son ran over to me and said, "Look Mum!" And there before us was a monument of a white Pegasus.

— *DEBBIE*

CHAPTER 20

Elements and Elementals

You can communicate with and influence the elementals who work with the elements. The great being in charge of water is Poseidon and under him is the elemental master, Neptune. He directs the water elementals, the undines, who move the flow of rivers, oceans and rain; and the mermaids, who look after flora and fauna.

The unicorns are in charge of air. The elemental master is Dom and the elementals are sylphs and fairies.

Archangel Gabriel is in charge of fire. The elemental master is Thor and the elementals are fire dragons and salamanders.

Lady Gaia is in charge of Earth. The elemental master is Taia and the elementals are pixies and goblins. Some of the elementals contain more than one element but none has all of them.

~ Sparkles in the Grass ~

Elementals are important to the future of the planet. It's reassuring to know that children intuitively understand the importance of their work.

• • • • • •

Growing up I was always fascinated by stories about fairies. I truly believed in them and used to sense their presence in the flowers. I now live in a home with a very powerful elemental vibration. I have always been able to feel it but it was delightful to have it confirmed by my grandchildren.

One sunny day my grandchildren came over, and we decided to play in the garden and look at all the flowers. One of my granddaughters said, "Granny, why have you got so many fairies in your garden?" Before I could reply she added, "Well, we need to help the fairies with their work so why don't we sing to the flowers?"

So that's what we did – we sang to the flowers and told them we loved them. Needless to say, my garden "blooms" with such brilliance that everyone comments on it.

— ELIZABETH ANN DCS

~ Stopping the Rain ~

The unicorns are in charge of the element of air. Although Jenny did not consciously ask the unicorns to stop the rain they responded to her request.

• • • • • •

I was at a week-long silent retreat, where we were camping. For the entire week it stormed. The rain lashed and the wind howled. On the last morning the rain stopped but it was damp and misty and everything was wet. The forecast was gloomy; there was no hope of change.

I decided to talk to the elements. I said, "Fair's fair. I don't want to pack a soggy tent. Please – I need sun and wind to dry it out. I'm going to have breakfast and help clear up so I'll be back in two hours to take down the tent."

The sun suddenly and unexpectedly came out. The wind started to blow gently. The tent dried and I was able to pack it away easily.

— *JENNY*

~ Sensing Fairies ~

What a wonderful example of connecting with nature spirits. Not everyone sees them but they will always find a way of letting you know they are there – you just need to ask and then pay attention, as Margaret did.

• • • • • •

I was in my garden one summer's evening. There was no wind and it was quiet and magical. I knew there were a number of nature spirits around; I could sense them and feel their energies – but I was unable to see them. I longed to have a glimpse of one. I asked if they could help me to see them to confirm their presence.

There was not a breath of wind that evening, but I noticed a leaf move as I looked at a clump of montbretia plants. Then the next leaf moved and the one beside it and so on. Soon the leaves of different plants were moving. Although I did not see any nature spirits, I knew it was the fairies making their presence known. It was great to sense their playful presence as they had fun waving the leaves for me.

— *MARGARET MERRISON DCS*

~ Guardian of the Land ~

Dragons are wonderful, protective and powerful fourth-dimensional elementals. Protecting the land as in this story is one of the many things that they do.

• • • • • •

There was an incident in a local hotel where a shot was fired during a break-in. The owner had small children and was very frightened, so called me in to help. I went into the hotel and cleansed every room. I also went to the garden and asked to speak to the guardian of the land. A huge dragon appeared and I asked what I could do to help protect the land. He told me to plant crystals in the four corners of the plot. I did so and the hotel has never had any more trouble.

— *SERENA*

~ *Playing with the Elementals* ~

When you love nature and the elements and honour them, then you can play with the elementals and they will respond.

· · · · · ·

I sat under a tree and appreciated it. Then a little breeze came and the leaves all tinkled and danced. I watched for a while, then asked the wind to stop; the air became still and the leaves were quiet. Then I asked for the wind to play with them again and the air immediately started to move again, making the leaves tinkle once more.

— *JENNY*

~ *Fairies Help* ~

Fairies, many of whom are highly evolved, can bring us healing as well as joy, lightness and laughter. They work with the unicorns and help with the growth of flowers.

· · · · · ·

I was going through a terrible time with illness. One restless night, I had a magical experience: I saw beautiful multicoloured fairies coming down from above. They sat one on each of my chakras and healed them. It was beautiful. I was asleep, yet awake. As a child I had always believed in the supernatural world, so for me it felt like a normal experience. I realize the world is a sacred and beautiful place and how lucky I am to receive such magical healing.

— *ANON*

~ *Communication with Nature Spirits* ~

Here is a story full of grace and wisdom as a human communicates with a tree and nature spirits.

· · · · · ·

Walking in the woods my attention was drawn to a sycamore tree. It felt sad, so I connected and asked if it would like healing. Its trunk was bent and distorted. I placed my hands on and tuned in. I became aware that the tree felt ugly. I spoke to the tree, saying it was truly beautiful. I looked with love and admiration at its beautiful bark, its branches and its leaves. I told it how wonderful it was that it had found a way to survive, despite difficult circumstances. It reminded me of myself and others who have grown through pain and difficulty.

I concluded the healing and said goodbye. I became aware of nature spirits heading towards me. Their energy was not good and they carried strange net-like devices. I asked what they were doing and they said they were harvesting energy from the trees. I sensed that they took what they wanted from the trees without asking.

I suggested that energy obtained through force would be of a lower quality, and if it were freely given the energy it would be more potent and they would need less. They considered this. One said, "The trees are not going to freely offer their energy." I didn't know how to answer this. A voice behind me said, "I will give you some of my energy." It was the tree I had just given healing to.

I returned to the woodland recently and noticed a beautiful tree and in astonishment I recognized it as the "ugly" tree – except now it was anything but ugly. It had totally transformed.

— *ELIZABETH HARLEY DCS*

~ *Connecting with Tree Energy* ~

Trees are gracious sentient beings, who hold the history and knowledge of their local area.

⁂ ⁂ ⁂ ⁂ ⁂ ⁂

I used to connect with nature and all the plants in my little courtyard. I planted a pine tree next to the house and it soon became very tall. I used to talk to it and hug it and it gave me messages that always helped me.

One day I went to the pine tree (I called it Piny) and asked it to help me with grounding. The message I got was "Wait and you'll get your answer." That evening I found on the internet an exercise that helped me and enabled me to ground. What amazed me was that it was Piny who had told me about it.

— *ANON*

~ *The Green Elf* ~

Connecting with the elementals can bring great laughter, healing, and joy into our lives, as Beverley's story demonstrates.

⁂ ⁂ ⁂ ⁂ ⁂ ⁂

I attended an amazing workshop with Diana Cooper. The highlight was when, following a meditation, we were rewarded with a room full of elementals. Diana said that each of us had an elemental sitting with us. An elf dressed in green jumped onto my knee, looking very happy and swinging his legs. As he looked at me my heart was filled with joy and my eyes filled with tears of gratitude. The unconditional love that poured into my heart was overwhelming! What a fabulous moment. How blessed we are working with angels and these other beautiful beings.

— *BEVERLEY*

~ *Transformation of the Ash Cloud* ~

As this story demonstrates, we can all make a difference and help everyone.

⁂ ⁂ ⁂ ⁂ ⁂ ⁂

My husband and I were due to go on a business trip and our business partners from all over Germany were to fly to Italy to take part. A week before the trip, the volcano in Iceland erupted and the ash cloud disrupted our flight plans. I thought if we were meant to go then we would be able to fly and if not then it would be fine. We could travel because the airports in southern Germany had opened again. However, our business partners from the north could still not travel.

I worked with the higher beings and the air elementals to clear the air. I asked Archangel Zadkiel to clear the air over Germany. I saw the cloud of ash being taken away and transformed in divine golden light. When it was done I thanked the angels and higher beings. After we landed in Italy I found out that the airports in Northern Germany had opened up again after I did the work with the angels and higher beings. I am so thankful to work with the higher beings for the highest good of all.

— *ALEJA DANIELA FISCHER DCS*

~ Fire Dragons ~

Fire dragons are beautiful fourth-dimensional elementals. They can reach into and burn up dark energies that angels cannot get down to.

• • • • • •

A group of us were releasing our negativity and we called in the fire dragons to burn up the lower energies. Afterwards one of the participants Katie Curtis gave me a drawing in which she depicted what she had seen when I called in the fire dragons. She had seen a huge dragon wind its body round the entire group and breathe flames towards us.

— *DIANA COOPER*

~ Hearing the Heartbeat of Mother Earth ~

This is a lovely story about connecting to Mother Earth or Lady Gaia (as she is often referred to), the mighty angelic being who is in charge of this planet. The more we connect with her heartbeat the more we become in tune with the earth. We can then open up to the great wisdom held within the inner planes.

• • • • • •

Early one August evening I sat alone on the beach at Hengistbury Head. I was relaxing listening to the waves, and fell into a dreamlike state. I had a sense of enormous space and was in a totally safe, enveloping darkness. I became aware of the deep volume and echo of Mother Earth's heart. It was a full connection and I was the heartbeat. It was enough to explode my soul and I can still imagine it – it was magnificent.

— *DEANNE SHEPPARD*

~ Working in Harmony with Nature ~

When you work in harmony with nature, you are connected to the elementals who help with the weather conditions.

• • • • • •

Because we have a farm we rely very much on the weather. Whenever I need to do jobs such as sowing seeds or fertilizing and I need a lot of water, I ask for it to rain. I then wait until I get the answer as to when I should do the work.

One Sunday I got the message to do the fertilizing and was ready to start. It looked as if it was going to rain but I said, "Please wait until I am finished and then it can rain." As I worked raindrops fell and I said, "Please wait – I am not finished yet." The rain stopped and it stayed dry until I was done.

As soon as I was home I said, "Now you can let it rain. Thank you." Immediately the rain started – and continued for two days. We got the exact amount of water we needed!

— *ALEJA DANIELA FISCHER DCS*

CHAPTER 21

Angel Orbs

For many years the angels have been promising us physical proof of their presence. As technology has developed they have been able to work with scientists; for example, they have impressed on them to create digital cameras that can record the sixth-dimensional frequency. Angels are actually seventh-dimensional so they have to slow down their vibration in order for even a digital camera to photograph them. When you capture an Orb on film you are seeing the sixth-dimensional "version" of an angel.

~ Archangel Orb ~

Angels and archangels gather in an Orb to help people and prepare them for illness and death.

• • • • • •

When my friend's mother, Mary, passed her photograph was placed on her coffin. This photo had been taken a couple of months before her passing. At the funeral my friend showed me the photo and I noticed that on her mother's cardigan was an Orb that contained many of the colours of the archangels. My friend said, "Yes, I wondered what that was." Mary was truly blessed by the angels. I believe they sent her that Orb containing all the love and light of the mighty archangels to be with her to prepare her for her death.

— *MARTHA MCMANUS DCS*

~ Orb ~

Angels send their Orbs as visible proof that they are giving healing.

• • • • • •

A new client arrived for a reflexology treatment. He told me he had cancer and was currently attending hospital for treatment.

I told him I was unable to offer reflexology until he had written permission from his specialist, and that his options were to cancel or have a reiki session instead. He decided to have reiki.

As we started I invoked the angels, especially the healing energy of Archangel Raphael. An Orb appeared when I worked on the area of his body where the cancer was. The Orb stayed visible for five minutes and was white and approximately 100 millimetres or 4 inches in diameter. This was amazing to see. I had no doubt the Orb was there to let me see that my client was being given all the help the angels – Raphael in particular – could give.

— *PAULINE GOW DCS*

~ *My Mother* ~

Here an Orb offers proof that a loved one is safe and well on the other side.

••••••

My mother passed away a year ago. I was wondering what to do with her ashes and if she was OK on the other side. I spoke to my mom and said, "Please give me a sign that you are OK and with Source. I am going to take a picture to show others." I took a photo of the altar where her ashes rested. When I looked at it there was the brightest Orb light shining over it and I knew she was being looked after.

— *CAROL DE VASCONCELOS DCS*

~ *Princess Pony* ~

When you see an Orb on an animal you know the angels are blessing it.

••••••

I had been thinking of buying a pony for myself but had not been able to find the right one. One pony advertised in the paper caught my eye but she was miles away at the other end of Ireland. Nevertheless I rang the owner and asked her to email photos of the pony.

On every photo there was an angel Orb on the pony. That was it – I bought her without even seeing her! Her name is Princess and she is the best pony I could ever wish for.

— *SUE WALKER DCS*

~ *Silver-Violet Flame* ~

When you combine the violet flame of transmutation with the silver flame of grace it is very powerful. When you invoke it with an "I AM" affirmation it is even more effective. I AM refers to your monad or original divine spark.

••••••

I was the mentor for Eileen who was studying on Diana's angel correspondence course, working with the silver-violet flame and Archangel Zadkiel. One day she walked round her garden saying the following affirmation for ten minutes: "I AM the silver-violet flame, I AM the flame of mercy, I AM the flame of joy, I AM the flame of transmutation, I AM St Germain, I AM Archangel Zadkiel."

Saying the affirmation made her feel joyful and at peace. Then Eileen noticed many Orbs, so she took a picture of them. The Orbs did not show up on the photos, but the second one she took showed a wonderful violet beam of light with a silver aura coming down from the universe and into her garden. What a great confirmation that Archangel Zadkiel and the silver-violet flame were working with her!

— *MARGARET MERRISON DCS*

~ My Child ~

As the frequency of the planet moves fully into the fifth dimension it creates an environment that allows more evolved psychic and sensitive children to incarnate. The following story is an illustration of these gifts.

• • • • • •

One day my son Mikael asked me if it was dark during the night as for him it never was – not even when he closed his eyes. I asked him what he saw and he said it was always purple or light blue and he saw spheres of different colours all around him even during the day. I didn't know what they were until I heard about Orbs; then I realized how gifted and sensitive he was.

— HÉLÈNE GONELLA

~ Orbs on the Farm ~

Smiley faces in Orbs are spirits that are being carried by the angels. Blue rings round an Orb indicate that Archangel Michael is protecting it. Large numbers of Orbs in your home suggest that it may be an angelic portal. This creates a beautiful resonance, which is what Roz describes in her story.

• • • • • •

After having fertility problems for years, in 2009 I had the most unexpected but joyful surprise when I discovered I was pregnant. I wanted to live near my family and in the countryside, so I was excited when I found a beautiful little farm.

I went to see it with my parents. My mom took lots of photos and when we developed them we saw Orbs all over the farm. When I enlarged the Orbs some even had smiley faces in them and some had blue rings round them.

I knew the farm was a magical, spiritual place and the right place for my son to grow up. The big day arrived on 19 May 2009; I went into hospital to have my son and again many photos were taken. One of my favourites is my mom in a surgical gown with an Orb right above her head.

Orbs are with us at the farm. I feel the presence of fairies in our garden. I truly believe my precious son Douglas is a gift from the angels. He is a happy healthy little lad, who has brought me and my family such joy and happiness every day since he was born.

— ROZ JORDAN

~ Orbs on a flight ~

This story is an amazing example of how one angel can hold a whole plane to keep it safe.

• • • • • •

On a flight from Málaga to Bristol we were told to keep our seatbelts fastened for the whole journey as bad turbulence was expected. I asked Archangel Gabriel to help and visualized millions of angels supporting the plane. It was no surprise to me that the turbulence settled, but what did surprise me was that when I looked out of the window I saw a perfect small circle, within which was a reflection of the whole plane. The colours were strong and yet the circle was transparent except the edge, which was white. I realized that it was an Orb. It stayed with us for the whole journey. I felt supported and incredibly connected with the angelic realms.

— *CHRISTINA*

~ Metatron Healing ~

Here is a simple but so profound story of healing through Orbs.

. . . . . .

I believe everything has a vibration, pulse and intensity that creates a unique rhythm. It's a song of the heart from every star, from every stone, from every aspect of creation. I was reading Diana's book *Ascension Through Orbs* when I came to the Orb of Archangel Metatron.

Metatron inspired me to communicate directly with him. I told Metatron about my pre-diabetes and asked if he could cure it. I felt his power and knew he had responded to my call. I thanked Metatron for his help and tested my blood sugar level. It was normal, lower than it has been since I was diagnosed. My blood sugar levels have remained normal since then and I can eat and drink whatever I want.

Thank you Archangel Metatron and thank you Diana and Kathy for the picture of Metatron's Orb. I communicate with him daily. He is a huge support to me.

— *KATHY FITZGERALD*

~ Orange and Green Light Beams ~

Here is a beautiful story describing how an Orb of Archangel Raphael, then one of Archangel Metatron, visit and actively radiate light.

. . . . . .

One beautiful Sunday morning, my father-in-law died. We went to see him and it was a serene moment. The next night I woke up and saw a bright green ball of light, the size of a football, hanging in the air beside me. It was glowing with platinum-like beams.

My first reaction was fear but I had the feeling there wasn't really anything to be afraid of. After a while I fell asleep, then woke again to see another ball in the air. It was orange and glowing with the same platinum-like beams. The next morning I woke up happy and full of energy.

— *TARJA SUHONEN*

~ A Ball of Golden Light ~

This story reminds us that the angels help with grief and to keep the one who has passed over in touch with those who are left.

. . . . . .

A close friend died suddenly, leaving a husband and baby son. Her baby and my baby were born only three weeks apart and I grieved for her as my dear friend and for her family. I also felt the loss of what could have been: enjoying our two boys together, going to the park, attending each other's birthdays, days out and all the other things we would never do.

Some months later my husband and I invited her husband and the baby over to stay. I looked after the babies while the men went out. I felt that my friend was around and had expected and hoped that since her baby was staying with me she would make her presence felt. But all was quiet.

I awoke during the night. Hovering in front of my chest was a ball of golden light. I recognized my friend's energy in it but it also felt angelic. I believe an angel carried her to see me. It felt so loving, like a big hug! I was so reassured.

— *SUSAN DCS*

~ An Amazing Display of Orbs ~

Magenta Orbs are angels of Archangel Mariel. Blue Orbs are Archangel Michael's angels, turquoise ones Mother Mary's. Green ones with red trim are those of Archangels Raphael and Metatron.

• • • • • •

I went for a walk with my friend through some vineyards. I had just finished Diana Cooper's book Ascension Through Orbs and thought, "That's all very well but seeing is believing!" As we turned up a pathway my friend said, "Do you see that?"

What I saw was phenomenal. It looked like the three strands of DNA in a magenta colour, swirling, hexagonal and in 3D. My friend has seen Orbs before but she said she'd never seen anything like this. There were also huge turquoise and deep-blue Orbs and clusters of green ones with red trim. Some moved slowly in front of us and above our heads. As one group of Orbs disappeared more would appear.

Ahead in an ancient olive tree was a big red Orb surrounded by four smaller ones, all red and flaming. I laughed and gave thanks for such a fabulous experience. I'm glad to say I now see Orbs very regularly – and of course I believe in them!

— *ANN*

~ Orbs of Healing and Protection ~

A story of angelic intervention to keep someone healthy.

• • • • • •

Over the last few months Orbs have been appearing in my photos and I have been feeling protected by them.

Ten years ago I had cardiac surgery, but I recovered fully. Recently I started suffering from heaviness in my chest and thought it was breathing related, but the doctor took an ECG and I was sent to the emergency room. Because of my Orb pictures, I knew I had strong angel protection. I prayed for help.

I was put on a drip and another EKG showed that I needed a cardiac procedure. I was fully prepared to hear that my arteries had narrowed, but was overjoyed and astounded when the doctor said, "The veins and bypass grafts are open and as pristine as when they were put in."

The doctor had no idea what caused the heaviness, but gave me a clean bill of health. I believe the angels intervened and protected me.

— *JEAN FERRATIER*

~ A Pleasant Surprise ~

Disappointment turns to joy when you realize that "blotches" spoiling photographs are in fact angels!

. . . . . .

A few years ago at our family Christmas, I took a lot of pictures with my inexpensive digital camera. I wanted to preserve the moment as our father was still around then and all the family was there.

When I got home I was disappointed to see lots of "blotches" on the pictures. I attributed it to poor lighting and a cheap camera. It was only when I read about Orbs that I realized the angels had shown their presence and I hadn't even known. What a reward! I can now look at those pictures and feel joy.

— *ELAINE*

~ Orb Inspiring ~

And here is a simple reminder that when you connect with angels through CDs, books, pictures or conversation, you are calling on them to show themselves.

. . . . . .

I had been listening to Orb meditation CDs, and that night I took the photo of the most amazing Orb; it fills me with joy and I find it so precious to look at!

— *JUDY HIGGINSON*

~ Confirmation from Orbs ~

Angels can help by confirming that you have made the right decision.

. . . . . .

I bought some curtains, but they were not right and I decided to take them back to the shop. I decided that it was easier to take a picture of them to show the shop staff than to try to explain what was wrong. I photographed the curtains and there was an Orb in the middle of the picture. It felt as if the angels were confirming that I needed to take them back!

— *KEVIN KELLOND*

~ Twenty-four Hours in the Arms of Angels ~

In this remarkable story a lady's kindness to a dying man is acknowledged by the angels.

. . . . . .

One morning I set off to work as usual. On the way I witnessed a motorbike accident and helped the rider to breathe until the ambulance arrived. He was unable to speak or move, but when I asked if he could see me he made a movement with his eyes to acknowledge that he could. He smiled the most beautiful, warm smile – a smile I will take to my grave – and he passed. I felt his soul leaving and it was beautiful. I felt honoured to be a part of his transit.

I own a café bar, so I had to carry on with my day. When I went to the bathroom, in the centre of the mirror was an Orb, white in colour with a slightly darker edge. I heard the name Derek, and over the course of the day I heard this name three times. When the police came to take a statement about the motorbike rider they me told me his name had been Derek.

That evening a medium gave me the message that I was surrounded by lights and was being given the thumbs-up sign. A man who passed recently with a chest condition was giving me his thanks and saying I had done a good job.

— *DAWN BRIDGWOOD*

~ Orbs in My Life ~

When people see Orbs they start to believe.

• • • • • •

I was having a hard time in my life. I found a little metaphysical chapel and started to go there to meditate. I would call on the angels to help me and ask them to give me signs that they had heard my prayers. Every time I asked I would find beautiful white feathers on my car, at work or on my porch. My dog brought me one on Mother's Day!

After a year of collecting feathers I asked the angels for another sign. At the time I was having to take pictures of my house for my insurance company and to my astonishment, Orbs showed on the pictures I took in my bedroom – where I meditate. I said thank you to the angels for that sign.

I have now taken hundreds of photographs in my bedroom and the Orbs come out whenever I ask them to. Many people have come to my house to get their picture taken with the angel Orbs. Sometimes I can take a photo and nothing happens until I ask the angels to appear in the next photo; then they always do. It is amazing to me. People go home as believers.

— *MARY STONE*

~ Angelic Reassurance for House Move ~

This remarkable story demonstrates how the angels help us in different ways and that if you act on it, it can help others move on.

• • • • • •

I am a realtor and I went to take photographs at a client's home. The couple had been in the house since the 70s and were sad to leave. I started to take my pictures and a huge Orb appeared. I kept taking pictures and the angel Orbs appeared every time.

I meditated and asked the angels who they were and they said the angels had brought the lady's mother and the gentleman's mother. The couple received an offer on the house but they were unwilling and didn't go through with it. The angels told me to tell them about the Orbs. I showed them the pictures and they both cried. I told the lady that her mother in spirit wanted to tell her that she was doing the right thing by selling the house, and that the gentleman's mother said she loved them and was proud that they were moving on. They were so happy: they signed the contract and moved on with their lives. I have sold over 600 homes and never seen anything like that happen before. Thank you angels.

— *MARY STONE*

~ Seeing Orbs with My Own Eyes ~

Orbs come in many shapes and sizes. It is always a great delight when you can see them with your physical eyes, not just in a photograph. Below is El's experience of this.

•••••••

Last week I saw an Orb for the first time. The glass door in the sitting room was open to the outside balcony and the Orb was outside; it was a dark night, with no lights around, so the Orb was very visible. It was a large bright-white, round, solid disc with a white band or ring of light about two or three inches wide surrounding it.

— *EL DCS*

~ My Healing Friend's Cone ~

Angel Orbs give pain relief.

•••••••

I had acute pains in the left side of my body, my left hand and left foot, which went on for two months. The pain was so acute that I felt very down and negative. One afternoon I was playing with my children, Gayatri and Erasmo, on the beach. Erasmo took some photos and in mine there was a beautiful colourful cone of light just below my hand.

A few weeks later my pains had gone, and thinking back I knew that they had disappeared when the Orb appeared. I am certain that it gave me the healing I needed.

— *CINZIA TAFFURI*

~ Come on Eileen ~

I love this story; it shows how Eileen Caddy is still doing her work in the spirit world.

•••••••

I arrived early at the DCS annual reunion at Findhorn. The sanctuary was empty so I went in and chanted some sacred chants. A huge white Orb with pink and gold lights in it entered and hovered in front of me. It poured energy into me. I found myself singing 'Come on Eileen'! I realized that Eileen Caddy, the founder of Findhorn, was in the Orb and she had come to see me. I felt overwhelmed.

Eileen impressed on me to take my singing bowls into the sanctuary and record them.

I knew I had to do something about the message. I asked if I could record in the sanctuary and was told that they could not spare the space for me to have it to myself, but I could record in there.

Another teacher accompanied me to operate the recorder, but as soon as I started she fell deeply asleep – well, more accurately her spirit left her body. In the wonder of playing in the sanctuary I lost all sense of time. I want to thank Eileen for guiding me and enabling me to produce my *Celestial Chanting* CD.

— *ROSEMARY STEPHENSON DCS*

~ *Archangel Michael's Orbs* ~

Here is a wonderful story of Archangel Michael's Orbs.

· · · · · ·

After attending Diana's class on preparing for 2012, I drove home elated and ready to return for the ascended master class.

That night I awoke, feeling a burst of energy enter my face then a big bursting sensation out of my solar plexus. I saw hundreds of interwoven Orbs like a curtain waving next to my bed. I rolled onto my back and saw that my entire ceiling was illuminated with blue energy. It was like a blue fire waving and moving around.

— *GLORIA PROPHET*

PART II

Angel Exercises and Visualizations

Grounding and Protection

Before asking for protection it's important to ground and protect ourselves each day – ideally every morning and evening. Here are some examples of how to do this.

EXERCISE 1: *Grounding and protection with Archangel Sandalphon*

To ground yourself make sure your feet are flat on the floor. This is even more effective if done with your bare feet in the grass.
1. Visualize roots going down from your feet into the Earth.
2. Ask Archangel Sandalphon to anchor your roots right down into the centre of the Earth.

EXERCISE 2: *Grounding and protection with Lady Gaia*

You may prefer to ask Lady Gaia, who is the great angel in charge of our planet, to ground you.
1. Visualize roots going down from your feet into the Earth.
2. See them going right down and wrapping round a great crystal in the centre of the planet.
3. Ask Lady Gaia to send her nourishment and love up through your roots into your body and into your life.
4. Relax for a moment and sense this energy coming up to you.

PROTECTION

Once you've grounded yourself, choose one of the following protection methods – or if you already have one of your own that you like, of course use that one.

EXERCISE 3: *Basic protection with Archangel Michael*

Every night before I go to sleep I do this exercise. I also do it in the morning; and I visualize this protection round my animals and loved ones too.

–   Ask Archangel Michael to place his deep blue cloak of protection over you and visualize the deep blue around yourself.

EXERCISE 4: *Invoking the Gold Ray of Christ*

Invoke the Gold Ray of Christ for your total protection. Say, "I invoke the love, wisdom, healing and protection of the Gold Ray of Christ" three times, then visualize a stream of gold light coming through you into the Earth.

EXERCISE 5: *Invoking Archangel Gabriel*

1. Invoke Archangel Gabriel.
2. Ask him to place a pure white bubble of reflective light over you so that all lower energies bounce back to where they came from.
3. Visualize yourself standing in this bubble.

EXERCISE 6: *To protect your home*

1. Invoke Archangel Michael to put a deep blue bubble of protection over your home.
2. Visualize this in place.

EXERCISE 7: *Protect your journey*

When you're in a car, whether as the driver or as a passenger, it is helpful to ask for angelic protection for yourself and others on the roads. Prayers when you give thanks as if you have already received what you request are very powerful, as they presuppose your faith that it has already been done.

–   "Thank you Archangel Michael for protecting my journey."

You may like to add any of the following:
–   "Please help me arrive safely at my destination by ten o'clock."
–   "Please find a large parking space for me by the entrance to the store."
–   "Please ensure I take the safest route."

Your Guardian Angel

Here are some lovely techniques to help you meet and deepen your connection with your guardian angel.

EXERCISE 8: *Connecting with your Guardian Angel*

1. Sit down in a quiet place. Take a few deep breaths and breathe out all tension.
2. Gradually relax your body from head to toe.
3. Ground yourself by feeling and visualizing thick strong roots, growing from the soles of your feet directly down to the very centre of the Earth.
4. Call upon Archangel Michael to protect you by placing his protective dark blue cloak round you.
5. Visualize a ray of white-golden light, coming from the universe, descending through your crown chakra, filling and purifying you completely and flowing down to the Earth.
6. Invoke your guardian angel by asking him/her to step closer to you.
7. Take time to feel, sense or see your guardian angel's presence.
8. Imagine your guardian angel smiling at you and radiating love that surrounds you and makes you feel safe. Know that your guardian angel loves you unconditionally.
9. At this point you can ask your guardian angel any question you need to in relation to your life , or simply ask whether they have a message for you.
10. When you have received your message or answer, thank your guardian angel.
11. Re-ground yourself by visualizing thick and strong roots growing from your soles directly to the very centre of the Earth. Absorb the Earth's energy a few times through your soles.
12. Tap the ground with your feet, wiggle your toes and fingers and when you are ready slowly open your eyes.

VISUALIZATION 9: *Find your Guardian Angel's name*

1. Find a place where you can be quiet and undisturbed.
2. Light a candle if possible to raise the energy.
3. Close your eyes and sit comfortably.
4. As before, imagine roots growing from your feet down into the Earth to ground you.
5. Ask for a deep blue cloak of protection to be placed over you.
6. Focus on your breathing and relax more with each out-breath.
7. When you are really relaxed and comfortable, sense or picture your guardian angel placing a golden light round you. Take time to feel this.
8. Ask your angel what his/her name is and quietly wait for a name to come to mind.
9. If you receive a name, accept it and politely thank your angel. If you do not receive your guardian angel's name, don't worry; it may come to you as you fall asleep that night.
10. You may also need to repeat this step a few times before you receive your guardian angel's name.
11. Open your eyes and return to the room.

3

Communicating with Angels

EXERCISE 10: *Tuning into the angelic wavelength*

The angels will find some way to warn you if you are in danger. However, it is much easier for them if you are already tuned in to their wavelength. Here is an exercise that will help you to tune in to. It is very simple to do and it only takes a few minutes – but it must be done every day.

1. Light a candle to raise the vibration and for something to focus on.
2. Look into the flame.
3. Say aloud or in your mind, "Angels, I wish to connect with you."
4. Wait a few moments, watching the flame. Notice how you feel and any thoughts that come to you.
5. Then make a very powerful affirmation. Say or think, "Angels I am connecting with you. Angels I am connecting with you. Angels I am connecting with you."
6. Close your eyes and again notice how you feel.

The following is a lovely angel song/chant by Rosemary Stephenson:

Calling angels, calling angels
Angels light, angels bright
Stay with me for ever, stay with me for ever
Day and night, day and night

EXERCISE 11: *Creating your sacred space*

The more you put into an exercise the more you get out of it. So you can do the following in a simple, quick way, or you can put energy into it by creating a sacred altar or by placing flowers, beautiful objects and high-frequency books in the space.

1. Light a candle and dedicate it to the angels singing over you.
2. Relax.
3. Sing an angelic song, chant or om or play a CD of beautiful music.
4. You may hear the angels singing as you do this.
5. When the music has stopped, listen in silence with your inner ears. They are singing over you whether you can hear it or not!
6. Thank the angels and expect good things to happen.

EXERCISE 12: *Automatic writing*

Before you start, state your intention of connecting with the angels and recording their messages while in meditation. If you wish to ask a question, write it on your paper or think it now.

1. Have paper and pen ready in a place where you can relax.
2. Light a candle to raise the frequency.
3. Imagine your roots going down into the Earth to ground you.
4. Ask Archangel Michael to place his deep blue cloak of protection round you.
5. Focus on the coolness of the air in your nostrils as you breathe in.
6. Follow your out-breath as it relaxes your body.
7. Continue to do this as you relax more and more and your focus turns inwards.
8. When you feel ready pick up your pen and start to write anything that comes to you. Do not censor it or think about it. Let the words flow freely from your pen.
9. When you feel you have finished thank the angels and come out of meditation.
10. Enjoy reading what you have written.

EXERCISE 13: *Using angel cards*

Working with Angel and Unicorn cards can give us loving guidance support and inspiration. The information below will help you create a sacred space in which to work with your cards.

1. Prepare a sacred space with a candle, flowers, incense, crystals – anything you like to raise the frequency.
2. Hold your cards respectfully in your hands as you think of your question.
3. Ask the angels to give you a clear answer.
4. Spread out the cards.
5. Choose one card with your left hand.
6. Read the card or look at the picture, then close your eyes and absorb the message.
7. Thank the angels.

Asking for Help

EXERCISE 14: *Ask Archangel Gabriel for clarity*

Archangel Gabriel is the angel to call on when you want clarity about a situation, relationship or your next step. You may need to do this exercise for a few days – or maybe even for several weeks – but it is very simple and he will give you an answer. Do not expect an answer to necessarily come to you while you meditate (although it may). Rather, treat your quiet time as a time when Archangel Gabriel can plant seeds in your consciousness to grow and flower when the time is right.

1. Find a space where you can be quiet and undisturbed.
2. Light a candle to raise the energy.
3. Close your eyes and relax.
4. Ask Archangel Gabriel to give you clarity about your next step.
5. Focus on keeping your mind quiet and calm.
6. When you have finished thank Archangel Gabriel and open your eyes.
7. Repeat this every day until you receive clarity.

VISUALIZATION 15: *Asking for a feather for guidance*

We are offered feathers by the angels in the physical world as a sign of their presence. But we can also receive messages and signs in our inner world. In this visualization you may receive a coloured feather. White is for purity. Blue is for healing. Deep blue is for communication and strength. Orange is for ascension. Gold is for wisdom. Pink is for love. Green is for balance.

Decide what your aim is for the exercise. Do you want the angels to touch you? Do you want guidance about an area of your life? Are you looking for clarity? Do you need to be given strength, courage or another quality?

1. Find a place where you can be undisturbed.
2. Light a candle to raise the energy.

3. Sit or lie comfortably.
4. Imagine roots going down into the Earth.
5. Ask Archangel Michael to place his deep blue cloak of protection round you.
6. Think of a situation, relationship or another area of your life in which you would like guidance or reassurance.
7. Hold out your hand, or just imagine doing so.
8. Ask the angels to help you by giving you a feather. Use your intuition to sense how big it is What colour is it?
9. When you have received a feather, stay open to receiving any other message.
10. Thank the angels and open your eyes.

EXERCISE 16: *Attracting what you want*

One powerful way of attracting angelic support and help for a situation is to write down or draw what you want. Always add the proviso, "Only bring this to me if it is for the highest good of everyone."

1. Light a candle and ask the angels to use the energy to help you.
2. Write or draw a picture of what you really want. Put energy into this.
3. Ask the angels to help you bring it about only if it is for the highest good.
4. You might like to put the paper under your pillow or burn it.

EXERCISE 17: *Release the old and bring in new*

If you are in the wrong relationship or job, or not on your spiritual path, you may be aware of a sense of dissatisfaction. If you are reading this and it makes you recognize that you need to wake up to a new life, here is an exercise you can do to help. Sometimes the adjustment you need is just a slight one.

- Write down on some paper all the things in your life that you feel bored or dissatisfied with.
- Burn the piece of paper and tell the angels that you are ready to wake up to the new.
- Write down on another piece of paper what you want in your life and put it under your pillow.
- Expect a guiding dream or, in your waking life, when you take decisions know that the angels are with you.

EXERCISE 18: *Guidance for the first step*

People often stay stuck in a situation or relationship; this is quite understandable, because every step you take towards change is painful or frightening or difficult in some way. If it was not hard you would already have taken action! So here is one way the angels can help you to make changes. And remember – every journey is taken one step at a time.

1. Write down your problem, e.g. I want to leave this relationship but do not have enough money and the children would be upset.
2. Write down or draw your ultimate vision, e.g. I am living in a lovely home where I are very happy and because I am happy, my children are happy and settled too.
3. Write a list of solutions or possible steps you could take towards this outcome, each on a different piece of paper. Then fold them all or screw them up.
4. Light a candle and dedicate it to the guidance of the angels for your next step.
5. Sit quietly, breathing comfortably while you hold the pieces of paper in your hands.
6. Ask the angels to help you choose the best next step for you. Then take one of the papers and read it.
7. Thank the angels.
8. Act on it.

EXERCISE 19: *Write a letter to someone*

If you have something you would like to say to someone why not write it down now? Ask the angels to take it and they will ensure that the other person receives the energy. It is never too late, not even if the other person is dead.

Do you wish you had told someone you love them or that you were sorry for something you said or did? Do you want to confess something and ask for forgiveness? Would you like to say thank you to your parents or friends who have passed or are too sick or senile to hear it?

- Simply write Dear ...   and tell them what is in your heart.
- Then sign it with your name.
- Ask the angels to ensure that the other person receives the energy of the message.

Remember to look out for signs from the angels that your message has been heard.

EXERCISE 20: *Ask your angel to talk to someone else's angel*

If you feel that the person you want to give a message to will not listen to you, you can ask your guardian angel to talk to their guardian angel, who can "slip" the message to them.

For example, your boss will not listen to you, but you can write via your guardian angel to tell him or her you deserve a rise in salary, or time off on a particular day or that you want to change your hours.

If your stepchildren or ex-partner or relative is blocking you out, write gently that you love them and want to change the situation.

1. Write Dear Angel …
2. Explain lovingly how you feel and what you would like.
3. Add that you would like your angel to pass this message to the other person's guardian angel.
4. Sign it with your name.
5. You may keep the letter or burn it.
6. Watch out for signs or use your intuition if you feel you need to do something.

Be an Angel

EXERCISE 21: *Asking angels to help others*

The more you ask angels to help those in need the more help you receive too. However, you must do this with your heart open with compassion. Always add the proviso, "That the outcome be for the highest good of everyone."

"Be an angel": act as if you had angelic qualities and help others today. Look out for people in need – maybe someone in a wheelchair or a blind person, or a beggar, or a parent struggling with children and shopping. Open your heart and ask the angels to help them.

VISUALIZATION 22: *Use your angel wings*

When your heart centre is open the energies radiate from you and can sometimes be seen or felt by other people as wings. You can ask the angels to help you develop your wings so that you can use them to comfort others. It is lovely to do this out in nature and even better if you have your bare feet in the grass or on the Earth.

1. Stand with your feet firmly planted.
2. Imagine your roots going down into the Earth.
3. Focus on your heart and on each out-breath imagine love flowing from you and creating magnificent wings around you.
4. Notice the shape, colour and size of your wings.
5. Reach out with your wings to enfold those who need comfort. You can allow the wings to extend as far as you wish.
6. Sense the love, peace, joy and comfort that you are able to pass to others.
7. When you have finished, allow your wings to merge back into your heart and know you can use them whenever you wish to.

EXERCISE 23: *Laugh and be blessed*

Angels love laughter, so have fun today and laugh a lot. Then open your arms and receive their blessings into your heart!

EXERCISE 24: *Act as if you were Archangel Michael*

1. Be aware that when you do this exercise with the proper intention Archangel Michael will be with you.
2. Stand tall and straight. Imagine you are wearing Archangel Michael's deep blue cloak. You are carrying his sword of truth in your right hand and his shield of protection in your left.
3. Walk as if you are Archangel Michael. Feel his power. Imagine yourself using his sword for the highest good, cutting away lower energies and helping those weaker than yourself.
4. Notice how you feel.
5. When you have done this for as long as seems appropriate, either remain standing quietly or sit and consider how you can use this energy in your life.

6

Cleansing and Releasing

EXERCISE 25: *Cleansing negative energy in a house*

Most houses can do with an energetic cleanse now and then!
Here are some of the things that will help to clear unwanted energy.

1. Light a candle.
2. Waft joss sticks into every corner.
3. Play singing bowls or even drums.
4. Clap your hands into every corner to break up stuck energy.
5. Open the windows to let the air blow through.
6. Om or chant in the rooms.
7. Call in the archangels and ask them to cleanse the space.

VISUALIZATION 26: *Letting go and handing something to the angels*

Angels cannot do their job properly if we are holding on to something or someone with our thoughts and emotions. We can hold people and prevent them from passing over, or stop people making the right decision or a child from growing up or a good business decision, because we are worrying about it.

Often the greatest gift you can give to the other person – and yourself – is to let go and hand it to the angels. Then you must refrain from thinking about it while they do their part.

1. Find a space where you can be quiet and undisturbed.
2. Light a candle to raise the energy.
3. Close your eyes and relax.
4. Ask Archangel Michael to place his deep blue cloak of protection over you.
5. Send roots down into the Earth to ground you.
6. Picture the person, situation, business or place and place it into the basket of a hot air balloon.

7. Visualize it rising up. Then cut the chains that hold it to the ground.
8. Ask the angels to take it for the highest good and see them surrounding the balloon.
9. Watch it floating into the blue sky and out of sight.
10. Open your eyes.
11. If you find yourself thinking about it, affirm "I hand this to the angels for the highest good." Then let it go again.

VISUALIZATION 27: *Cutting cords to a person*

Before you do this exercise, decide who you want to let go of. Remember that uncording can only change things for the better, for only lower emotions form cords. You may find that when the cords are released you see the person differently and become closer; or that you feel emotionally free to step away. Whatever happens is always for the highest good of all. Archangel Michael ensures that.

1. Find a place where you can be quiet and undisturbed.
2. Light a candle to raise the energy and transmute the old.
3. Sit with your eyes closed and imagine roots from your feet connecting you deep into the Earth.
4. Breathe gently until you feel relaxed.
5. Invoke the mighty Archangel Michael and sense him coming to you. Sense or see him place his deep blue cloak of protection round you.
6. Visualize the person you wish to uncord from sitting in front of you. Tell them gently what you propose to do.
7. Sense where the cords are between you and what they look like. Are they thin wire or thick rope; black and sticky like treacle or clinging like tentacles? If you cannot sense or see them, just relax and trust Archangel Michael to do what is necessary.
8. Ask Archangel Michael to cut the cords away with his sword of truth and dissolve the energy right down to its roots.
9. When this is finished imagine yourself and the other person standing under a shower of light and being totally cleansed.
10. You may find that you are wearing different clothes in the image.
11. See the other person walking through a gate onto a golden happy road.
12. See yourself walking through a gate, close it behind you and find yourself on a beautiful golden road, up a hill to a higher path.
13. Thank Archangel Michael and open your eyes.

VISUALIZATION 28: *Cutting cords to a house, business, idea, project or anything else*

Before you do this exercise, decide what you want to let go of. If it is an idea or project you may like to choose a symbol to represent it. It is possible that you may feel a little tired or emotional after this exercise. Plan the exercise for a time where you can have space and time to quietly reflect. Archangel Michael will ensure that the outcome is always for the highest good of all.

1. Find a place where you can be quiet and undisturbed.
2. Light a candle to raise the energy and transmute the old.
3. Sit with your eyes closed and imagine roots from your feet connecting you deep into the Earth.
4. Breathe gently until you feel relaxed.
5. Invoke Archangel Michael and sense him coming to you. Sense or see him place his deep blue cloak of protection round you.
6. Visualize in front of you whatever you wish to uncord from, or its symbol.
7. As before, sense where the cords are and what they look like. Are they thin wire or thick rope, black and sticky like treacle or clinging like tentacles? If you cannot sense or see them, relax and trust Archangel Michael to do what is necessary.
8. Ask Archangel Michael to cut the cords away with his sword of truth and dissolve the lower energy right down to its roots.
9. When this is finished imagine yourself standing under a shower of light and being totally cleansed.
10. You may find that in the visualization you are now wearing different clothes.
11. See yourself walking through a gate onto a golden happy road. Open your arms for the new and better to come to you.
12. Thank Archangel Michael and open your eyes.

Healing

EXERCISE 29: *Giving healing with Archangel Raphael*

If you want to give someone formal healing with Archangel Raphael, here is a way to do it.

1. Prepare your space for this sacred work.
2. Light a candle to raise the energy.
3. Ask the person you are healing to sit or lie down and help them to feel comfortable, safe and relaxed.
4. Place your hands on their shoulders; this opens their feet chakras and helps to ground them.
5. Place protection round both of you.
6. Say a little prayer to dedicate yourself in service to your friend or client and ask that the divine will be done.
7. Invoke Archangel Raphael and be very still while his energy comes into your hands.
8. If you are good at picturing colour, visualize emerald green passing through your hands to the person you are working on. Don't worry about this if you can't picture it.
9. Place your hands on each of the 12 chakras, or 1 inch (2.5cm) above them. Or alternatively place your hands wherever your intuition guides you.
10. When the energy stops flowing, cut yourself symbolically from your partner and thank Archangel Raphael. Then sit quietly, holding the vision of their divine perfection.
11. When your partner opens their eyes both of you should drink a glass of pure blessed water.
12. Share what you both experienced if this feels right.

EXERCISE 30: *Prayers to heal a relationship*

If you are in a difficult situation with a friend or a partner and feeling frustrated, angry, sad, weak or helpless, there are beautiful prayers you can offer to the angels.

Find your own words, expressing first of all your aim for a loving relationship with the other person (if you do wish to continue it and truly believe that that would be good) and then your aim for a solution to the highest best of everyone involved.

Here is a sample prayer

Dear Angel,

please help me/us finding a loving solution for the highest good of everyone included in that situation.

Thank you for your help!

— 8 —

Spiritual Practices

EXERCISE 31: *An Angel Journal*

This exercise is very simple. Buy yourself a journal, the most beautiful you can find.
– Each morning ask the angels for signs of their presence.
– Write them down. You may be amazed!
– Remember to thank the angels when you go to bed.

EXERCISE 32: *In the shower*

Blessing water brings it into the fifth dimension, which raises the frequency of your aura and the cells of your body.

1. When you are in the shower bless the water with the words, "I love you. I bless you. I thank you."
2. Then call in the unicorns and sense them showering you with light.
3. Call in Mother Mary and ask for her divine feminine to fill your aura.
4. Call in Archangel Butyalil the cosmic angel.
5. Call in Archangel Metatron to hold you on your ascension path.

VISUALIZATION 33: *Fifth-dimensional chakra alignment*

Every night when I go to bed I do the following. When you become more familiar with the exercise you will find you can practice it quickly.

1. Close your eyes and relax.
2. Ask the unicorns to touch and balance each of your twelve chakras and bring them into alignment in the fifth dimension.
3. Then focus on each of your chakras in turn as follows:
   – Focus on your Earth Star chakra below your feet.
   – Focus on your base chakra.

- Focus on your sacral chakra.
- Focus on your navel chakra.
- Focus on your solar plexus.
- Focus on your heart chakra.
- Focus on your throat chakra.
- Focus on your third eye.
- Focus on your crown chakra.
- Focus on your causal chakra just above your head.
- Focus on your Soul Star chakra above the causal.
- Focus on your Stellar Gateway.

4. Finally ask the angels to sing over you while you sleep to hold you in the fifth dimension.

EXERCISE 34: *Dreaming about angels*

The angels connect with us while we are asleep but usually we do not remember these dreams. You are more likely to remember the experience when you are sleeping lightly. Water is the medium of dreams and a full bladder means you sleep less heavily and get up during the night. You may find the following helps; and the more often you do it, the more likely you are to start remembering your dreams.

1. Affirm during the day that you wish to dream about the angels.
2. Eat lightly at 6 p.m. and nothing after that.
3. Drink a lot of water and make sure you bless each glassful.
4. Leave a pen and notepad by your bed.
5. Let your final prayer be that you connect with the angels during sleep.

EXERCISE 35: *Empowering our voice*

Hearing psychically is a function of the throat chakra. Here are some things that will help the chakra function more effectively.

1. Practise saying what you really feel.
2. Archangel Michael is in charge of this chakra, so ask him to help you raise the frequency here.
3. Breathe Michael's deep blue colour into your throat ten times each morning and night.
4. Listen to hear what others really mean.
5. Speak to empower others and help them feel good.
6. Trust in self.
7. Honour the magnificence of who you truly are.

9

Comfort

EXERCISE 36: *Transmuting emotions with stones*

Rocks and stones hold ancient wisdom. They absorb and release energies and can take in and transmute your feelings.

1. Hold the intention of finding a stone that will take your sadness. Ask the angels to help you with this. You may find one in your garden, a park, the forest, in the mountains or by the sea.
2. Blow on the stone to cleanse it.
3. Ask the angels to bless it.
4. Hold the stone in your hands as you think about your sadness. You may feel the stone absorbing your feelings.
5. Thank the stone when you have finished.
6. Either bury it in the ground or place it in water so that the elements of earth or water can transmute the feelings you have placed in it.
7. Breathe in positive qualities of joy, happiness, love and tranquillity.

EXERCISE 37: *Invoke the angels to bring comfort*

An invocation is very powerful and the purer, clearer your intention the greater the response from the higher realms. Take as long as you need for this invocation and allow the archangels to help you. You can also call in other angels if you wish.

1. Find a place where you can be quiet and undisturbed.
2. Light a candle and dedicate it to the angels bringing you what you need. Mentally tell them.
3. Sit comfortably and breathe gently.
4. Picture roots going down from your feet deep into the Earth.
5. Invoke Archangel Michael; picture his deep blue cloak of protection being placed round you and know he is looking after you. Breathe in the deep blue.

6. Invoke Archangel Gabriel and sense his pure white light flowing round you bringing you hope. Breathe in the pure white.
7. Invoke Archangel Raphael and feel his emerald healing light surrounding you. Breathe in emerald green.
8. Invoke Archangel Uriel and allow his gold light to give you confidence. Breathe in gold.
9. Invoke Mother Mary and allow her aquamarine light of compassion and comfort to touch you. Breathe in aquamarine.
10. Relax in the energy of these archangels and allow them to help you.
11. When you have finished thank the archangels.
12. Open your eyes and return to the room knowing the angels are assisting you.

Working with
Animals and Birds

EXERCISE 38: *Tune in to an animal*

If you have an animal at home or work that you can tune in to, that is excellent. If not, think about an animal you know. This may be a domestic animal that belongs to someone else, or a wild one you have seen in a zoo or on a television programme.

1. Sit quietly, outside in nature if possible.
2. Ask Archangel Michael to place his deep blue cloak of protection over you and your animal and feel it going round you.
3. Focus on your breathing until your mind is still and quiet.
4. Tune in to the animal's feelings and thoughts.
5. Send it a message of love and peace or hope.
6. You may receive a message back from your animal.
7. Ask the angels what messages they want to send through you to your animal. Then pass them on.
8. When you have finished bless the animal and open your eyes.

EXERCISE 39: *Draw an animal*

When you draw you access your right (intuitive, creative) brain and unexpected ideas or thoughts may come to you. You do not have to be good at drawing! It is fun to do this with others and share what your drawings mean to you all when you have finished.

1. Get paper and pens ready.
2. Light a candle.
3. Ask the angels to work with you as you do this.
4. Draw any picture you want to that contains animals. There may be one animal or several different kinds.

5. When you have finished, look at your animals and sense what messages they have for you. Are they free? Are they safe or endangered? How are they treated by humans? What is their habitat like? How do they feel?
6. Thank the animals and the angels for coming to you.

Note that you can do this exercise with birds instead; you may like to ask yourself the following questions. Are they flying free? Floating peacefully? Trapped in a cage? Sitting on a fence? Being battered by rain? Hiding in a tree?

EXERCISE 40: *Tune in to the birds*

– Go out into nature where it is quiet and sit on a bench or in the grass or lean against a tree. Ask that the birds bring you messages from the angels.
– Make your mind as still as possible and listen to the birds. Try not to think. Just be.
– Then watch the birds and again try not to think, just observe.
– Be open to any messages from the birds.
– When you have finished bless them and be aware that your channels to the angels have been purified.

In Conclusion

I hope that you feel inspired and excited by the stories in this book. Most importantly I hope you have that "knowing" inside you that angels are everywhere – and particularly that your guardian angel is with you. Both birds and butterflies are messengers for the angels and carry some of their beautiful energy, and you know that birds and butterflies surround us – so angels really are with us all the time.

I love the way the angels help us in our daily lives. My granddaughter is very sensitive to energies and atmosphere. She phoned one evening because she felt unsafe, so I suggested that we ask Archangel Michael to help. She loves Archangel Michael she agreed readily. We visualized his lovely blue cloak of protection going round her, her puppy, her mother and father and brother and the house. By the time we had finished she felt fine and was totally relaxed; and even from a distance I could sense a total shift of the energy in the house.

Children are particularly receptive to angels, archangels, unicorns and all the elementals. If you know a child, do read some of these stories to them. It is a wonderful way to introduce them to their invisible helpers and is also a great boost to their spiritual path. Trust that you will choose the story they need to hear and you never know – they may bless you for years to come!

As I write this, my dog Venus and my kitten Ash-ting are playing together on the sofa beside me. They are pretend-biting each other and tumbling all over the place and from time to time stopping to lick each other. They are best friends and it is heart-warming to watch the affection and love they have for each other. The cat runs up to Venus as soon as she appears and rubs himself against her. The dog rushes round the garden to look for Ash-ting if it is time to come in and often won't come in until she has found him. Then the two of them race in through the back door together. Every morning and evening I ask Archangel Fhelyai, the angel of animals, to put one of his angels on duty with each of them. I visualize the dog and cat with a yellow circle of light around them and I know they will be looked after. Archangel Fhelyai also helps them to keep their relationship close. Angels are around wherever there is love between two creatures: whether they are animal or human.

Remember that the angels are with you as you read these pages. They pour light onto you and help you to absorb the messages. The angels have told me that this book will help to provide a link between you and the angelic realms.

I offer you this book with love.

Contributors to this Book

M uch gratitude to everyone who has sent in stories of their experiences. While it has not been possible to list every contributor here, further information on teachers and workshops with the Diana Cooper School can be found on the website of the school: *www.dianacooperschool.com*

UNITED KINGDOM

Janis Attwood
Diana Cooper School Angel Teacher
England
Email: *janscuisine@gmail.com*

Lindsay Ball
Teacher Diana Cooper School
England
Email: *info@lindsayball.co.uk*
www.lindsayball.co.uk

Rowena Beaumont
EFT, Angelic Reiki teacher
England
www.rowenabeaumont.com
www.angelicreikiassociation.co.uk/
RowenaBeaumont.html

Eloise Bennett
Principal Teacher Diana Cooper School
Wales
Tel.: +44 (0) 1437 711404
Mobile: +44 (0) 7977 583224
Email: *seraphinatempleoflight@*
btinternet.com
www.seraphinatempleoflight.com

Diane Hall
Teacher Diana Cooper School
England
www.dianehallsbooks.com

Elizabeth Harley
Reiki, Master Teacher Diana Cooper
School
Scotland
Tel.: +44 (0) 1343 830052
Email: *elizpeace@live.co*
www.reikitraining.org.uk

Karelena MacKinlay
Teacher Diana Cooper School
Scotland
Mobile: +44 (0) 7976 525455
Email: *km@beingatone.co.uk*
www.beingatone.co.uk

Margaret Merrison
Principal Teacher Diana Cooper School
England
Email: *margaret@unicorn*
centre.co.uk
www.unicorncentre.co.uk

Elizabeth Ann Morris
Principal Diana Cooper School
Scotland
Tel.: +44 (0) 7904 182542
Email: *ann@elizabethannmorris.com*
www.elizabethannmorris.com

Krystyna Napierala
England
www.london-angels-olympics.com

Jillian Stott
Deputy Principal and Principal Teacher
UK with the Diana Cooper School
England
Tel.: +44 (0) 1926 851898
Tel.: +44 (0) 7989 676 648
Email: *jillianstott@btopenworld.com;*
jillian@authenticfengshui.org.uk

Jill Webster
Scotland
Email: jill@jillwebster.com
www.jillwebster.com

AUSTRIA

**Martina Maria Seraphina
Kammerhofer**
Teacher Diana Cooper School
Austria
Tel.: +43 (0) 664 497 77
E-mail: martina@balance-des-lebens.at
www.balance-des-lebens.at

CYPRUS

Susan Rudd
Master Teacher Diana Cooper School
Cyprus
Tel.: +357 (0) 97648218
Email: *spiritandsole@hotmail.com*
www.spiritandsole.com

FRANCE

Ann Quinn
France
Email: *hqelec@gmail.com*

GERMANY

Rama Regina Margarete Brans
Teacher Diana Cooper School
Germany
Email: *info@cometorelax.de*
www.cometorelax.de

School of Divine Light
Aleja Daniela Fischer
Teacher Diana Cooper School
Germany
Tel.: +49 (0) 8284 928 95 93
Fax: +49 (0) 8284 928 95 92
Email: *aleja.d.fischer@web.de*
www.schoolofdivinelight.de
www.schoolofdivinelight.com

Cornelia Maria Mohr
Teacher Diana Cooper School
Germany
Tel.: +49 (0) 9120 8285
Email: *praxis.c.mohr@t-online.de*
www.mohrcornelia.de
www.dasinnerezuhause.de

IRELAND

Mariel Forde Clarke –
City of the Tribes
Teacher Diana Cooper School
Galway, Republic of Ireland
Tel.: +353 (0) 879185421
Email: *iggyc@gofree.indigo.ie*
www.marielscircleofangels.ie

Sue Walker,
Custodian for Mother Earth
Master Teacher with the Diana Cooper
School, Reiki Master/Teacher
Tipperary, Republic of Ireland
Tel.: +353 (0) 87 2186148
Email: *suewalker@eircom.net*

ITALY

Franziska Siragusa
Teacher Diana Cooper School
Italy
Email: *angeldolphins@gmail.com*
www.angeldolphins.com

SLOVENIA & CROATIA

Marjetka Novak
Teacher Diana Cooper School
Angel Academy of Awakening® and
Angel Touch of Awakening®
Ljubljana, Slovenia
www.svetangelov.com

SOUTH AFRICA

Jenny Hart
Somerset West, South Africa
Tel.: +27 (0) 828908789
www.sacredharthealing.wozaon
line.co.za

Hettie van der Schyff
c/o Hettie Nawa
Holistic Healing & Teaching
South Africa
Mobile: +27 (0) 82 4960 145
Email: *3g.hettie@gmail.com*
www.holistichealingsa.co.za

SPAIN

Pauline Gow
Teacher Diana Cooper School
Spain
www.spirituallightacademy.com

Penny Wing
Master Teacher Diana Cooper School
Spain
Email: *pennyjon@live.com*
www.pennywing.com

UNITED STATES

Carol Guy
United States
Ordained Minister, Angelic Counselor,
Life Fitness Coach, author; founder and
host of Earth Angels Radio Network.
www.carolguy.com
www.earthangelsradio.com
www.aperfectbodyforme.com

Tammy Marinaro
Brennan Healing Science® Practitioner
New Jersey, USA
Mobile: +1 (0) 7814 790016
E-mail: *Corexpressions@yahoo.com*
www.corexpressions.com

Christy Richards
Teacher Diana Cooper School
United States
Email: *Corepeace@gmail.com*

Angel of Light Cards

BY

DIANA COOPER

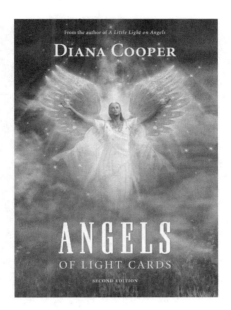

Each of the 52 Angel Cards included in this deck represent a different Angel quality, and can be used for guidance, inspiration and affirmation. The cards will help you tune in to the higher vibrations of the Angels, and allow you to feel the helping hands of these beings at all times. Following the inspiration of the Angels will raise your consciousness, which will automatically help you attract to yourself people and situations of a higher vibratory level and release old negative thought patterns. Carry these cards with you wherever you go and use them to remind yourself of the presence, guidance and help of the Angels in your life, always and everywhere. You are never alone or lost when the Angels are with you.

Set of 52 cards + 2 instructions cards
in desktop presentation stand with slipcase – ISBN 978-1-84409-141-6
Pocket edition: *set of 52 cards + 2 instructions cards*
in tuckbox – ISBN 978-1-84409-171-3

The Keys to the Universe Cards

DIANA COOPER
& Kathy Crosswell

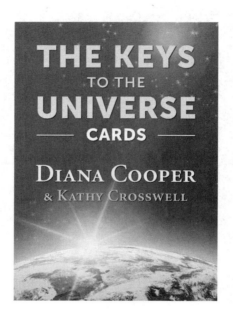

The perfect accompaniment to The Keys to the Universe book, these beautiful cards help seekers on the path of enlightenment. There are 50 keys — 48 of which enable readers to unlock the secrets of other realms, such as the animal or natural kingdoms, the elements, archangels and other angelic beings, cosmic masters, and wisdom centers; and two Golden Cosmic Keys, Hollow Earth and Sirius, which allow attunement to the wisdom of the cosmos. Two cards with specific instructions and explanation for use of the deck are included.

*Set of 52 cards + 2 instructions cards
in desktop presentation stand with slipcase
ISBN 978-1-84409-609-1*

FINDHORN PRESS

Life-Changing Books

For a complete catalogue,
please contact:

Findhorn Press Ltd
117-121 High Street,
Forres IV36 1AB,
Scotland, UK

t +44 (0)1309 690582
f +44 (0)131 777 2711
e info@findhornpress.com

or consult our catalogue online
(with secure order facility) on
www.findhornpress.com

For information on the Findhorn Foundation:
www.findhorn.org